MW01046866

READER RESPONSES FROM THE EVERYDAY WORLD:

Levi Switzer, youth counselor: "This book will appeal to anyone... it has ideas and concepts that you can put into practice in your own life no matter what your life situation looks like. Whoever you are, you will gain something from reading it."

Martin Hooernart, corporate attorney: "This is a great gift for anyone who is facing a significant challenge in their lives or who needs a kick-start in achieving their dreams."

Robert Burns, ret. managing partner, New England Financial: One of the best books that I've ever read. It should be mandatory reading for every sales organization in both the United States and Canada...and for every business as well.

Penny Reiger, adminstrative assistant: Everyone, even if not in a serious impossible/I.M. Possible situation should give it a read. The "One Sock Process" is so helpful in every situation whether it is dire or not.

Ryan Williams film director, producer: "Jamie has presented a battle plan for how to win the greatest war any man ever fights—the war within himself. It's grounded in realistic expectations and scientifically backed principles that separate it from simple self-improvement titles. I plan on implementing a number of the concepts right away."

Shawn Egan, industrial foreman: "First thing I did was use the One-Sock Process to finally get my refrigerator cleaned. The One-Sock Process alone is worth the price of the book."

Deb Flohr, homemaker: "I got so emotional by the time I was halfway through the book. I thought, 'Why didn't I have this information sooner?' I am so thankful I have it now. Not just for me; every member of my family is going to get a copy."

Matt Gilson, college grad, entrepreneur: "This book is basically giving people the tools they need to reinvent their lives if they choose to do so."

Diane Sams, executive assistant: "Every teenager should be given this book upon their entrance to High School. Everyone going through a divorce or job loss needs to have this book in their hands."

Adriana Aguilar, manager: "I would like to see your book translated to Spanish so I can send it to friends in Venezuela. I believe that your book will make a significant self-development to anyone who reads it, because it has the mirror effect. While you read each chapter you will find yourself identified. Your book is perfect to do group book discussion because people can share experiences."

Kathryn Davis, author, editor: I've been going through a challenging time ... and have been smiling at the powerful positive message in your book, realizing I can use what I'm learning every day in my life, and feeling lighter and stronger minute by minute."

What an exciting time in the age of information! Neuroscientists Bryan Kolb and Ian Whishaw helped pioneer the way for a new understanding of the human brain and its potentials.

Norman Doige has brought neuroscience into individual stories and outcomes, organized around the dramatic process of neuroplasticity.

Eric Kandel has won the only Nobel Prize in all of psychiatry for his pioneering work on growth and potentiation of synapses in memory consolidation, a metabolic pillar of neuroplasticity.

Other authors, including Dan Siegel, have extended the field in relational directions: the neurobiology of 'we', and the metabolism and growth of neural tissue through the process of relating to one another.

Jamie DeNovo has managed to create a model, a formula, which fuses the complexities of neuroscience, the creativity of metaphor, and the practicalities of life: I.M.Possible! This represents an incredible system anyone can access and apply—a rare achievement in our field. Jamie has managed to encase the neurobiology of hope with a procedure for growth and change. I.M.Possible is a gift to all of us who struggle with the impact of our own version of the impossible.

Dr. Roy Turner, MD, FRCPC
Dept. of Psychiatry, Rockyview Hospital
Associate Professor University of Calgary

I.M.POSSIBLE MUSCLE®

FOR THE MIND

The Power To Achieve Success
When Success Seems Impossible

by JAMIE DeNOVO

with DR. BRYAN KOLB

Edited: by Pat Kozak, Stephanie J. Beavers and Jamie DeNovo
Special Edits by: Dr. Roy Turner, Carl Macdonald,
and Kathryn Lynn Davis

Published by Global Dreamers Guild, Inc.

ISBN 978-0-9877330-9-2

This book is dedicated to first to my number one hero and husband, Scott, who embodies the true spirit of I.M.Possible, and to my children, Chance, Kirstie and September and grandchildren, Nicolas and Nathanael, who never stopped believing I could do the impossible.

My second dedication is to you the reader.

I can do that – make a second dedication, because in the realm of I.M.Possible boundaries can be recreated. I dedicate this book to every person who grappled with a problem for which there seemed no solution and achieved success anyway – but especially to anyone still in the arena, like me, battling to achieve a worthy goal against overwhelming odds.

Authors Note:

I cannot sufficiently express my gratitude to Dr. Bryan Kolb, for so graciously giving his time and expertise to mentor and support the creation of this book and its processes.

Long considered one of the world's most influential neuroscientists, Dr. Kolb has been described as one of the founding fathers of behavioral neuroscience. Among his many national and international honors is membership in the prestigious International Neuropsychology Symposium called the Group of One Hundred, which gathers together the most eminent behavioral neuroscientists in the world. Dr. Kolb is author or co-author—often with fellow researcher Ian Whishaw—of seven books, including two standard textbooks, An Introduction to Brain and Behavior and Fundamentals of Human Neuropsychology, now in its sixth edition, translated into five languages.

Acknowledgments

I would like to thank the following people, who gave so generously of their time, stories, insights and knowledge during the making of *I.M.POSSIBLE MUSCLE FOR THE MIND*. Each of you contributed fibers of encouragement and support during the years these processes were being developed. All of you are heroes. If I've missed anyone, I sincerely apologize. I will rectify the omission in the next book.

Anna Blankert	**Louie Malloy**
Armand Vos	**Lynette Watson**
Alexandria Victor-Morgan	**Martin Hooernart**
Cara Holditch	**Paul King**
Carl Macdonald	**Larry & Beth Horowitz**
David Coleman	**Laurence Kirshbaum**
Diane Sams	**Levi Switzer**
Dr. Bryan Kolb	**Ralph Palmieri**
Dr. Elizabeth VanArkel	**Robert F. Kennedy Jr.**
Dr. Roy Turner	**Richard Merritt**
Duane & Lisa Egan	**Ryan Williams**
Ernie Tillman	**Saladin Patterson**
James Christensen	**Shawn Egan**
Jason Alexander (Book cover)	**Teresa Gillies**
John Alm (and the C5LA)	**Tim Houghton**
Kim Mason	**William Sudah**

Very special thanks to:

Ed Sardachuk, and the boys, Grant, Marc and James, for all the times you've been there for me over the years

Les Hewitt for pointing me in the right direction

Steve Harrison, for shutting off the Extra Mile meter

Jack Canfield, for whom there are no words adequate to express my gratitude, but with whom I don't need them

And to **Patty Aubrey**, who gave me the shirt off her back. It's my favorite shirt in the whole world.

You are I.M.Possible heroes from the inside out.

Contents

Foreword by Dr. Bryan Kolb, PhD, FRSC

When Jamie came to see me, she wanted to find out whether there was a credible fit between the unusual concepts she had for this book and the findings of neuroscience.

Despite our differing methods, we both shared a common goal in our work: to find new ways to help more people help themselves—starting from wherever they are now—and to maximize their opportunities for a happy, healthy and productive life.

One of the real challenges for me as a neuroscientist is to translate basic facts about brain-behavior relationships to the general public. Thus, when Jamie approached me about helping with her project, my interest was piqued and I listened to her story. It soon became clear that Jamie had found a means of taking basic information that neuroscience has learned about the brain and introducing it in a new way, so the general population can use it.

If you think about accomplishing your impossible dreams or goals, you've got to change the brain. Because you are your brain. Thoughts and behaviors reflect brain activity. Different types of thoughts and actions are correlated with particular patterns of brain activity. These patterns must be changed if adverse or counterproductive thoughts and actions are to change. *I.M.Possible Muscle for the Mind* is the first approach I've seen that helps people to break this process down into tiny increments, and can get you thinking in a different way. In doing this, you will change your brain. It's not hoo-ha. The real issue is, "Does this method actually get you thinking or acting differently?"

Changing behavior is like starting a train - it's really hard to get it moving. But, once the train is moving, even if there are some dips and bumps, the momentum is there to move forward.

Progress is best made in small steps that build. Jamie has captured this concept and applied it successfully to provide a recipe for a novel form of cognitive behavioral therapy. If you can see light bulbs going on in people's heads, you've reached them. I believe when people read this book, light bulbs will go on.

Bryan Kolb, PhD, FRSC.
Professor of Neuroscience, Board of Governors Chair in Neuroscience,
Canadian Centre for Behavioral Neuroscience
University of Lethbridge

Introduction

"Most of the things worth doing in the world had been declared impossible before they were done."
—Louis D. Brandeis, Associate Justice of the United States Supreme Court

Have you, or has someone you care about, ever grappled with thoughts such as those in the list below? If so, *you need this book.* If not, you lead a charmed life—so far.

- *I've stopped believing. There's no hope.*
- *I can't get there from here.*
- *I don't even know how to start. I may as well give up.*
- *People like me don't succeed.*
- *People expect me to succeed. I can't try this in case it fails.*
- *This has changed my life. I'll never be happy again.*
- *I was born this way. I'm helpless to change anything.*
- *Life has passed me by. It's too late.*
- *Any of the 'Terrible Toos: I'm too… important/ unimportant, rich/poor, fat/too thin, pretty/ugly, confused/dumb…*

By the time you are finished reading this book, you will never again have to remain powerless in the grip of the above words and thoughts. *I.M.Possible Muscle for the Mind: The Power To Achieve Success When Success Seems Impossible* was written to open up a world of new I.M.Possibilities for every person grappling with seemingly impossible obstacles to happiness or greater achievement. The concepts in this book will work for you regardless of race, background, occupation, financial or social standing.

What is *I.M.Possible*™? It's a vital new look at what used to be *Impossible*. In the first chapter you will learn exactly what it is, and why it can change your life. But for now just say it like this: "I Am Possible."

Chicken Soup and I.M.Possible Muscle

Inspirational stories. How do they make you feel? The *Chicken Soup of the Soul* book series has sold over 500 million copies, which is a strong testament to the power of example to provide comfort, hope and motivation. Who wouldn't love to be one of those success stories? On the other hand, it can be very difficult to keep slogging ahead when our efforts seem to be futile. When feelings of inadequacy spiral into frustration and despair, it becomes harder and harder not to begin thinking of failure as our inevitable long term outcome. Over a period of years, my inspirational achievements had morphed into a nightmare where none of the conventional methods for overcoming could penetrate. The specialist who ran a series of brain tests and scans said the severity of the PTSD (post traumatic stress disorder) from which I was suffering, was similar to that seen in combat veterans. Although circumstances and degree may vary, sooner or later we are all faced with challenges that leave us feeling in some measure like we are trapped in a war zone with no adequate means to push through to the other side. Under such extreme conditions, I realized that if I was going to push through to a new success story, I'd to have to develop a new kind of muscle – an I.M.Possible muscle for the mind.

"Aha moments aren't limited to the uncovering of a blinding new fact that no one has ever presented before. They are also found in a kind of learning that carries in it a strong element of excitement. You suddenly understand something you've known all your life, but in a new, more powerful way..." —Jamie DeNovo

I.M.Possible Muscle For The Mind uses an absolutely unique approach to overcoming apparently insurmountable obstacles to advancement and achievement. Now anyone can develop break-through thinking and behavior skills. This book will act as your guidebook and personal coach in the sense that it teaches you how to build and strengthen your own I.M.Possible Muscle in moment-by-moment steps—not complex or huge leaps. You will be given tools that offer a *personal and immediate* means to experience positive change. Use the processes to accomplish anything from basic chores you've been putting off, to achieving life-changing goals. With practice, you will gain greater ability to reshape the *impossible*, to realize a dream, and to act as an inspiration and strengthening force for others. It's onward and upward. Your best is yet to come!

A Glimpse Through the *Impossible to I.M.Possible* Doorway

'Overcoming the impossible' is like building and training muscle. *The more we do, the more we can do.* Increase your abilities, and change your outcomes, using simple processes that build, train and reshape brain patterns. With repetition, such changes retrain or reshape circuitry of the brain and produce constructive behaviors or skills that replace self-defeat. Change in behavior will lead to change in results, which in turn leads to a change in outcome. In this way, formerly seemingly impossible obstacles may be overcome, and individuals are equipped with a cogent set of basic tools they can utilize anytime to navigate

adversity and confusion, and achieve optimal victories even under very challenging circumstances.

The best exercise programs are designed to work you up to the next step, and to cross-train and maximize gains, as you go along.

Similarly, the information in each of the chapters of this book is designed to interlink and progressively provide long-term, adaptable exercises and tools for working through many types of impossible barriers.

Today neuroscience helps us understand how, at any time throughout life; we can strengthen and reconstruct I.M.Possible Muscle®. With deliberate practice, you will find yourself increasingly able to push beyond restricting or self-weakening *impossible* thoughts and behaviors.

Just imagine. As old boundaries give way, you will discover new potentials. In getting past old limitations, you will create new worlds of opportunity for yourself and those whose lives touch yours!

> "Athletes become stronger the more they work out and train towards their goal. They can condition themselves and their muscles to respond reflexively through practice and technique. The brain works the same way. You can re-shape your thinking, through practice, to make you stronger, happier and more resourceful."
> —Dr. Bryan Kolb, pioneer in the field of

Weak Spots and Hot Spots

Emotions like despair and anger have a paralyzing effect on our I.M.Possible Muscle. How so? They override and inhibit brain activity in regions that could otherwise generate solutions. Here's the good news. *Although we cannot stop emotional triggers, we can train our brain to deflect them when they hit.* How? I.M.Possible Muscle exercises included in this book are designed to help you develop that crucial strength. As you learn how to redirect your focus, your brain will respond. It will activate regions that help stabilize your emotions and enable you to think and act far more productively.

For example, in Chapter 9 you will experience for yourself how mentally changing your pronunciation of *Impossible* to "*I. M. Possible*" can dramatically change your approach to challenging situations and your outlook toward perceived limitations. Warm up for success and ward off the spiral into negative emotions, as you learn to reset thoughts of impossible to I.M.Possible!

When You Hit a Wall

I.M.Possible Muscle For The Mind will lift you beyond the walls of your current mental 'box. Imagination and novelty are the foundation of genius. Discover in Chapter 5 how you can increase these I.M.Possible Muscle superpowers to break away from routine, cyclic or dead-end thinking and push ahead to breakthrough successes. Learn how to go beyond thinking outside the box to a world without boxes- the wonderland in your mind!

What can you do if you find it impossible to push productively through exhaustion, frustration and chaos? Chapter 11 will introduce you The One Sock Process, a revolutionary micro-process for achievement even when you are overwhelmed or overloaded! Many readers found this to be the most powerful tool in the book.

Even if you are initially skeptical, if everything else you have ever tried has failed, you will soon find that by understanding *how to make tiny progressive changes*, you can actually advance in ways you never thought possible. The I.M.Possible processes offer you an immediate and continuous means to strengthen and transform your weakest links. These basic tools can also be used to achieve greater success with any other personal or professional development, educational, motivational programs and/or professional or medical therapies!

Whoever you are, whatever your circumstances, you can personally experience positive results as you build your I.M.Possible Muscle fiber-by-fiber, moment by moment. Just as I did, you can likewise develop the ability, not only to survive the effects of trauma or life-altering challenge, but to rise above it and achieve success in ways that once appeared impossible.

You will find you absolutely can believe and achieve impossible things.

You *can* change your life, starting in the very next moment.

"If you limit your choices only to what seems possible or popularly accepted, you disconnect yourself from what can truly be achieved, and all that is left is a compromise." — Robert Fritz

---

By the Way...

I.M.Possible Muscle For The Mind: The Power To Achieve Success When Success Seems Impossible is not just another book to read, then stick on the shelf. It was specially designed to give you maximum, ongoing personal benefit. To that end, a variety of means have been incorporated to exercise your I.M.Possible muscle while you are reading the book. The processes will get your brain working on higher levels and imprint key concepts in your working memory. Based on scientific brain and behavior principles, these have proven invaluable during my own impossible times. Let yourself feel and act as like a champion in the making - an explorer of uncharted territory. The ability to try something new, when appropriately directed, is an I.M.Possible superpower. (Why and how revealed in Chapter 5).

I Want to Know Now

Are you a bit ADHD when reading? Looking for a fast fix in the first few pages? I.M.Possible growth requires a blend patience and curiosity, so this is a good place to start. While quick fixes are the order of the day, the results don't last long, or provide quality long term outcomes. Yes, you can skip to any section and begin, but each chapter is like the stairs on the front cover – it serves a specific underlying purpose. Which is? To progressively lead you to the next level, equipping you with key insights and essential knowledge (your inner Scientist), and stimulating your imagination circuits (your inner Visionary Dreamer). Each section prepares you to make far more powerful use of the tools and exercises as you get to them!

Could You Say That Again? I.M.Possible Muscle Reps

> **For Short-Term Memory: Repeat to Remember**
> **For Long-Term Memory: Remember to Repeat**
> —John Medina, Brain Rules

Throughout the book you will find that a number of key concepts are repeated. This wasn't done to annoy you. Repetition embeds primary points in your mind. You don't want to close the book and, a week later, think, "There was some really good stuff in there but I don't remember it." Think. Why is it critical to do reps when building physical muscle? The same principle applies here. By *re-reading key points in various forms, you will make a stronger connection to the information and increase your ability to retain and apply it in your daily life.*

The Wonderland Quotes – Mental Flexibility & Stretch

What can we possibly learn from the characters in Alice in Wonderland? You'll be surprised! Each chapter in *I.M.POSSIBLE MUSCLE FOR THE MIND* is prefaced with a quote taken from *Alice in Wonderland* or its sequel, *Through the Looking Glass*. The quotes tie to universal attitudes, behaviors or principles discussed in that chapter. The novel nature and use of the quotes will you to look at familiar situations in a new light. *Discover why thinking novelty and in metaphor rank as an I.M.Possible superpowers in Chapter 5.*

The importance of learning to perceive the world in a fresh way is clearly a part of the generally accepted theory of creative thinking. If creative thinking is the novel association of existing concepts in memory, then it follows naturally that it is useful to create a storehouse of concepts. - de Bono, E (1992) Serious Creativity. New York: HarperCollins Publishing

Write In This Book Exercises

Write in This Book section came about because I write in all my books and I want you to feel free to write in yours. Why?

I don't know what I think until I write it down.

Making notes or marking key points helps us to apply and quickly re-find those points. Behavioral psychiatrist, Dr. Roy Turner, graciously assisted with creating this section. According to Dr. Turner, research confirms that:

(1) *Writing a daily plan of activities increases the probability of doing the activities* an

(2) *Writing helps us organize our thoughts and consider them more clearly. It focuses our brain and activates circuits that generate higher levels of thinking.*

(3) *Writing is one of the strongest means for developing change in the brain, leading to permanent and durable long-term change in thinking and behavior.*

If you are uncomfortable writing in your book, or want to keep a more detailed written journal, separate workbooks are also available at www.jamiedenovo.com or www.i-m-possiblemuscle.com [1]

Please, however, be clear on this: Processes alone, of any kind, will not create personal success or fulfillment. They will serve you in much the same way that gear, coaching and exercise assist us to achieve physical goals. The way you use those tools and your willingness to practice with the intent to improve will, of course, affect the quality of your final result.

In order to grow, I.M.Possible muscle requires movement away from *comfort zones*, moving away from some *controls*. I had to keep practicing until I could let go of what I had built with old tools in order to build something more substantial, more able to weather storms and the winds of change. The results more than repay the effort. The new skills help me, just as they will you, in every aspect of life: spiritual, mental, moral, personal and professional—you name it. I am finally on higher ground and still climbing. After all, it was the climb that helped me forge a way for others. Now we can all to climb higher than any of us thought possible.

I.M.Possible begins where you are right now, at this very moment. ***You don't even have to believe at first in order to get results.*** Practice and you will achieve. Belief will come. There is a bonus in this approach. Whether you believe or don't, if your belief is faulty, you will now have a means to test, to make adjustments and move past obstacles to achieve the ultimate goal.

---

[1] *WRITE IN THIS BOOK*, Global Dreamers Guild Inc., First Edition, 2012.

So get started, I.M.Possible dreamer, whoever and wherever you are. I.M.Possible is not just transformational, it's addictive. As seemingly impossible challenges become I.M.Possible victories, your first impossible thing will prove to be the first of many…

"If we did all the things we are capable of, we would literally astound ourselves."
—Thomas Edison, inventor

My researches included interviews with many people who had faced overwhelming adversity and major setbacks while in pursuit of an 'impossible' dream. To achieve an I.M.Possible success, each had to let go of a familiar way of thinking or acting, and take on a rebuilding process involving definite, identifiable patterns. *Just as many fibers interact and come together in definite ways when building strong, agile physical muscle, you will learn how to identify, then develop and strengthen the fibers that underlie your personal ability to achieve I.M.Possible things!*

Portions of the interviews appear throughout the book. The interviewee names are not recognizable in every household. None relied on wealth or connections in achieving goals. Some faced severe financial hardship. All met with heartache, failure and discouragement along the way. They had to push through fear and discomfort. But each has attained a worthy goal (or goals) that, at one time, appeared to be impossible.

The overviews below encapsulate the background for some of those I.M.Possible interviews. You will find excerpts from these throughout the upcoming pages. All interviewees shared their experiences with the goal of helping others to understand:

1. The power of I.M.Possible Muscle training,
2. How we increase [or decrease] its strength,
3. How to maximize your own potentials for positive change and new accomplishments.

Dr. Bryan Kolb - *He dreamed of being a world-class badminton player. Reality didn't agree, so he studied law instead. In the course of his studies he found his true calling: Neuroscience. With the indomitable spirit that is a hallmark of his character, young Dr. Kolb put his budding career on the line to develop what later became the first university courses in neuropsychology. From ground zero, within a small, relatively unknown university, he and his associate Dr. Ian Whishaw went on to establish the Canadian Center for Behavioral Neuroscience (CCBN). Today CCBN boasts sixteen neuroscientists, more than one hundred graduate students, post-doctoral fellows and technical staff, and is recognized as one of the leading neuroscience research centers in the world. At the age of thirty-eight, Dr. Kolb suffered a stroke and was faced with the possibility that he might never see or work again. At age fifty-*

two, he began his first horseback riding lessons with the dream of entering and performing in the realm of impossible-seeming equestrian show maneuvers.

Scott Q. - Scott's dream was to become an airline pilot even though his chances didn't look good. As a child, Scott was small and sickly, and picked on by bullies. He repeated fifth grade and was believed to have a learning disability. Working nights in his teens, Scott saved money for flying lessons. He proved to have such a natural ability he was allowed to fly solo after only six hours of instruction. His lifelong dream came to an end when eye testing revealed minor color blindness. Disqualified from becoming a commercial airline pilot, Scott studied electronics. He struggled to learn according to the way his teacher taught, and barely earned his professional certification. Fast forward twenty years. Scott is, in many respects, a real-life counterpart to the fictional character 'Q' in the James Bond series. Recognized as one of the best in his elite profession, Scott creates world-class, high-tech wireless systems for observation and intelligence gathering. I think of Scott as the King of I.M.Possible. Not only did he overcome impossible odds to succeed, but he must continue to overcome the impossible daily on many different levels in order to meet the critical needs of his clients.

Jess Mirran - Jess's dream was simply to be happily married, raise a family and work in some capacity to help others in need, especially children. But to Jess, this seemed an impossible future. Beautiful inside and out, Jess could never see herself that way. When she was a child, she hated her reality so much she used to wish she could be someone else—anyone else. Plagued by childhood sexual abuse and low self-esteem, she was shy and easily dominated by other people. She never had the confidence to stand her ground or achieve her own dreams. Jess became so depressed she tried to commit suicide and woke up in a hospital psychiatric ward. Today? Jess is happily married to a man who adores her. She has two teenage children and is a vibrant Bible teacher who makes a positive difference in the lives of nearly everyone she meets. With the right spirit, Jess teaches them, nothing is impossible.

Tim Houghton - Today, Tim is Vice President of a leading international security corporation. A few years ago, however, this executive took on a battle he would never have dreamed possible. Tim had been a senior homicide detective with UK's Scotland Yard and crime scene manager on the elite Specialist Investigations Branch, travelling the world, working with such organizations as MI5, MI6 and the FBI. But his demanding career was taking its toll on his personal life so he and his wife decided to make a life change and move to Canada. Given his status with Scotland Yard, Tim never doubted that his credentials would be valuable in Canada. Even the best investigators can make mistakes. Tim's reality turned upside down as he awoke to the realization that he had planted new roots in a distant country that refused to give him a break. With no job, no friends, no telephone, no credit and a house to pay for, Tim and his wife began to rebuild their identities and their lives. His story of transcendence and self-reinvention is an epic example of the micro-processes underlying the transformation from impossible to I.M.Possible.

Ryan Williams - *Growing up in Utah, Ryan dreamed of becoming a famous movie director. He started with zero connections and roughly the same amount of money. In an industry that is notoriously difficult to break into, the odds of having a film production go into the media mainstream are comparable to those of all athletes hoping to make the Olympic team. Ryan beat the odds. While he's not quite famous—yet—Ryan is making his living doing what he loves, something many people only dream about. He's even picked up a few awards along the way. Also against the odds, Ryan has managed to stay real in a world that is every bit as strange and unreal as Alice's Wonderland. Despite each new challenge, he is moving ever onward. Ryan has just completed a movie for entry into the Sundance Film Festival. We'll be rooting for him.*

Lynette Watson – *As head nurse at the Hoffman Center for Integrated Medicine, Lynette faces challenges similar to every mom trying to balance career, family and personal growth. Among these is a battle familiar to many, including me. Lynette has struggled with the inability to say no to chocolate and sweets, though she knows only too well the high toll junk food takes on our minds and bodies. The majority of us can empathize with her plight, especially in our world where sweets and fatty foods are often synonymous with comfort and love, and when living in the [current] moment often trumps living for a future moment. Today however, Lynette is winning her personal battle, thanks to her I.M.Possible Muscle-building toolkit.*

James Christensen - *Born with a love for fantasy and fairy tale, this renowned artist didn't think he could make a living with artwork inspired by myths, fables and imagination. So James took other work and showed people only those paintings he thought they would like. At the age of thirty-eight, he finally decided to take the journey through I.M.Possible territory. James finally sold his first fantasy-themed painting at the age of forty-three. The rest is history. Today, James Christensen's artwork is sold and exhibited in galleries throughout North America. He has won awards and received commissions by publications such as Time Magazine and OMNI Magazine. His story may sound like something out of a book, but it is in fact evidence of the power of fairy tales to connect with us in the real world.*

Saladin Patterson - *Growing up in Alabama, Saladin dreamed of being an IT engineer. He earned top grades in school and, confident in his future, entered MIT. An identity crisis set in as he realized that he was in a new and different league. Worse yet, Saladin found he might not be suited for the engineering career he had dreamed of since childhood. Afraid to disappoint his family and uncertain of which way to go, Saladin had to make some hard choices. Self-honesty, flexibility, and a determination to do whatever was necessary to find his true calling, were I.M.Possible strengths that carried Saladin through a voyage of discovery. Research, preparation, practice and improvement enabled him to rework the impossible and eventually carve out a new a place for himself - as a writer for the hit television series 'Frasier'! From his first I.M.Possible thing, Saladin moved to the next, becoming a writer and executive* *producer for the comedy series Psych, which became, at the time of printing, USA network's longest running series on air.*

(Author's note: My family and friends are glad Saladin didn't settle for engineering. *Psych*, in my opinion, was one of the most entertaining shows on television; one of the few I would recommend to anyone. Feel-good and yeah, unapologetically silly, *Psych*'s enduring success proved audiences don't need gratuitous sex and violence to be entertained. And, no, I am absolutely not being paid to say this.)[2]

THE INTERVIEW FILES: CHANGING REALITY   DR. KOLB

JDN: I don't like the term *self-help*. It's overused and just not inspiring. The I.M.Possible building Muscle program has a different dynamic. It is much more empowering to think of change as self-reinvention—because we're always re-inventing ourselves. It's more exciting to think of yourself as a work of art.
DR. KOLB: That's a good way to put it. Life is about change. Things change, life changes. We get older, we learn, we change. Everyone is a work in progress.
JDN: And whenever we change, we're creating something new in ourselves. When we're hit by something that takes away a piece of us, we can choose to tear the rest down, to sit and cry in the ruins. Or we can say, *"So I lost this; what do I have left? What can I invent with the tools I still have to work with?"* And we can begin to rebuild.
DR. KOLB: That's what the process is. It happens all the time, so accept it. Work with it. And there are ways we can make it easier to do that.

Impossible says "What have I done?"
I.M.Possible says "What will I do?"

[2] http://tv.msn.com/tv/article.aspx?news=850960

"There is no use trying, "said Alice; "one can't believe impossible things."
"I dare say you haven't had much practice," said the Queen.
"When I was your age, I always did if for half an hour a day.
Why sometimes, I've believed up to six impossible things before breakfast!"
—Through the Looking Glass, Lewis Carroll

1. An I.M.Possible Inspiration

"To shift the boundaries of 'impossible', think I.M.Possible. Imagine like a child, think like a scientist and practice like an athlete." — Jamie DeNovo

Have you ever achieved or experienced something so wonderful you can hardly believe it has happened? You might have thought, "At last! This is a reality!" or "Yes!—I've done it!" Did these events boost your confidence? Increase your optimism and energy? Could you look back and recognize an inspiration or strength that arose from the struggles that threatened to overwhelm you? Without doubt, you were able to face other challenges with greater strength, thinking to yourself something like this: "I've achieved this victory, despite the odds against me. I can handle this too." What made you *feel* this way? When a personal goal becomes a reality, emotional reward is produced by the brain. Each time our efforts and capabilities are reinforced and validated, we are motivated to strive for greater levels of achievement.

Imagine how much more we could accomplish if we could always remain forward-moving, positive and able to take whatever life throws at us! Such energizing attitudes aren't difficult to maintain if you have a safety net, unlimited resources at your disposal, or when failure won't matter much one way or another. But it's a herculean task to maintain that outlook when you are not in a fail-safe position, perhaps having to function productively under extreme adversity or opposition. When we feel utterly defeated or powerless, or when failure could prove devastating, how can we develop the qualities required to lift the I.M.Possible out of the impossible?

Most of us have grappled with conflicting emotions. I've certainly run the gamut. On attaining seemingly impossible victories, the re-energizing power of validation and creation have filled me with absolute confidence that I could accomplish anything I set out to do! On the other end of the

1

scale, I've suffered injustices that engulfed me in anger, grief, and the painful conviction that all hope was gone.

1. An Impossible Situation

Ironically, it was during one of the darkest times that I began a soul-wrenching struggle to reclaim a meaningful life. After many years spent painstakingly laying the groundwork, my husband and I had established a top-tier reputation for our small but elite company, which was also successfully engineering a break-through technology. Having pushed through immense barriers time and again, our goals began materializing and the company hurtled into a growth crisis. Backed by investment money, I travelled to Washington, D.C. to set up a branch office, working incredibly grueling days and nights, while my husband remained in Canada to manage technology operations. Unbeknownst to us, the seeming windfall of investment capital was irresistible to officials in a position of trust, as was the technology itself for others. We were defrauded of both. Treachery, greed, corruption and betrayal came in guises we could never have foreseen or imagined. How do you recover from such a thing? I don't mean simply financially; the damage inflicted in such circumstances extends far beyond dollars. And how do you recover the ability to trust when the very systems set up to help and protect fail to do so? When impossible takes on such proportions, and looms all around, how do you even begin to re-shape for the better?

Such an exercise proved to be far more difficult than any physical exertion I have ever done. *Far* more difficult. But it led me to create a universal micro-blueprint for self-reinvention (The One Sock Process). Yes, it was a long, daunting journey through *impossible* territory that drew forth the inspiration from which this book evolved. Like Alice, through her dark slide down the rabbit hole, I eventually overcame disbelief. Despite mistakes, confusion, frustration and fear, I ventured on, and so discovered a hidden doorway—one that opened up the way to a new and amazing wonderland.

2. An Impossible Dreamer

I have always been a *What if* thinker. What does that mean? *What if* thinkers keep alive inside themselves, a healthy curious streak that urges them to look past *What is* (the obvious or expected), and to wander with childlike wonder into the world of *What if.* In this realm, the boundaries defining *impossible* can be reshaped from obstructive walls to windows through which we can look beyond all barriers. Only within this mental framework, can such windows open to allow something new to enter our real world—something once believed to be impossible. In fact, it is only through a willingness to venture into such a world that we are able to bring into existence new knowledge and new achievements – many of which had been thought to exist only in the pages of fiction and fantasy.

From 'What If' to 'What Is'

Through the world of *What if*, we are able to discover or recreate the world of *What is*, as you will find exemplified in the experiences and interviews included throughout *I.M.Possible Muscle For the Mind*. 'What if' thinking lead scientists Kolb and Whishaw to create the first human-behavioral neuropsychology courses, Scott Q. to develop his unusual niche in the security intelligence sector, Saladin Patterson to discover his writing genius, and Jess Moran to rise above her past and make possible the life she'd dreamed of as a child.

> "Some men see things as they are and ask why. Others dream things that never were and ask why not."— George Bernard Shaw, essayist, playwright

I first read Lewis Carroll's *Wonderland* tales as a child, but throughout the years, the stories continued to hold a special fascination for me, as they do for many adults. One phrase in particular came to mind during difficult times: "Start with one, practice, and soon you'll be up to six impossible things before breakfast." To one who, thankfully, had never stopped thinking in terms of *What if*, this fantastic concept had a ring of truth.

Although not in the ranks of Einstein or the Wright Brothers, my own experiences taught me that each time I achieved a win in the face of colossal opposing odds, I was increasingly able to manage the next hurdle. Hard lessons learned along the way, including the setbacks and struggles, were used to mold strengths and qualities that helped build the foundation for some future breakthrough.

This appeared to hold true for other achievers, past and present, whether they were famous and larger than life, or everyday people in their own private lives. In fact, the phenomenon held true for *any* success achieved by *any*one, under conditions perceived to be impossible.

Though I didn't have scientific evidence at the time to show why my hypothesis worked, I concluded that a person's ability to do what was

3

impossible was, indeed like muscle development: the more you work it, the more you can do. The less you practice, the less you can do.

3. An Impossible Inspiration

> *"Familiar things happen and mankind does not bother about them. It requires a very unusual mind to undertake analysis of the obvious."*
> Alfred Whitehead, mathematician, philosopher

Returning to Alice's conversation with the White Queen, I analyzed the thinking and results cycle of their opposing viewpoints. Reflect on the words *"I can't believe that. It's impossible."* Do you notice how disbelief is immediately linked to non-action? *"There's no use trying."* And how practice ties to belief...and progress? Undeterred by the whimsical source, I followed the trail of reasoning through cause and effect using contrasting approaches of Alice and The Queen. The result was astounding. As you can see from the Belief Chart located after Chapter 10, I was able to trace the self-fulfilling processes of both success and failure with simple but profound clarity. Such is the power of metaphoric thinking, as you will find in Chapter 5.

"Any fool can know. The point is to understand." —Albert Einstein, theoretical physicist

Such deductions went beyond mere hypothesis. They were rooted in fundamental natural laws of cause and effect. The I.M.Possible Muscle-building steps seemed to provide a real-world basic blueprint for achieving any kind of goal, from small to large, and for maneuvering productively through the myriad daily details, challenges, setbacks and detours en route.

"There is nothing as powerful as an idea whose time has come." – Victor Hugo

Before investing the time in writing an inspirational, personal development book based on such a novel approach, I obtained feedback from people of diverse ages, backgrounds and cultures. I was also determined to out expert professional opinions and guidance. And while there were many successful mainstream authors who would likely be interested, I'd learned through hard experience that it was going to be tough to find one who would support a newcomer with a new approach to personal achievement; one who would reach people—all people— on a level that the traditional experts had overlooked? After all, I wasn't one of *them*; I was from the lay people (that is, from the real world targeted by many of those experts who don't actually live in it).

Then I thought of David Coleman, better known as America's Dating Doctor. I'd met him several years before at a conference where he was a guest speaker. I wrote to ask if I could fly out for a meeting and get his feedback on a book I was writing. David agreed. It was testing time! I presented him with my story and draft material for my envisioned books.

David's reaction? "It's brilliant. I can't believe no one thought of this before. Anyone can incorporate this into their life. You have to write this book! I'll help you create workshops and change lives all over the world."

> *"Unless you undertake more than you can possibly do, you will never do all that you can." —William H. Drummond, poet*

What encouragement! An award-winning motivational speaker in my court! One more I.M.Possible thing accomplished. It was nothing short of amazing. Every action and accomplishment represented a fiber added or strengthened in my I.M.Possible Muscle and gave me new hope that I could achieve my much bigger goal. Each step completed, no matter how small or large, kept me believing. I realized that this is how people create and renew motivation to carry on, even when times get tough. Which was a good thing for me, as there were still a good many 'impossible' times ahead before *I.M.Possible Muscle for the Mind* would become a completed, published reality.

4. *An Impossible Obstacle*

I next undertook a study of the science behind I.M.Possible Muscle-building, in order to provide documented evidence for my assertions that this unusual blend of fantasy elements with daily reality could be as powerful a tool for others as it was for me. It was essential to make sure the platform I used was grounded in science fact and absolutely credible. The more I researched, the more evident it became that I was on to something. The micro-blueprint I was developing to rebuild myself could be customized and used by anyone else struggling to surmount their own seemingly insurmountable obstacles.

Despite life-long study, research and experience, I was now facing another formidable challenge. In order to bring this information to the rest of the world, I was going to need a highly credible collaborator with recognized professional credentials. Who would work with me, a first-time author with no Greek letters after my name?

Spearheading all the latest books on brain and behavior, self-development and change, were a broad spectrum of field specialists, from medical doctors, neuropsychologists, psychiatrists and researchers to talk show hosts and motivational speakers. I could not find a single instance where a foundational neuroscientist had personally collaborated on any of these mainstream motivational books, let alone on one with an approach as unconventional as mine.

Being the first has historically proven to be a double-edged sword. As Australian writer, Barry Jones, so aptly put it: *"If you have the same ideas as everybody else but have them one week earlier than everyone else then you will be hailed as a visionary. But if you have them five years earlier you will be named a lunatic."*

The only comfort I could find in this train of thought was a firm conviction that my favorite scientist, Albert Einstein, would have cheered me on. In his words: *"Any intelligent fool can make things bigger, more complex, and more violent. It takes a touch of genius—and a lot of courage—to move in the opposite direction."* That's the kind of scientist I needed to reach—one with an Einstein mindset! But, I needed something more.

> **"All who have accomplished great things have had a great aim, have fixed their gaze on a goal which was high, one which sometimes seemed impossible."**
> —Orison Swett Marden, writer

My scientist also had to be of the *neuro* variety, (involving study of the anatomy, physiology, biochemistry and pharmacology of the nervous system). Additionally, he/she needed to specialize in the areas of both brain and behavior. To raise the bar even higher, I wanted to work with one of the best. Hmmm. Despite a wide network of friends and acquaintances, I had never travelled in scientific circles. I had not one contact to introduce me. What were the odds I'd meet my match? In Einstein-speak: *astronomical.* But not *impossible*!

5. An Impossible Venture

In the true spirit of I.M.Possible, on April 10, 2010, I put my theories to the ultimate test. Through chill winds and pouring rain, I drove one hundred miles from Calgary to Lethbridge, Alberta, Canada, to a meeting with the scientist I hoped would become my mentor. In keeping with my determination to find the best in the field, I had chosen to approach one of the world's foremost neuroscientists: Dr. Bryan Kolb, PhD, FRSC, Professor of Psychology and Neuroscience. Co-founder of the Canadian Centre for Behavioral Neuroscience (CIBN), Dr. Kolb had developed novel training courses for behavioral neuroscience, co-wrote textbooks that were now standard in universities throughout the world, gave lectures globally, had hundreds of claims on his time every day, and according to a Centre administrator, was booked for up to two years in advance. With no prior claim to fame, no financial sponsor, and no introduction but my own, here I was, planning to ask this international icon, "Will you please collaborate with me on a book that blends fairytale and metaphors with scientific fact to give everyday people a blueprint for building their I.M.Possible Muscles?" The whole thing, as I thought about it, could have been a scene from Wonderland itself. In my imagination, I saw little Alice standing on my left shoulder, telling me I was crazy to try such an impossible thing. On my right, the White Queen kept whispering I.M.Possible words of encouragement into my ear. I brushed Alice to the floor and stuck with my mission. I was fully prepared to present my case to Dr. Kolb.

As I entered the busy halls of the daunting Centre for Behavioral Neuroscience—at that moment, to me, the dragon's lair—my courage almost failed me again. Can you blame me? Let's face it. I was venturing into his world, for all practical purposes, as an anonymous nobody. The distinguished Dr. Kolb is not only acknowledged amongst his peers as 'one of the founding fathers of behavioral neuroscience'[1]; he is also credited with fundamental research contributions regarding the nature of *brain plasticity*. [You may recognize this now universal term, which is a simple way to describe the reorganization of brain circuitry that occurs throughout our lifetime, in response to experience.[2]]

Dr. Kolb, himself, was seemingly no stranger to exploring new territory. Would this work in my favor or against me? (You'll learn more about his *impossible* battles throughout this book.) On the plus side, I hoped his own experiences with adversity might make him more approachable, more empathetic. On the minus side, all his victories were heady stuff. Increasingly, arrogance and inaccessibility seem to be characteristics that accompany great success. As Einstein had done in the realm of physics, Dr. Kolb had redefined the boundaries of impossible in the realm of the human brain science. Well, I would give it my best.

---

[1] http://www.cifar.ca/bryan-kolb; http://ccbn.uleth.ca/detail.php?record=25
[2] Bryan Kolb, Robbin Gibb, and Terry E. Robinson, "Brain Plasticity and Behavior," *Current Directions in Psychological Science*, 12, no. 1 (2003): 1-5.

The outcome of my personal version of the White Queen vs. Alice? My meeting with Dr. Kolb stretched from one hour to three. Gifted with not only a brilliant intellect, but a lively curiosity and sense of humor, Dr. Kolb listened with patience and genuine interest. Occasionally stumbling with nervousness, I explained the inspiration for and premise of *I.M.Possible Muscle for The Mind:* increasing one's ability to do the seemingly-impossible can be likened to building strength and ability in physical muscle.

- The more you practice in the right way, the more you build.
- The more you build, the greater the growth
- The more you do, the more you *can* do.

Dr. Kolb and I discussed the impact of mentally transforming the word *impossible* to *I.M.Possible*, and he recounted some of his own impossible-to-I.M.Possible stories, some of which are included throughout these pages. Finally, we reviewed the scientific validity behind the White Queen's 'six impossible things' quote that had inspired the *I.M.Possible* project. I asked questions such as the following:

JDN: *In the first part of this quote, Alice says, "I can't believe that." The White Queen tells Alice, "Try again. Draw a long breath and close your eyes." How do those actions help us in overcoming problems and challenges?*

DR. KOLB: *Closing your eyes helps to filter out distractions and focus your mind visually. Taking a long breath also helps you to redirect your thoughts. It engages your diaphragm muscle, which is situated below the chest, which allows more oxygen to get to your brain. This creates a feeling of relaxation and well-being and can help you to think more clearly.*

I showed Dr. Kolb the Belief Flow Chart I'd created. Was it was neurologically sound? (See the Belief Flow Chart in the middle of this book on pages 128, 129.) He confirmed this chart is an accurate representation of the cause and effect cycles producing success or failure, and accurately traced the relationship between thoughts, behaviors and outcomes. By the end of the meeting, we had agreed that Lewis Carroll's Wonderland Tales contained metaphors for principles that all the great writers, artists, scientists and inventors—past and present—followed consciously or unconsciously as they grappled against stupendous odds to reset their own boundaries for 'impossible'.

6. An I.M.Possible Outcome: The Dreamer and the Scientist

Finally gathering my courage, with pounding heart, I put the fateful question to Dr. Kolb. I began, "Against impossible odds, you wrote the first book on a subject that didn't exist and created a course that didn't exist. You revolutionized the thinking of neuroscientists. Now, I'm trying to create a book, using an approach that has never been used, to bring that science to the world of everyday people. It will revolutionize the way we think." I took the fateful plunge, "Will you mentor me?" As I waited, breathless, he looked thoughtful and then replied in his understated way, "This sounds like fun. I'm on board, happy to help." I almost fainted.

> "When I examine myself and my methods of thought, I come to the conclusion that the gift of fantasy meant more to me than my talent for absorbing positive knowledge,"
> —Albert Einstein

The fact that Dr. Kolb not only granted me the interview but agreed to mentor me on this project is testimony to the power of attempting the Impossible. I am grateful to him for taking the leap to conjoining imagination with knowledge. That other great scientist, Albert Einstein, would have applauded.

CREATING REALITY: WHEN YOU DON'T BELIEVE   DR. KOLB

Self-help books and motivational seminars pound away at us with the message "Success starts with belief. Just BELIEVE enough and you will achieve. BELIEVE. BELIEVE." The conversation quoted at the beginning of this chapter inspired me to challenge that assumption. The White Queen tells Alice to practice first, and then she (Alice) would believe. I consulted Dr. Kolb about this concept.

JDN: What if I've been hit so hard in life that I've built all these self-defeating pathways in my mind? What if I've become very cynical—so much so that I've lost belief? Should I just shoot myself in the head and end it all? Or, is the Queen's advice to Alice neuro-scientifically accurate? If you don't believe you can do a particular thing? Can going ahead and practicing actually still produce results? Can practice help you to turn doubt into belief or success?

DR. KOLB: Yes, because practicing is changing the brain. For example, when you first pick up a musical instrument to play, it feels like the first day in rehab class. Fingers can't do that. Your mouth can't do that. But by practicing you change those regions of the brain that control your fingers and your mouth. If you are learning to play the piano, the brain areas controlling both hands are changing, getting bigger. When you first start, you feel like you have two left hands, all thumbs. It doesn't matter if you believe or don't. If you just keep practicing pretty soon you're playing a little ditty or a little refrain, and you're going, "Wow, I can do this!" Because you actually change your brain with each little move. And the more you do it, the more each increment becomes automatic. So, once you've got the pathway, you don't have to build it anymore. It becomes auto-conscious. Then, you build to the next level from that one. So the practice itself changes the brain. It doesn't make big changes instantly. And it can revert back pretty darn fast if you don't keep it going. That's why you have to do it over and over.

JDN: So the White Queen, a.k.a. Lewis Carroll, is right. With the right practice we can do many things that appeared impossible when we began. *Because, as you practice, your brain changes. When you make progress, you begin to believe.* Now you are at a higher motivational level and a higher skill level than before. As you repeat this process, the transformation evolves. And this is how you achieve your first I.M.Possible thing. Is that correct?

DR. KOLB: Yes. The more you practice, the more permanent it will become. But as you said, you have to practice regularly, in the right way.

JDN: Voila! There it is. Don't pull the trigger.

CREATING REALITY: WHEN YOU BELIEVE   **DR. KOLB**

JDN: How is belief backed by practice? How is it achieved from a starting point of discouragement or disbelief? And how does belief accelerate learning?

DR. KOLB: You're getting reward now with each small success. It's like learning to play the piano and actually managing to play a piece flawlessly. There's a lot of reward in that, which is going to bring us back for more. It's the whole process of learning. The reason that we learn things is because we get reward, whether it's endogenous or external, for having succeeded in something. Interestingly, it's not just the results that spur us on. The reward, in itself, does cause the release of neurochemicals in the brain that will make [the brain] more receptive to change. For example, once I came to realize I could lope a horse and not have it run away, it became a lot easier to do that, but until I came to realize I wasn't going to lose control, I had a heck of a time. Of course, little girls get on horses and they just want to go fast. But I wasn't a little girl. I was a 50-something man who knew that he could get hurt. So, it is not until we've found and activated these circuits, that we can really let ourselves fully do this. As we practice and progress, it gets less and less difficult to do so.

JDN: So, another lesson here is: No matter who you are, it takes time to re-create yourself. True, it's easier when you're very young and pliant. You're not self-conscious. Spills and mistakes don't have the same embarrassment factor as they do when you're older. But that's the law of the way it is.

DR. KOLB: Yes. We've just got to deal with it, accept it as part of the process, if we want to achieve. Life never stops being a work in progress if you want to grow.

> *"All the great achievements of history have been made by strong individuals who refused to consult statistics or to listen to those who could prove convincingly that what they wanted to do, and in fact ultimately did do, was completely impossible."*
> —Eric Butterworth, minister, author

I.M.POSSIBLE WRITES IN THIS BOOK

This book is meant to be an I.M.Possible tool for YOU. **WRITE IN IT.** Underline, circle or highlight areas of interest. Make notes in the margins. Make a separate goal and progress journal for reference as you go along. Backtrack to any part of the book at any time. The exercises are made to imprint and cross-train. Discover what works for you! You don't have to color inside the lines when you are in I.M.Possible territory. Begin…right…now.

Impossible to I.M.Possible: Combine the imagination of your inner dreamer with a scientific approach: curiosity and desire to learn.

Your Name Here: _____

Imagine, then write down, something you would really like to do -- but fear you haven't got the ability to achieve. It can be a big goal or you can begin with a smaller one. Start with one early and simple step you can take. It's the I.M.Possible process! Work in any order you choose. (Principles for achievement don't change but the steps we must take, in order to get to our end goal, often do). Challenge yourself to use the I.M.Possible processes you will learn throughout this book to break through impossible territory. See how far you can go into the wondrous new world of I.M.Possible.

1. **Impossible Goal: (recreate as I.M.Possible)** – *Write it as though you were going to achieve it, even if you don't believe right now.*

2. **Impossible Inspiration: (recreate as I.M.Possible)** *Imagine people, places, environments, events, books, research articles; write down everything and anything that might give you inspiration on how to begin achieving the above. Don't be afraid to try something new!*

3. **Impossible Obstacle: (recreate as I.M.Possible)** *Identify any one obstacle, the first that you will face, as you move toward your goal.*

4. **Impossible Endeavor: (recreate as I.M.Possible)** *Imagine, plan and undertake an action that will help you to overcome the above obstacle. Do research, ask other people, consult a variety of sources and don't be afraid of trial and error.*

5. **Impossible Outcome: (recreate I.M.Possible Outcome)** *What have you achieved as a result of the above? Repeat these steps using processes you learn in this book.*

When you improve a little each day, eventually big things occur. When you improve conditioning a little each day, eventually you have a big improvement in conditioning. Not tomorrow, not the next day, but eventually a big gain is made. Don't look for the big, quick improvement. Seek the small improvement one day at a time. That's the only way it happens – and when it happens, it lasts. - John Wooden, basketball player and coach. Nicknamed the "Wizard of Westwood". Won ten NCAA national championships in a 12-year period—seven in a row—as head coach at UCLA, an unprecedented feat.

Alice: "I simply must get through!"
Doorknob: "Sorry, you're much too big. Simply impassible."
Alice: "You mean IMPOSSIBLE?"
Doorknob: "No, impassable. Nothing's Impossible."
—Alice in Wonderland, Lewis Carroll

2. I've Got an I.M.Possible Muscle?

"There comes a time in life when to get where we have to go—if there are no doors or windows—we walk through a wall." —Bernard Malamud, novelist

I-M-POSSIBLE / I.M.POSSIBLE: Adjective: [pronounced: I-Am-Possible or I-M-Possible]
I.M. (Possible) is an acronym for I Make (Possible),
1. A process or force through which the impossible (not doable) becomes possible (doable),
2. A successful outcome or result formerly thought to be impossible, unable to exist, be done or performed.

I-M-Possible Muscle/I.M.Possible Muscle (Both terms are acceptable): (Def.) A metaphoric 'creator' muscle characterized by the ability to break down the impossible into I.M.Possible elements and make possible a successful outcome. This muscle can generate force sufficient to move humans individually or collectively to a favorable outcome under conditions that appear to render such an outcome impossible.

****

I.M. Possible Muscle. We can't see it, but we have all have one. This muscle is capable of feats far beyond the combined abilities of every other muscle in our bodies. I.M.Possible Muscle gives each of us the capacity to move a mountain, re-sculpt a life or hold immovably on our own course in the face of adversity and opposing forces. Although the underlying basic processes are the same for everyone, this muscle will perform in unique ways for every human being on the planet, giving each of us differing means and abilities with which to push past seemingly impossible boundaries.

Whatever your personal preference—I-M-Possible Muscle or I.M.Possible Muscle—in this book the term is written as *I.M.Possible* and *I.M.Possible Muscle*. Whether written I-M-Possible or I.M.Possible think of the I.M. as an acronym for "I Make Possible!" Although the trademark and web domains necessarily require the I-M-Possible format, the term appears here as I.M.Possible to more effectively train your brain reset the word *impossible* to a condition you have the potential to alter. By the time you have completed this book, you will already be feeling the effect. You will think of 'impossible' in the same way again. Your I.M.Possible Muscle will be primed to immediately transform the word *impossible* to *I.M.Possible* and to reshape the conditions that are blocking your ability to advance.

How Can a Muscle Break Through the Impossible?

Have you ever felt trapped inside your own boundaries? The feeling that we are in an impossible situation can overcome us in many different ways. To name just a few: We may feel physically trapped in a home, neighborhood, relationship, workplace, or community that we desperately want to leave. We can become emotionally locked in by tradition, habit or expectations (either our own or someone else's). Physical or mental conditions, spiritual despondency or disillusionment, finances, the past, or even a culture or way of life can cause us to feel we are imprisoned and helpless to break free. Yet, there is a means available to you to cope and overcome.

Your I.M.Possible Muscle is actually a creator muscle, designed to learn, analyze, transform and create new realities. These qualities equip us all, as human beings, to produce outcomes that may have at one time appeared impossible. I.M.Possible Muscle has unique properties that enable it to:

1.   Remake or re-create itself,
2.   Create that which did not formerly exist,
3.   Interact synergistically with others' I.M.Possible Muscles.

A combination of brain, heart, courage and spirit, this invisible muscle is the world's greatest and most available untapped new energy source.

I.M.Possible Muscle: Picture the Invisible to Do the Impossible

How can working with a muscle we cannot see produce such powerful results? Physical efforts often give us the satisfaction of seeing immediate, visible physical results. As we develop this muscle, we can perform, transform and create at levels beyond the realm of mere physical strength or obvious capability. Additionally, your I.M.Possible Muscle is designed to reward you internally each step of the way, motivating us and increasing our abilities on many different levels.

> *"Ordinary people believe only in the possible. Extraordinary people visualize not what is possible or probable, but rather what is impossible. And by visualizing the impossible, they begin to see it as possible."* —Chérie Carter-Scott, author

Where, Exactly, Is My I.M.Possible Muscle?

I.M.Possible Muscle represents the combined mental capabilities and biological potentials in every human being that, when progressively worked and strengthened, can lift us into a miraculous creative zone so powerful, we can accomplish feats that once seemed impossible. By visualizing these interconnected elements as a muscle and muscle fiber, abstract concepts take a familiar form we can visualize and work with to achieve real-world results.

Think of your I.M.Possible Muscle as a blend of muscle and miracle located in your head. Your own unique brain is the core component of your I.M.Possible Muscle. The visual image is personal to you. I picture this muscle as shaped like a brain, but capable of being enlarged or reshaped with practice and flexed to perform difficult feats. The more it is trained, the more you can call on this awesome muscle to pull your goals and dreams towards you or to push away obstacles that would otherwise lock you in an impossible or futile position.

"Nature arms each man with some faculty which enables him to do easily some feat impossible to any other." —Ralph W. Emerson, essayist, lecturer, poet

Of course you know your brain isn't literally made of the same muscle matter as skeletal muscle, but the two are analogous in other scientific and practical real-world ways. What makes this mental muscle so extraordinary is its astounding range of capabilities and power. Your I.M.Possible Muscle can make you stronger than any situation or circumstance you have to face. How? Each physical muscle, no matter how well trained, eventually reaches the limits of what it can do. Your I.M.Possible Muscle power does not! It not only influences the action of every cell, muscle and organ in your body, it also has the ability to make endless internal connections, reorganize, heal, become smarter, stronger and more skillful, and adapt to changing circumstances!

15

"Researchers at the Cleveland Clinic Foundation conducted a fascinating experiment where for 12 weeks (five minutes a day, five days per week) a team of 30 healthy young adults imagined either using the muscle of their little finger or of their elbow flexor. Dr. Vinoth Ranganathan and his team asked the participants to think as strongly as they could about moving the muscle being tested, to make the imaginary movement as real as they could. Compared to a control group—that did no imaginary exercises and showed no strength gains—the little-finger group increased their pinky muscle strength by 35%. The other group increased elbow strength by 13.4%. What's more, brain scans taken after the study showed greater and more focused activity in the prefrontal cortex than before. The researchers said strength gains were due to improvements in the brain's ability to signal muscle."[1]

I.M.Possible Muscle is composed of more than just the brain. It also encompasses our growing I.M.Possible internal and external resources as we increase and refine our knowledge, skills, networks, relationships and achievements. Like all muscle, the more you develop your I.M.Possible Muscle, the stronger and more powerful it becomes. The more you practice, the more you do. The more you do, the more you can do.

Think of it! No other species on the planet is imbued with the insatiable creative spirit, intellect, imagination and drive that characterize our I.M.Possible Muscle. We can puzzle out meaning and solutions, make reasoned error corrections, and develop an endless variety of alternative ideas. It also enables us to develop an external network of people and resources outside our immediate circle.

Have you ever felt weak, inferior or in any way disadvantaged? This feeling will change! I.M.Possible Muscle growth and capabilities do not depend on physical body stature, social standing or IQ. You can develop your I.M.Possible Muscle, and a changed perspective, regardless of whom, or where, you are in life. *Put the processes into practice as you read. Write in this book. You will achieve more than you had imagined!*

"Impossible is like a great big cauldron. You know that some of the things swirling around in there are truly impossible, but it doesn't stop you from reaching in, fishing around and pulling out the things that are not really impossible, things you can actually make happen if you go about it the right way." —Ryan Williams, Film Producer

[1] *Neuropsychologia 42, no. 7 (2004), 944-56.*

What Makes I.M.Possible Unique?

"It is the word...which builds the universe and commands its power." – G. H. Bonner

I.M.POSSIBLE is a new and powerful term, representing a force that breaks through mental 'impossible' territory to uncover solutions that did not previously exist. As you go through the upcoming exercises you'll become aware of the impact of everyday words on your brain. You will understand why a shift to I.M.Possible thinking can make a significant difference in your thoughts, behaviors and outcomes.

I.M.POSSIBLE

~~POSSIBLE~~   ~~IMPOSSIBLE~~   = NEW BASE POSSIBLE

The brain cannot light up networks simultaneously for both *possible* and *impossible* in a coherent way. The two represent opposing concepts. I.M.Possible is the concept that will allow neural networks to bridge the two.

Possible ↔ Doable. Achievable. Open-ended. Impersonal. Possible can refer to either a positive or negative outcome. Such as "It is possible to win the lottery if I buy enough tickets." Or "It is possible to lose all my money trying to buy tickets to win the lottery." There is still enough of a natural safety net associated with this word to activate brain circuits associated with certain areas of our personal mental comfort zone.

Impossible ↔ **Not possible**. Unchangeable. Closed. Not negotiable. Impersonal. Impossible signals a mental no-go zone. "This wall is not going to move." "No possible solution here."

I.M.Possible ↔ I will Make way for a new Possible. A melding of above two distinct and opposing states, requiring a different circuitry process. A battle cry and personal declaration of commitment and accountability, characterized by willingness to explore every avenue, transitioning mind*set* to mind*shift* in order to wrest new realities from the realm of *impossible* things. Discomfort is necessarily going to be part of the process.

Clearly, working with what is possible is absolutely necessary, and does play an essential role. But dependence on 'possible' thought networks won't connect you with your ultimate potential. As we practice building I.M.Possible Muscle and our brain becomes familiar with the full meaning of

17

the term 'I.M.Possible', we will build increasingly stronger networks between those two main 'impossible' and 'possible' panels. We will be able to 'light up' and connect ideas that couldn't be reached from either place alone. "Rethink possible" is a useful concept for thinking in the context of existing platforms. But to actually break new ground, whether personal, professional, spiritual, social – *any area at all* - you must rethink the *impossible*.

In an essay addressing the ability of humans to predict the future, Sir Arthur Clarke, British author, inventor and futurist, summed up the I.M.Possible mindset when he stated: *"The only way of discovering the limits of the possible is to venture a little way past them into the impossible."*[2]

"There is no upper limit to what individuals are capable of doing with their minds. There is no age limit that bars them from beginning. There is no obstacle that cannot be overcome if they persist and believe." —H.G. Wells, sometimes called the father of science fiction.

I.M.Possible is an Action-Oriented Word

I.M.Possible doesn't wait for someone else to start. Rather, it is a force that *makes* things happen. Rather than sapping our strength railing against impossibilities, a well-developed I.M.Possible Muscle will respond by reconstructing the word *impossible* as I.M.Possible, that is, I-Make-Possible. One of the ways in which it does this is through pulling focus *away* from what cannot be done right now, *toward* what must be done. Next, it moves us to search out and do what *can* be done in the next moment, breaking the task down into manageable I.M.Possible elements.

"We could accomplish many more things if only we didn't think of them as impossible."
– C. Malesherbes, French statesman, minister, council for King Louis XVI

I.M.Possible Muscle is a force that can be progressively trained to kick in and get your brain in working in new ways when there is no one there to rescue you—no watchful enabler, safety exit, or sympathizer or rescuer's rope to keep you from falling too far. It is only by doing our own exercise and hard work, even when painful, that real growth takes place.

I.M.Possible signals the commitment to a personal moment by moment exploration and transformation process. Make that commitment now and step into the wonderland of I.M.Possible.

---

[2] Arthur C. Clarke, "Hazards of Prophecy: The Failure of the Imagination" in *Profiles of the Future* (New York: Harper & Row, Rev. ed. 1973).

I experienced this in a literal way a number of years ago when my husband and I began bicycle riding for exercise and recreation. Although the city had many beautiful bike trails, it was situated in a river area full of steep hills. Ours were racing bicycles, not mountain bikes, and so, not ideal for climbing. I hadn't been on a bike in years. My stamina wasn't the best. In fact, it was pretty pathetic. The first time out, I felt awkward on the bike and pedaled about five blocks before I began to complain. Lungs burning and legs were exhausted, I found myself in a major discomfort zone. I soon gave up, disgusted and mad. My husband, surely the world's most patient man, assured me I had done wonderfully. He said I had taken the first step—I tried. He encouraged me to try again each day. We could turn back at any time. I committed to a bike ride each day on those terms. I listened to upbeat music as I rode. Thus equipped, I reentered my discomfort zone and unconsciously began to build I.M.Possible Muscle. Astoundingly, each day I improved. My discomfort began to fade away as I morphed through the I.M.Possible zone. That first painful day, had someone told me within two months I would be riding my bike 15-20 miles at a time, looking for steep hills to climb, I would not have believed it. I was able to pedal my road bike to the top of hills so steep, I passed regulars from the local gym walking their mountain bikes to the top.

The I.M.Possible Zone

I.M.Possible Muscle takes you to impossible places but it doesn't leave you there. Impossible is a checkpoint at which you must face the facts which allow you to move in a forward direction. Travelling past any checkpoint requires a willingness to go through the necessary official 'exercises' in place to determine your eligibility for passage. Similarly, I.M.Possible Muscle-building processes were designed to most effectively move you through impossible zones of defeat - which you will soon recognize as a discomfort zone - and onto the next leg of your journey. Impossible checkpoints can be as daunting as an attempt at passage through North Korea. There is an instinctive reaction to look for a shortcut or a fly-over, or simply turn back. To continue moving forward past the impossible checkpoint, you will have to practice some new behaviors, work hard and make changes. (Sorry, this is not going to be sudden glory.) Achievement at this level always involves some discomfort and/or confusion, although seldom as perilous as a jaunt through North Korea. Nonetheless, the same principles for optimal success hold true no matter what your ultimate I.M.Possible goal.

> *"There is no greater joy than that of feeling oneself as a creator. The triumph of life is expressed by creation."*
> —Henri Bergson, philosopher

How Does I.M.Possible Muscle Change Your Life?

By progressively working your I.M.Possible Muscle, you will find the discomfort zone getting less and less uncomfortable. Just as happens with physical muscle, you will suddenly experience a growth spurt, gaining new strength. The discomfort zone will increasingly give way, allowing you entry into the new world you have opened in, and to, yourself. Energy and confidence will soar as you lengthen your mental stride. In the I.M.Possible zone, the motivation to do more increases. Eventually you will hit a sweet spot – that magical point where all the I.M.Possible efforts seem to merge, allowing you to break through to a victory that once seemed unattainable. The feeling is as though you could fly…

I'll never forget the first time I felt what it was like to be in what top performers and athletes call 'the zone'. We'd been cycling for some time and I was exhausted. Still a few miles from home, I sipped some water, relaxed into the tunes and kept going. I began to feel stronger, apparently getting my second wind. Riding on, an amazing phenomenon occurred: There came over me a physical, mental and emotional unity that can only be described as a natural high. My senses, physical strength, agility and riding technique meshed into perfect sync. I no longer felt tired. The feeling that I could go forever took over. It was like a form of flying.

When you get into the zone, old limitations and distractions fall away. Everything comes together in a way that seems like pure magic. You don't need to be an athlete for this to happen. Getting into the zone is not limited by age, or to one area of endeavor. The zone can be achieved by anyone in any area of life.

Hollywood film producer Ryan Williams says of this ultimate I.M.Possible zone: *"I know exactly what you're trying to describe. That's a zone that's fun to be in. And it's a real place. You see it in all walks of life. There's a sacrifice to getting in that zone and when you get there, it's precious. That is the place where the really impossible things happen."*

"I was no longer conscious of my movement; I discovered a new unity with nature. I had found a new source of power and beauty, a source I never dreamt existed."
—Elizabeth Fry, first woman to circumnavigate Manhattan Island against the tide and in record time

I.M.Possible Muscle – The Ability to Fly

"Aerodynamically, the bumblebee shouldn't be able to fly, but the bumblebee doesn't know it so it goes on flying anyway." —Mary K. Ash,

Does it seem like fantasy or science fiction to believe that you personally have a muscle that can be built by practice and that will help you break through the impossible? Although not physically designed for aerial mobility in the sense that birds and insects are able to fly, the miraculous way in which the human brain is designed equips each of us with a far more expansive means of flight. In fact, the Wright brothers trained their I.M.Possible Muscles so well, these two men were able to defy the odds and prove they actually *could* fly:

"In 1903 The United States Army was trying to develop an airplane but the plane wouldn't fly. The New York Times wrote, maybe in '1 million to 10 million years' they might be able to make a plane that would fly. Meanwhile, the Wright brothers were also experimenting with various flying machines. It was just eight days after the U.S. Army failure and the prediction of the New York Times that the Wright brothers were successful in flying the first manned plane." [3]

"The Wright brothers flew through the smoke screen of impossibility."
—Charles Kettering, inventor, engineer, businessman

Despite disbelief in high places, the Wright brothers succeeded in reshaping the boundaries of impossible. They, and everyone else who has achieved success against enormous odds, cultivated a distinctive mental *'impossible'* reset ability: "It's *I.M.Possible. I* will *make* a way for a positive outcome."

Said Orville Wright, *"If we worked on the assumption that what is accepted as true really is true, then there would be little hope for advancement. If birds can glide, why can't I?"* Orville wasn't simply big talk and dreams. To his *I.M.Possible* attitude, the Wrights added the necessary *I Make Possible* actions. Their successful invention of the airplane provides us, who are still struggling, with some apt metaphors for the power of I.M.Possible Muscle. In fact, we see in these two visionaries a spirit similar to that of Lewis Carroll's Alice, as she encountered each new facet of Wonderland:

"That's very curious! But everything's curious today." —Alice in Wonderland
"Isn't it astonishing that all these secrets have been preserved for so many years just so we could discover them!" —Orville Wright, aviation pioneer, on his view of the real-world Wonderland

---

[3] http://wrightbrothers.info

Whatever is yet not demonstrated as possible, but cannot truly be proven impossible, provides new frontiers for exploration and discovery for trailblazers. You don't have to invent or even own a flying machine or live a story book life. To create any new outcome, pioneers and trailblazers begin inside themselves. Wonder is a state of mind.

We all have a metaphysical ability to reshape our own wings, broaden our wingspan, teach others to fly and even journey beyond the physical boundaries of the earth. I.M.Possible is a wonderland open to *you*. You can, at any time, build your I.M.Possible Muscle and venture in. Your first I.M.Possible Thing will be only one of many...

Imagine → Practice → Believe → Achieve

WRITE IN THIS BOOK: *List from one to six impossible-seeming obstacles, small to large, that you would like to overcome. Check back on this list occasionally as you move forward in building your I.M.Possible Muscle. (The first time you break through an old barrier you will have gained a greater ability to achieve the next victory. One Impossible Thing conquered; two Impossible Things, and so on. With each item you are able to check off your list as completed, you will experience new strength in your I.M.Possible Muscle.)*

☐ **1.**

☐ **2.**

☐ **3.**

☐ **4.**

☐ **5.**

☐ **6.**

What other responsibilities must you attend to while working towards your I.M.Possible goal? *(Obviously, your physical health is one; family may be another, and so on.) The list is for you to determine. Only you can choose your priorities. Some may change along the way; others will always be core to your success at any point in life. List these responsibilities in order of priority as they relate to your goal.*

"Above all challenge yourself. You may surprise yourself at what strengths you have, at what you can accomplish." – Cecile M. Springer, chemist, entrepreneur, consultant

*"So either way I'll get into the garden,
and I don't care which happens!"*
—Alice, Alice in Wonderland, Lewis Carroll

3. I.M.Possible Beginnings

"Everyone who got where he is has had to begin where he was."
Robert Louis Stevenson, novelist, poet, essayist author of Treasure Island and Dr. Jekyll and Mr. Hyde

During the odyssey to re-create large parts of my life, I felt somewhat like a baby in an adult body—beginning at the beginning, not much to work with, and not sure of how to go on. Ironically, it was from babies that I gained some valuable insights on transforming impossible to I.M.Possible.

****

What do the following people have in common: Albert Einstein, Edmund Hillary, Navy SEALs, Alice in Wonderland and a baby? Each follows the same approach to impossible situations.

You're probably thinking, 'How could a baby possibly be a role model for building I.M.Possible Muscle?' From newborn to toddler, it certainly appears that infants don't do much to earn their way in life. The truth is, babies actually work very hard—in ways you might never have considered. In fact, it's during this time of seeming helplessness that the building of I.M.Possible muscle begins.

How so? Cast your mind back to your adventurous pre-school years. Or, if memory fails you, observe any child of pre-school age. Infants often cry because they are insecure. They have an imperative need for constant external rescue and reassurance. But as babies grow and develop new abilities, they become a little more confident and a little less uncomfortable with new people and situations.

When pre-toddlers watch bigger people stride around, they realize they aren't yet able to move in that same manner. But at that age, we didn't fixate on what we *couldn't* do. From early babyhood, we progressed toward the goal of walking by unconsciously practicing and developing the skills necessary for independent movement. We gradually gained enough strength and

23

coordination to attempt standing. We would get part way up on shaky little legs, and then fall when those unsteady legs buckled. We might have been scared and cried as a result, but as soon as we realized we weren't really hurt we would try again… and again… and again. Progress was all over the map, our movements often clumsy. There were times of frustration. But excitement and hope grew with every new success. With practice we experienced better results. Our confidence and determination grew. Then one day, it happened. We stood firm, our legs held, and we took those first two steps on our own!

What happened after that? Having achieved that milestone, we were then able to believe in the next impossible thing—walking. Step by tiny step, belief, ability and confidence grew. We kept trying. Little legs grew stronger, steps surer, and one day, the next impossible thing becomes a reality. Baby is walking!

Success is a natural outcome of the struggles and growth—literally the ups and the downs—we experience as newcomers to the world of human life. Fear or discouragement from falls is fleeting. Helplessness gives way to tiny victories that, one by one, moment by moment, culminate in the inevitable achievement of our goal. At this time, defeat is a temporary condition. To a baby, failure means try again or try another way. So confident do many little ones become, they believe they can do anything. Toddlers want to fearlessly climb, touch and explore everything in their world. They are generally heedless of danger or consequences. Everything we did when we were very young was filled with elements of the new and exciting. We were always reinventing ourselves. Life was a learning process and a creation process.

And do you know it still is? True, we are now older. Over the years we've accumulated boxes full of reality checks, whereas for most toddlers, that reality hasn't yet set in—they rarely think of anything as impossible. Their miniature I.M.Possible Muscle is in full swing. If we are capable of walking today (or had the capacity to walk at some point in our lives), this is basically how we accomplished it. Think about it. We started out thinking only of where we wanted to go or what we wanted to make happen. Despite the falls, scars and scrapes, we believed that progress and eventual success was worth the bumps, growing pains and even the occasional broken bone. Each time we would get back up and try again, we often did so with a new set of skills or knowledge.

24

As adults, many of us have lost that confidence and endless determination we had as toddlers. We may wonder what happened to it all. Much has probably happened in our lives to make us doubt ourselves. We may have become inflexible in areas where our thinking really should be 'flexed.' Our adult I.M.Possible Muscle now has weak spots that are lazy, injured or only partially developed. Somewhere along the way, we may face setbacks that put us at square one. Many of us don't have anyone to nurture or pick us up when we fall or to help us believe. Or if we do, they may not know *how* to help us.

Often we have to be our own rescuer. I have had to come to my own rescue, independent of outside human help, beginning from childhood. I've earned the right to tell you that, even if you are alone, if at this moment you have no other human being to pull you up or believe in you, an I.M.Possible victory *is* possible. It can be done. In actuality, all of life's decisive battles are fought first and foremost from the inside. I am not saying that we can overcome any obstacle on our own. Far from it. How successfully you fight, however, and whether or not you open yourself up to receiving the very help or knowledge you need, will depend on how you build, exercise and direct your I.M.Possible Muscle capabilities.

"All things are difficult before they are easy." —Thomas Fuller, churchman, historian

---

As long as you are alive, you remain involved in learning and self-creation processes that are ever-changing and ongoing. But it is up to you to make the decision to flex your I.M.Possible Muscle and develop the weak areas so you can better handle these processes. Each I.M.Possible quality put into practice weaves into and strengthens muscle fibers that work more effectively to lift you closer to new breakthroughs.

Our brain is like a master muscle that is working constantly to form, stabilize and re-create our realities each day. It is not naturally designed to give up, to fail and stagnate in hopelessness. The human spirit or life force does not thrive by languishing in *impossible*. From

> *"Your next interaction hasn't happened yet, therefore anything that has happened in the past has nothing to do with it. Leave the past behind and enjoy the moment like a newborn babe."*
> —Lance C. Beste, Beste-People

conception, we were designed for growth, learning, curiosity, enthusiasm, discovery, creating. We innately need to be doing and moving toward a higher goal. Human beings were constructed for purposeful activity and accomplishment, not only for oneself but for the benefit and happiness of others. Your particular role can only be determined by you alone—through struggle, adjustment and perseverance. Free rides won't take you anywhere worth staying. Remember, even a baby has to go through its own tiny, painstaking processes to create the possible from the formerly impossible. You can feed it all the best foods, have love, support and encouragement but what if, during this time, the little one just lay there, happy to be spoon-fed and carried from place to place? Could its muscles ever develop and grow strong? Would the child be able to suddenly walk independently? Of course not! In order to grow in physical abilities, baby must do the practice and hard work itself.

Baby-Step: It's Still the Way through Impossible

Achieving any kind of progressive success, including winning your own impossible battle, has another significant parallel with learning to walk. It's accomplished tiny step by tiny step. It is important to remember that people do not achieve the impossible in one leap any more than a toddler was born with the ability to walk. Mount Everest was not scaled in one step nor did humans land on the moon using the first rocket made. Sir Edmund Hillary, the first climber to reach the top of Mount Everest, said in an interview:

"I never had a vision to climb Mt. Everest. As with everything else, it just more or less grew. I started in the New Zealand Alps and I got more competent, and I climbed harder mountains there…. It was a growing process and a learning process. Never, in my early days, did I ever think of attempting to reach the summit of Mt. Everest." —November 1991 interview, American Academy of Achievement

Throughout history, mountain climbers, astronauts and many other everyday people—including babies—have proven that, with much work, impossible can be broken down and reshaped to achieve the I.M.Possible. In every instance, victory consists of all manner of tiny steps, forwards, backwards, up and down. And each victor would tell you they fought their hardest battles from the inside.

> *"It is not the mountain we conquer, but ourselves."*
> —Sir Edmund Hillary

As you practice moment by moment to develop your own I.M.Possible Muscle, your choices for building muscle fiber will increase in both size and number. With every new thing you do, you are reinventing yourself. With every old habit changed, you are creating new outcomes. **No matter where you are in life, you can always become more than you were the moment before.** When you have taken the first steps towards your impossible thing, your confidence will grow and the next

26

step becomes easier. Like the child who has finally learned to walk with confidence, you will one day run like the wind!

"'You're off to Great Places! Today is your day! Your mountain is waiting. So... get on your way!" —Dr. Seuss, "Oh The Places You'll Go!"

CREATING REALITY: NEVER TOO LATE   DR. KOLB

JDN: Dr. Kolb, there are a lot of parallels between the process of building I.M.Possible Muscle and your experience in learning to ride and train horses. Is it ever too late to recapture the feeling of *"Oh my goodness, I'm just starting out and I'm making progress! This makes me happy. This is exciting"*?

DR. KOLB: I didn't start riding horses until I was fifty-two. At the time, I was skeptical. Nobody thought it was going to be possible for me to start something so dangerous so late [in life]. I remember the first time I saw a spin, the horses flew around and around, rotating on one hind leg. As fast as you imagine a horse can go, double it. My eyes popped out of my head. I said, *"I can't believe they can do that."* I decided it was something I really wanted to learn how to do. So I had to start at square one—at pre-beginners, so to speak. I am certainly not an expert and, although I am still improving thirteen years later, I've far exceeded any expectations I ever had. But it took ten years to reach that level.

Because the first step is to get the horse to take one step. And then it just seems to take forever. But that's just a perspective. It just takes time and allowing yourself to go through the processes. One of my co-workers used to keep in his office a cartoon of this baby in diapers sitting there bawling and underneath it said, "But I wanna be famous now!"

"But I wanna be famous now!"

JDN: For people who like to be good at something right away, the learning curve is a tough one to endure.

DR. KOLB: It is a tough one for sure. And when you're surrounded by people who already do it so well, you feel pretty inadequate. But you have to look past that and say, "They once were like this. They may not remember it but I know it's true." Am I going to be able to ride in the next world equestrian games representing Canada? Of course not! Did I ever think that would be the case? No. I'm happy if I can do the pattern right, I don't fall off, and the horse doesn't run away. I think that's realistic.

JDN: At one time you thought that would have been impossible, didn't you?

27

DR. KOLB: Absolutely. My initial thoughts were, *"There's no way I could do those patterns. There's no way I could get the horse to do that. Especially at my age."*

JDN: And for us watching in the audience, watching you, we wouldn't know you ever felt that way. We wouldn't be sitting there saying, "Oh, he could never ride in the World Equestrian Games." We'd just be in awe, thinking, "I wish I could do that. But I couldn't. That looks impossible."

DR. KOLB: But it's not. It's what you've termed *I.M.Possible.*

I.M.POSSIBLE MUSCLE POWER EXERCISE: *Key points you'd like to remember from this chapter:*

Alternatively: Think of a skill you have already learned at this point in your life.

Now break down that particular skill into the tiny steps (including falls or setbacks) that you had to go through in order to achieve or develop that skill. This practice (breaking down a final accomplishment into micro-steps) is an exercise you will find to be invaluable throughout your life - and as you read upcoming chapters.

"People seldom see the halting and painful steps by which even the most insignificant success is achieved." —Anne Sullivan, American teacher, companion to Helen Keller

*"Take care of the sense
And the sounds will take care of themselves."*
—The Duchess, Alice in Wonderland, Lewis Carroll

4. I.M.Possible Science: Creating Reality

"It is astonishing what an effort it seems to be for many people to put their brains definitely and systematically to work." —Thomas Edison

Anorexia and diet pill addiction were two of the I.M.Possible battles I fought and won in my early twenties. Although the warning signals were flaring, I didn't have the necessary understanding to interpret them correctly. I ate very little, led a high-stress life (married, at the time, to an abusive alcoholic), smoked mega-cigarettes, drank umpteen cups of coffee daily, was addicted to diet pills, and exercised religiously. Young and seemingly strong, I took my body and mind for granted, believing they would never let me down. I didn't think I needed to have more than a basic understanding of how this was accomplished from the inside. Such knowledge seemed to be of practical value only in the realm of doctors. My reality check arrived when I collapsed and was hospitalized for two weeks. I was very angry at my body, feeling it had betrayed me. The doctors disagreed, saying, "You must have an exceptionally healthy constitution. Considering what you've put your body through, it's a miracle you're alive." I still didn't get it. Fighting to reclaim my health, I began to study natural medicine and nutrition versus pharmaceuticals. With this newfound wisdom came a blinding glimpse of the obvious. In all those years prior, I had never really understood that my body's ability to grow, heal, excel, and respond to the demands placed on it, were directly affected by everything—in any form—that I fed into or refused to feed it. This simple knowledge base made a life or death difference in my ability to overcome the addiction, and to my future.

As I consulted with Dr. Kolb for this book, I realized that I had been taking my mental functions for granted in much the same way. Such lack of awareness had affected my life on many levels. Like the body, the brain functions according to systematic processes. What I'd been feeding (or not feeding) into my brain directly affected the quality of the output. As before, I realized that the insights I was gaining could make a huge difference in the quality of my life. But, to know is one thing. To do is another. So now what?

****

Brain books targeting the mass market are all the rage these days. As a member of that mass market, I had found, and continue to find, much of

29

the science intriguing and even useful. But at some point, the ocean of material started to become information overload. When that happens, if you're like me, you start losing track of even the valuable stuff. Too, mixed in with the good was a lot of gimmicky-seeming hype. Doing random brain exercises for the sake of stretching my brain was clearly a clever marketing angle but didn't translate into anything of practical value. Most of us have pressing responsibilities tugging at our sleeves every moment. If there is any kind of serious crisis or trauma added to the mix - (the story of my life) - mind games just don't cut it. I remained interested, but uncertain as to just how all this brain information could make any difference to the average person.

Thanks to the unremitting patience and support of Dr. Bryan Kolb, and Dr. Roy Turner, input from various other experts, years of multi-faceted research—and slogging it out in the trenches of hells bowels with crap raining down on you; I've been able to figure out how we, in the everyday world, can immediately and powerfully make use of a basic understanding of how our brain works. My eventual success was grounded in an underlying faith as demonstrated through reality, self-sacrifice, endurance and deliberate practice. As I did, you can discover for yourself that you have more power at hand than you realize on any given day, and at any given moment.

So where do you begin to build the fibers of a solution in any challenge? Literally, inside your head. Why? Our thinking processes create the foundation for everything else we do. And the quality of our long-term outcome is determined by the makeup of the underlying foundation.

I.M.Possible Muscle: Needed at the Steering Wheel

Have you ever watched an episode of the *Worst Drivers* television series? The show provides compelling examples of how behavior choices and lack of knowledge affects—and can forever change—the reality of, not only the drivers, but those unfortunates around them. While we watch and cringe, unskilled drivers climb into a vehicle and careen through the course. They crash into obstacles, terrify passengers and pedestrians, grind the gears, burn out the clutch, blow the tires, stall the vehicle—all the while furiously swearing and blaming the car. We are amazed. The real source of the trouble is obvious. Even the best-designed vehicles can't overcome bad driver input. It's common sense! Unless you have at least a basic understanding of an automobile's design and processes, and know how to steer and redirect it under adverse conditions, sooner or later you are going to run into serious trouble. You might even take someone else with you. Everyone can see it except the bad drivers. Only when faced with extreme consequences, do they admit the need to change their thinking and behavior.

There is a somewhat unfortunate analogy between how we often manage our brain and these bad drivers. Many of us are careening through life behind the figurative wheel of our powerful brains, or are coasting along on a kind of auto-pilot mentality. Even though we're more or less keeping it on the road, we hit ditches, spin our wheels or smack into obstacles that could have been avoided. We set ourselves up to burn out, blow up or stall. I was no exception. However, with a few basic lessons and some practice, you will find, as did I, you have much more control of your vehicle and a lot more power under the hood than you thought. You might even come to enjoy the process of active driving over dependence on autopilot.

What Does it Mean to Create Reality?

"To know something about how your brain works is the beginning of being able to use it, maintain it, fix it, modify it and make it your servant rather than your master."

"We all create reality as we go along in life," states Dr. Kolb. "I start with what I'll call the brain hypothesis. That is, you are your brain. The main function of the brain is to create your reality. Because in the absence of a brain, there's no reality. And that reality is fragile in many ways, because it's based on your experiences."

Why is reality so fragile? The way each of us experiences life is subjective and constantly undergoing change. On many different levels, the way we interact with life each day (or the way life interacts with us) can alter the way we experience reality. Today's choices impact tomorrow's reality. As we think and act, we each create the reality of the person we are as well as the person we will become.

How do we do this? Our brain organizes around extremely complex network interactions. The three very basic brain functions are to:

1. **Generate knowledge** (i.e., thoughts, memory associations, sensory information),
2. **Produce behavior** (i.e., associative thoughts, actions, feelings),
3. **Create reality** (i.e., results: our reality, what we internally experience as well as our concrete external outcomes).

31

This system of organization creates our current reality, the ongoing creation and re-creation of our inner world over time. It's a circle of cause and effect. Consider a simple example: When we awaken each day, we begin to make choices. The questions in the next paragraph represent just a few of the options we might consider as the moments and hours pass. Our choice of response directly creates or influences the next reality we experience.

Will I get up or sleep some more? Am I happy, sad or bored? Will I go to work or will I stay home? Or will I look for a new job? Will I spend time with my child or get a sitter and go out with my friends? Will I get some exercise or sit on the couch and watch TV? Will I try doing this differently? Or will I stick with routine? I can do this, I can do that, or that, or this. I will choose this. This will become reality.

Keep in mind the three basic cause-and-effect brain principles outlined previously. How does each play a role in the way you personally experience your social and environmental reality? Apply these principles as you go through the book and in daily living. It will help you really *get* how, consciously or not, we personally create and can change many facets of our reality. Knowledge produces behaviors produces outcomes. Faulty knowledge equals faulty outcomes. With the *right* knowledge, we each gain a far greater ability to create I.M.Possible outcomes in our own reality.

Why You Are Your Brain

Your brain can truly be characterized as your I.M.Possible Muscle. Why? The brain not only reflects many of the characteristics of physical muscle, it acts as the master control center for all you do, think and feel. How does it accomplish this?

With the help of the nervous system, the brain is connected to networks within itself and the rest of our body. Nerve networks carry messages from our brain to, and from, all other parts of the body. Our thoughts and movements all interact in a synchronized, interrelated manner. So although any action in itself may appear simple, such as when we walk, dance, talk, chew, hug, smile, wink, or frown, many different brain regions are engaged. The most insignificant-seeming acts can affect us in powerful ways we don't consciously realize! From our thoughts, actions, facial expressions, muscle movements and emotions to what we look at, listen to, read—even our environment- each generates internal responses that act like a link in a chain of 'cause and effect' behaviors – and of course, outcomes.

Similarly, we seldom consciously think about how we use, misuse or neglect our muscles, unless we are actively training or working out. The cumulative negative impact generally doesn't hit home until we're forced beyond our comfortable range of movement or strength. This happened to me when I quit running and exercising for several years. One day, two friends talked me into running a marathon with them. I chose the 5k run, which should have been a breeze. To my horror, I had to struggle to keep going shortly after I began! Worse yet, I'd neglected to equip myself with water, or even motivating tunes. My lungs were burning, heart pounding, and legs ready to give way. If it weren't for a dogged determination not to collapse in front of all the onlookers, I would have given out long before the finish line. Of course, I suffered painful after-effects for days afterward, while my two fit friends were just fine.

Do you see the correlation to I.M.Possible Muscle? There is a cause and effect relationship between how effectively we manage challenge and chaos and the way we manage our own brain on a daily basis. Do you recognize how your thoughts, our actions can influence your outcomes? As with a driver and his vehicle, our mental input choice and quality will determine the extent to which we are able to shift and guide the output quality of your life.

How Do We Change Our Reality?

How do we, as humans, alter our reality for the better or even, for worse? How do we change direction? And how can we break free from a cycle of negative outcomes? Here is how the process works from within: Habitual or ingrained behavior is a result of patterns in time. These patterns consist of thoughts and actions. Our beliefs shape our thoughts. Our thoughts feed our beliefs. It is very important to realize that our thoughts *can* be changed. In order to create new thoughts and beliefs, however, we need to break the pattern. How can we do this? Try reverse change tactics. *If we change our actions, this will lead to a change our thoughts, which will in turn alter our beliefs and associated behaviors.* All of these things are connected, and can be reshaped with time. *One thing leads to another.* Not only does altering the brain change our behavior, altering our behavior changes our brain. It's quite amazing, really.

Your brain has the capacity to rewire itself and/or form new neural pathways—if you consciously do the work to make it happen. As with physical reshaping, neural changes require focused repetition and activity to reinforce new learning and produce new results.

If you understand basically how this process works, you will have a greater ability to alter 'impossible' behaviors. As you learn to think creatively and become aware of *how* you think (called *metacognition*), new brain pathways will develop. You can break out of old cycles, where responses are habitual, determined directly by past experience (referred to as *experience-dependent categorization*). New experiences will replace those which once dominated your thinking.

For most people, changing ingrained thoughts does not come naturally or easily. Often, the harder we try to think differently, the more rigid the categories become. Depression and Posttraumatic Stress Disorder (PTSD) are two prime examples of this. Having experienced both at severe levels, I can tell you firsthand that there *is* a way to rebuild thoughts and be productive once again.[1] It is surprising just how many areas of life can change for the better when we learn to identify and alter thoughts that have been giving our brain all the wrong signals.

During the writing of this book, I met a young woman, we'll call her Melanie, who believed that everyone looked down on her because she had a learning disability. Melanie worked in a major cosmetics store, was competent with the products and interacted well with customers. Despite the fact that she had worked at the store for two years, newer employees were regularly given preference over her in working hours, training and department choices. Melanie felt others often took advantage of her, but felt helpless to change anything. She became increasingly depressed and had very little self-confidence. Although facing severe ongoing financial struggles, Melanie was afraid to speak up for herself in case it made her situation worse instead of better. The cycle didn't seem to have a way out—that is, until we met and she gained some insight into how the brain works. Given this new knowledge, Melanie realized how past experiences influenced the way she thought of herself, and how this affected others. In brief, here is how she was able to change her reality: For years, Melanie's thoughts had trained her brain to categorize herself as a learning-disabled person. I pointed out that we all have weak spots in one way or another when it comes to learning or memory functions. She was, in fact, exceptionally quick at picking up new ideas, especially in areas that were important to her. Melanie was constantly underestimating her ability to learn new things because her self-concept included, "I have trouble learning anything new." She saw herself as someone who would always be at a disadvantage to so-called normal people. So to avoid their disappointment, she would always warn them in advance and excuse herself for being inferior.

In coming chapters, you will come to see how our self-concept is directly tied to goal achievement. So when we focus on helplessness, our

---

[1] The processes in this book will be helpful in any situation; however, it is important that anyone suffering from severe depression, for any reason, also seek qualified medical and/or crisis assistance.

brain processes align to support that input. Melanie had created brain networks focused on supporting a reality in which the dominant factor was her learning disability. With repeated use, those neural (brain) pathways strengthened and spread, while the networks that could lead to more positive outcomes remained undeveloped. By habitually telling others that she had a learning disability, Melanie was not only reinforcing that reality in her own mind, she was setting up her co-workers' minds to expect less from her and treat her accordingly.

Once she became aware of how she was creating this reality, Melanie used this knowledge to begin to create a new one. She was able to stop speaking to others about being disabled. As her actions changed, her self-talk (thoughts) changed, her focus changed, and with it, her brain networks. Melanie's achievements and confidence increased, producing a positive change in self-concept. This caused her to interact differently with her co-workers. The outcome? Within a few months, Melanie's relationships with her manager and co-workers improved greatly. She was given more hours and put in charge of the skincare department.

"The world as we have created it is a process of our thinking. It cannot be changed without changing our thinking." —Albert Einstein, theoretical physicist

While your or my weaknesses may differ from Melanie's, we are all alike in this respect: *Change does not happen spontaneously. Ingrained thoughts and habits have deep pathways.* We must work at creating and sustaining the change. Before that can take place, however, here's the cold, hard truth. Until we become conscious of the manner in which we deceive ourselves, we will continue to make choices based on faulty beliefs. Until we come to see how our thoughts naturally travel along the path of least resistance, and we are willing to risk doing something differently, we will continue to think the same unproductive thoughts and repeat old, outmoded patterns of behavior. We will miss out on insights and solutions that can only be found outside one's familiar way of thinking or responding.

Dr. Kolb sums up the practical science of creating reality:

"Change has to take place in order to become real. You cannot do nothing and expect a change is going to take place. If, and only if, change takes place, then it transforms how we experience reality. This is how you create your reality day after day, changing it or keeping it the same. If you think the way you normally think, you will act the way you normally act. And nothing will change. Your outcomes will follow the same pattern. That's reality."

How to Break the Cycle Before It Breaks You

So how do we change our reality when we are stuck in rut? Remember: *Behavior is a result of patterns in time.* This simple concept holds a key to breaking free from habits that hinder growth and breakthrough. When you get stuck in self-defeating behaviors, it seems impossible to change your reality for the better. What can you do to break a self-defeating cycle of thinking and behavior? *Break the pattern.* And keep on breaking the pattern. The first step? Do something differently from the way you normally would. What effect does this have? It initiates change in your brain. Dr. Kolb explains:

"You can start anywhere. If you have a new thought, and tomorrow you can remember that thought, then your thought changed your brain because it remembers something. To remember something, the brain has to be changed; otherwise it (the thought) doesn't exist."

Yes, every moment you are thinking, acting and feeling, you are changing your brain or keeping it the same. Doing the same things in the same way, over and over, creates nothing new. In fact, it generates change-resistance. Breaking a thought or behavior pattern is like breaking a circuit. Your brain can then switch to activating circuits that generate new thoughts and actions, stimulate mental flexibility and produce alternate solutions. Upcoming pages will provide coaching and exercises to help you do this. To free oneself from a repetitive cycle requires practice. With time and repetition, new brain maps will form, overwriting the old, moving you past former limitations.

"Running through the same thinking patterns forms an imprint on our brain. If you continue to reinforce changes in the way you think, new branches and connections in the brain will grow; the many links that correspond to your old ways shrink. For a very simple example, if you repetitively flexed your right hand over several days, the brain area for it would expand because more neural connections would have formed. But if you stopped doing this, and then switched to flexing your left hand, the brain area or brain map for your right hand would shrink because you were no longer using it, causing the map for your left to grow instead." – Dr. Kolb

Anyone Can Build I.M.Possible Muscle

Is it ever too late to begin? Absolutely not! According to Dr. Kolb, brain research evidences that you can, at any age, train or retrain your I.M.Possible Muscle to:

- *Uncover more of your inborn potentials, learn new skills, improve your learning ability,*
- *Discover new aspects of life and in yourself,*
- *Solve problems, move on, or overcome past difficulties, achieve goals,*
- *Reduce risk of conditions such as depression and severe anxiety,*
- *Increase your ability to recover from illness and injury, including brain damage,*
- *Decrease harmful effects of stress and depression.*

I.M.Possible *begins with exploring new thought avenues, new ways of acting in a given situation.* By reading this book and doing the exercises, you have begun. Try using some of the techniques in the course of your day. If the outcome is positive, repeat the process, imprinting the pathway in your brain. As you do so, it will take less effort for your brain to get there again. Eventually, you will find you have re-created your old reality, defeated a pre-existing weakness, and gained greater I.M.Possible Muscle power!

JDN: If I make the challenge, "You can change your life starting in the next moment," it's not just words? You really can?
DR. KOLB: Yes, you really can...

CREATING REALITY: MAKING MEMORIES   DR. KOLB

DR. KOLB: Here is an example of how someone or something becomes part of our reality in our personal world—how we create our reality. If I ask you to visualize your grandmother, I presume you can?
JDN: Yes, easily.
DR. KOLB: So how is it you can do that? Especially when your grandmother has not been alive for some time. It is because whatever regions of the brain you used to look at your grandmother, you've now turned these on again. It is easy for you to do this because the reality of her is stored in your long-term memory. How do the people in our lives become real to us? They have become imprinted on our brain through repeated exposure and experience. The frequency and intensity of our exposure and experience also affects the nature of that reality. That is why reality is so subjective.

The metaphor I use in class is: You've got Jack and Jill. They're on the little hill and Jack's got a pail of water. He stands on top of the hill and he dumps it down the hill. How does it go down the hill? In a sheet? No. It goes down the hill, making little rivers. Jill's at the bottom, she collects the water, brings it to the top and says, "Jack, do that again." So Jack dumps it again. Lo and behold, the water remembers the route. It takes the same route down the hill. And it does it over and over again as long as Jack repeats the same behavior.

You create reality in the same way. You construct neural pathways and frames of reference that generate knowledge and emotions as a by-product. Take, for example, the first time I see your face. That sensory experience goes through my brain and creates a pathway as it does so. If I never saw your face again or for a long time, I might not remember it. It might have a very fleeting sense of reality for me. But if I saw it again fairly shortly afterward, the same route is taken. So, what's happened here is the reality of Jamie DeNovo for me is now created by the change in brain structure caused by the experience. The more we interact, the more real we become to those who interact with us. The same processes hold true in all areas of life.

This may help you to understand why, hear about the death of someone you don't know, you won't experience the same emotions as you would if you knew the person well. The event doesn't hold the same reality for you. To take it a step further, the reality of the death would be processed differently in the brain of someone who loved the deceased person than it would be in someone who hated the person. The frames of reference for the deceased would generate different responses in the brain, which might, in turn, result in a variety of behaviors. One person's experience of the deceased may cause him to have feelings of sadness or grief, send flowers or attend the funeral. Another's experience of the same person may give rise to feelings of satisfaction or relief.

CREATING REALITY: A PILL IS NOT A SKILL   DR. KOLB

JDN: The chart in your textbook[2] shows that over 50% of the population battles some form of depression in their lifetime. That's huge. Depression and negative thoughts make everything feel impossible. How can we turn these into an I.M.Possible win?

DR. KOLB: Any feeling you have or reality you have created is a result of circuits that produce feelings. Take, for instance, sad and happy. Imagine the two. How can you shift from one to the other in your mind? What you have to do is realize that the happy circuits are there, you just haven't accessed them. To do so requires some kind of facilitator, which might be a book like this, which can help you to change your thoughts and actions. It might also need some other kind of therapy or pharmaceuticals to prepare the brain.

JDN: But pharmaceuticals and talk therapy just prepare our brain. We still need to produce the thoughts and actions.

---

[2] An Introduction to Brain and Behavior, 3rd Edition, Worth Publishers, Pp 592

DR. KOLB: Yes, absolutely. The drug or therapy talk itself won't do it.

JDN: So, the two biggest success tools we have are thoughts and actions, right? Or going for help, which is an action choice.

DR. KOLB: It's an action choice. The biggest factor in that is, if you go for help, you have to be prepared to accept it. Many people don't accept it. They go for it and then they're resistant to it. You have to be in a state that you're ready to receive it. Maybe that requires pharmaceuticals. But the pharmaceutical is not healing you. You're healing yourself.

JDN: It may be helping to equip you, but it's not doing the work.

DR. KOLB: Right. For instance, as part of therapy for people with strokes, we can give drugs, but the drugs are relatively ineffective without therapy while under the action of the drug. The drug is merely the facilitator to help the brain change. A lot of therapists don't get that. I think they're starting to. There's the whole idea that, *"I've got this physiotherapy,"* and, *"I'm seeing a therapist, so I'm doing my part."* The drug may or may not be helpful because what we're really trying to do is get *you* to change your brain. The brain processes are the key. Pharmaceuticals might provide something that makes the brain easier to change, that could facilitate or assist the therapy. But things can happen while under the spell of the drug. One problem is, when you're no longer on the drug, the brain becomes less plastic.

JDN: If you are taking some kind of drug to help you to heal mentally or physically, and you're not aware that you must also be changing your thoughts and actions, is it harder in the absence of that facilitator to maintain the same level of function? Would it make it easier in the absence of the facilitator if you've already been working to change your thoughts and your actions in conjunction?

DR. KOLB: Yes, absolutely.

JDN: More therapists need to inform their patients. When a doctor hands out an anti-depressant, he doesn't tell the patient, *"Look, this is just equipment. You've got to make some changes."*

DR. KOLB: There's an assumption encouraged by the pharmaceutical industry: we can fix this by just turning on a switch. It isn't so. In fact, all the data suggest drugs are no more effective than cognitive behavioral therapy. In spite of what the pharmaceutical companies will tell you, the number of people who respond positively to anti-depressants is far less than 100%—much, much less. Why is that, do you think?

JDN: So that people who take antidepressants without trying to change their behaviors will need more and more of a drug or will keep switching drugs?

DR. KOLB: Right. You need to do the therapy in conjunction, because the drug only facilitates the changes in the brain circuits. But the drugs themselves are not the answer. People just aren't aware of that. They don't get it.

39

JDN: They will after they read this book. The message is clear: You have to input conscious thought changes, and practice productive behavioral changes, to go with the drugs and the therapies, or it's not going to stick.
DR. KOLB: That is absolutely correct. It's not going to stick.

WRITE IN THIS BOOK: *Think of (imagine) a situation in which you would normally react with anger or impatience. What do you anticipate? What are your associations and images? What were the actions?*

Now visualize yourself in that same situation with this goal in mind: being calm and patient. What would you say differently?

How will you act differently, consistent with the goal?

What can you anticipate will be different about this outcome? (Become aware of how thoughts and actions affect your outcomes, shape your reality and become memories).

Make a deliberate choice and create reality in the next moment.
How have your words or actions brought a new facet of life into being?

"**True imagination is not moving the blocks of our reality from one spot to another; rather it is the pouring forth of an entirely new reality according to the wellspring of the dreams within our hearts.**" —Robert Tennyson Stevens, developer of Mastery Systems

"What is the use of a book
without pictures and conversations?"
—Alice, Alice in Wonderland, Lewis Carroll

5. Metaphor & Novelty: I.M.Possible Superpowers

5a. The Genius Power of Metaphor

"If a picture is worth a thousand words, then a metaphor is worth a thousand pictures." —
Dan Pink, motivational expert, author of 'Drive'

> ➤ *"Even when it's explained, I don't see it."*
> ➤ *"I really can't see how this applies to me."*
> ➤ *"I just can't picture it. It'll never work."*

Do you find it hard to remember new information? Or to use the knowledge you do have in a practical way? Is it hard to call up the right bit when you really need to put it to use? In the age of distraction, our attention is all over the map. I can't remember if I locked the car two minutes ago. Not surprising when you consider that:

* 90% of the all the data generated in human history was generated in the last two years.[1]

* The average American consumes 34 gigabytes / 12 hours of information per day – outside of work

* In the US, people who text send or receive an average of 35 texts per day

When routine ways weren't working, I looked for alternate means to not only understand, but transform essential knowledge into mental pictures and memory cues, so my brain could readily recall and apply the information with relative ease? It was while searching for an answer to this enigma in my own chaotic life that I stumbled on a solution in a most unexpected place.

---

[1] http://www.sciencedaily.com/releases/2013/05/130522085217.htm Source SINTEF

In the fantastic world of *Alice in Wonderland* I discovered the magic and power of metaphors and novelty.

What Is a Metaphor?

Metaphors can be words, pictures, stories or other types of symbolism used to parallel or represent reality. The essence of metaphor is, in the simplest of terms, a comparison that shows how two things that are not alike in most ways are similar in an important way. Metaphors create a picture in our minds to help us visualize or 'see' abstract concepts. They also provide a means for understanding something new – by connecting it with something familiar.

How powerful is the combination of words and mental images? Sven Lidman was a Swedish lexicographer whose idea to use illustrations with textbooks took European lexicography to new heights. Concerning the power of combining words with pictures, Lidman said, *"Through the picture, I see reality. Through the words, I understand it."*

The Genius of Metaphor Thinking

What does breaking through the *impossible* have to do with metaphors? Metaphor thinking is a powerful I.M.Possible strengthening device because it stimulates various brain spheres for higher-level processing, called *high-level perception*. One of the most important properties of high-level perception is that it is extremely flexible, giving humans the ability to think and reason in many different ways.

> *"The greatest thing by far, is to have a command of metaphor. This alone cannot be imparted by another; it is the mark of genius, for to make good metaphors implies an eye for resemblance."*
> —Aristotle, Greek philosopher

Metaphor thinking is an exercise that can stair-step us to insights we might never have grasped otherwise. Tremendous amounts of research have been done on whether computers can make the kind of intuitive leaps that would lead to breakthroughs and creative works similar to those made by human scientists, artists, writers and inventors. In all cases, even using the most sophisticated computers, the findings have been negative. Why? Because computers are unable to perform true high-level processing. They cannot independently reason and make connections between abstract concepts.[2] In other words,

---

[2] David J. Chalmers, Robert M. French, Douglas R. Hofstadter, "High-Level Perception, Representation, and Analogy: A Critique of Artificial Intelligence Methodology," *Journal of Experimental & Theoretical Artificial Intelligence* 4, no. 3 (1992), 185-211.

computers are limited to working with whatever information humans put into them. They do not have this unique power of your I.M.Possible Muscle.

Metaphors are very useful for switching on the "Aha!" light bulbs in our minds. We suddenly make sense of something that didn't make sense to us before. Such vivid emotional and intellectual connections remain in our memory, working at both conscious and unconscious levels.

You will find this book is filled with metaphors. One of the key reasons that every reader will take away something of value from it is because information is presented in ways that make it easy to 'picture' the concepts in terms of something visual which we can readily relate to events or situations in daily life. The association of ideas can be easily brought to mind.

Think back on just a few examples: in Chapter 2, building and training muscle is used to parallel building and shaping outcomes. In Chapter 3, babies help us understand the importance of micro-steps. Dr. Kolb used the metaphor of Jack and Jill in Chapter 4 to describe how our brain forms memories and behavior or thought patterns. What differences would you have found in reading the factual information if metaphors had not been used?

> **"Images and stories activate vast brain networks more than plain information, but we're more likely to connect to images and stories that are familiar."**
> —Dr. David Rock. author

The Power of Stories to Help Us Get Real

Fairy tales, illustrations and parables are types of *extended metaphors* that have been used throughout human history to teach children lessons in life. If you just lecture a child to get a point across, he or she will forget your words in five minutes. If you give them the same information in the form of a story, they will be able to repeat the story back to you with embellishments of their own. Psychologist Irmgard Thiessen observes, *"Fairy tales have messages on different levels and leave the metaphors open for interpretations…Children learn value systems and develop a sense of well-being by listening to stories. Life-values, such as honesty, loyalty, self-control, politeness, patience, and caring, are implanted in the personality of the child through these tales. They become a motivator for good or bad behavior, promote a sense of well-being and provide resources for coping with upsets in future life."*[3] As adults, our minds really

---

[3] Irmgard Thiessen (1988). *The Importance of Metaphors in Fairy Tales in Promoting Egostrength Values and Well-Being.* [Washington, D.C.] : Distributed by ERIC Clearinghouse, 1988. Paper presented at the Annual Meeting of the International Council of Psychologists (Singapore, August , 1988).

don't work all that differently. Captivating stories create vivid mental pictures that make information come alive and imprint its concepts on our minds. Just as we open storybooks and find life lessons reframed in the words, we can find life experiences mirrored by metaphor in all types of literature. The most powerful communication devices are filled with it.

The most compelling teacher in history, Jesus Christ, continually used illustrations to get his point across and reach the hearts of listeners. For instance, the eventual fate of the man who built his house on a sand foundation is contrasted with that of the one who built his house on a foundation of rock. This simple,

> *"Imagination is more powerful than knowledge, for knowledge is limited to all we now know and understand, while imagination embraces the entire world, and all there will be to know and understand."*
> —Albert Einstein, theoretical physicist

powerful metaphor using a common scenario helped people of all backgrounds get the sense of the consequences of basing their lives on choices that ultimately brought only temporary or illusory security vs. those that would prove to be of solid and enduring value.

Imagination, Knowledge and Metaphors

Imagination, when sparked with knowledge, can suddenly illuminate an insight or release a potential that may have been hidden for ages. Lewis Carroll's stories, rich in metaphor and [I.M.] possibilities, have been around for nearly one hundred and fifty years. I've read the stories and seen the movies at different times throughout my life, but it wasn't until 2007 that I saw the concept of an I.M.Possible Muscle in Carroll's works. *One thing leads to another.* This new perception then stimulated

> *"The significant problems we face cannot be solved at the same level of thinking we were at when we created them."*
> —Albert Einstein

higher thought processing, leading to a scientific analysis (as discussed in Chapter 1) of the White Queen/Alice conversation for confirmation of cause-and-effect principles found in the real world. My brain network continued to expand as I interacted with the additional brain network, Dr. Kolb…and so on. The more I practiced, the more I learned. The more I learned, the more I grew and the more I could do. This book grew into being only *as the work was being done.* It evolved. Each step opened way to the next.

The eventual outcome was the development of a micro-process that modernized and built upon previous science and wisdom, one that could be customized for personal achievement.

In the meantime, I began to decode other lines and scenes from Carroll's *Wonderland* tales[4] to reveal readily adaptable, fun-to-use principles for building I.M.Possible Muscle.[5] Successful completion of this task involved practicing what I preached. To crack the codes effectively, I had to power exercise using curiosity, openness to learning, imagination, knowledge, logical reasoning, experience, feedback and research. Did it take a tremendous amount of time, effort and perseverance? Yes. Was it worth it? Absolutely! I hope you agree.

CREATING REALITY: PICTURE THIS	DR. KOLB

JDN: Why are the *Wonderland* and *I.M.Possible Muscle* metaphors so powerful for helping us understand and remember abstract concepts?

Dr. KOLB: A key point here is visualization. Because if you just try to remember words and you haven't used some sort of, I'll use your word *metaphor*, it's quite difficult. For example, when I was a post-doctoral fellow, we had people who were amnesiac and one of the things we tried to get them to do was to learn word associations. Say you show them a picture of an apple and a train, or a book and a tack. These things are meaningless in a sense, right? [There's] no association. What we would do is say, *"Imagine a train running over an apple."* Now you've got a train steaming along and squishing an apple. You can visualize that. You can do the association. Or a tack stuck in the cover of the book. And so on. The amnesiacs started showing better memory, because they suddenly realized, "Oh, I see it. I can remember it." It's a whole different strategy and it works. The same thing is true here. If you have the image, the illustration ties to the words. It's going to be much easier to recall—which is your whole point.

It Worked for Me. Why It Will Also Work for You

All cause and effect is governed by an orderly and interwoven set of universal laws and principles. Understanding these relationships helps us to network the information with other areas of life. The metaphors in this book vary so people with differing interests and backgrounds can get the idea. But once you start looking, you'll find they're everywhere.

---

[4] *Alice's Adventures in Wonderland* (1865) and *Through the Looking-Glass, and What Alice Found There* (1871) by Lewis Carroll (Charles Lutwidge Dodgson).
[5] Jamie DeNovo, *The Wonderland Code* (Global Dreamers Guild Inc., 2012).

Metaphor Wonderland

> *"I know this world is ruled by infinite intelligence. Everything that surrounds us— everything that exists—proves that there are infinite laws behind it. There can be no denying this fact. It is mathematical in its precision."* —Thomas Edison. inventor

Consciously or not, Lewis Carroll, in his fantastic *Wonderland* tales, provided a visually captivating, eternal resource pool of metaphors that can serve as memory cues. These metaphors not only have a common, familiar source, but their novel use for personal daily living stimulates our powers of creativity, renews a sense of wonder, and provides a dash of humor, all of which signal the release of feel-good neuro-chemicals. There is even a metaphor representing the value of metaphors: says the Duchess to Alice in Wonderland: *"Tut, tut, child! There's a moral in everything if only you can find it."* The Duchess's words are a simple way to remember that we can use any situation to build our I.M.Possible Muscle if only we know how to look at it.

By now you will have noticed there are Wonderland *quotes* prefacing each of the chapters of *I.M.Possible Muscle For The Mind*. Have you been able to identify how each quote is tied to universal attitudes, behaviors or principles that we encounter daily? If not, go back and try the exercise. You may be surprised at the connections you are able to make with situations that arise in the real world. The fantastic nature of these metaphors, and the absence of stereotypical applications, opens the way to identify in unique way with different characters at different times. We can interpret each metaphor in many ways and circumstances.

> *"In all aspects of life...we define our reality in terms of metaphors and then proceed to act on the basis of the metaphors. We draw inferences, set goals, make commitments, and execute plans, all on the basis of how we in part structure our experience, consciously and unconsciously, by means of metaphor."* —George Lakoff and Mark Johnson. authors

Metaphors and Emotions

Metaphors help us to take in knowledge and exercise thinking ability at a deeper and more emotional level. Stanley Kubrick, regarded as one of the greatest filmmakers of all time, said of metaphor usage, *"Metaphors are very powerful things. They are cognitive super conductors that allow us to process and comprehend complex, metaphysical and conceptual ideas with succinct efficiency. Moreover, the power of metaphor goes beyond just the condensing of information and allows for emotional weight to be embedded into meaning.*[6] Big business and politicians know the significance of this fact. When we view their commercials, they want us to remember and connect to their product, even if it has no factual value to us. They know that the only way to get people to buy into their way of thinking is to tap into us on an emotional level. This approach works so well that advertisers spend billions of dollars each year creating highly visual ads and campaigns that work on our emotions. This same principle holds true when we want to change or take control of our own thinking and behavior. Unless we can find a way to lock in emotionally on what we learn, it's harder to buy into it. Without this emotional attachment, even the most valuable knowledge is just not going to stick with us in a meaningful way.

Go back to the problem we face in trying to retain information in working memory. How can metaphors help imprint ideas in our mind so we recall and relate to them in our own world? To help you see for yourself, let's revisit a *Wonderland* scene and break it down for real-life application. What does the conversation below reveal about ways in which we might unconsciously create, or influence, our own positive or negative outcomes? (For a hint, refer to the Belief Flow Chart in the middle of this book, pages 128 and 129.)

Alice: *There is no use trying. One can't believe impossible things.*
White Queen: *I daresay you haven't had much practice. When I was your age, I always did it for half-an-hour each day. Why, sometimes I've believed as many as six impossible things before breakfast.*

Can you see how the above *Impossible* conversation between the Queen and Alice contrasts two different attitudes towards the same difficulty? Let's take a closer look at these viewpoints.

1. **Alice:** By the time she had had this exchange with the White Queen, Alice had already experienced many things she had once thought impossible. So, why would she now insist one couldn't believe in impossible things? Why was she unwilling to try—to use some extra initiative in order to allow for this particular impossible thing? Because Alice's brain was still defaulting to the same impossible frame of reference generated by her old experiences of reality. Anything that

---

[6] Mike Jones, "The Power of Metaphor," mikejones.tv,
http://www.mikejones.tv/journal/2012/2/6/the-power-of-metaphor.html.

seemed impossible was an automatic cue that signaled, "Stop here. Nothing can be achieved beyond this point." (Interestingly, by the end of the stories, Alice has retrained her brain.)

2. **The Queen:** The White Queen's attitude was based on a contrasting frame of reference. She had developed neural networks that Alice had not. As a result, her mental and emotional responses to encountering the seemingly *impossible* differed from Alice's. The White Queen had a strong ability overturn impossible thinking, while Alice's kept trying to lean on past experience. The White Queen had built and strengthened her I.M.Possible Muscle through deliberate effort (i.e., practice) and progressive outcomes (i.e., results). In time, she had grown confident enough to tackle as many as six impossible things before breakfast.

At this point in her journey through Wonderland, Alice hadn't had to consciously work at originating an I.M.Possible outcome. She marveled, and then accepted when the impossible gave way around her time and again, but readily fell back on old attitudes as soon as she developed a new comfort zone. Alice was merely an *Impossible* participant while the White Queen was, in contrast, an active expert. The two were speaking different languages, reflecting the mental state of each. Alice was saying and thinking *Impossible* and the Queen was replying and thinking *I.M.Possible.*

Do you see how this conversation can be lifted out of fantasy and put to powerful use in your own world? The White Queen's advice follows a neurologically sound formula, and contains essential steps, for triumph over seemingly insurmountable odds.

> "If one particular style of thought stands out about creative genius, it is the ability to make juxtapositions between dissimilar subjects. Call it a facility to connect to the unconnected that enables them to see things to which others are blind."
> —Michael Michalko, author

If, for some reason, you can't (or won't) think in terms of metaphors, sadly, you'll miss I.M.possibilities and insights that you would not be able to gain any other way. More importantly, the dynamics of metaphor and novelty trigger our creative and thinking capabilities at basic and powerful levels. And, as I'm going to emphasize over and over again, the willingness to exercise our curiosity and imaginative powers is the beginning of achieving the I.M.Possible.

Impossible Things. Are they really impossible - or can they be achieved in ways you hadn't dreamed possible?

CREATING REALITY: A POWER METAPHOR	SCOTT

SCOTT: When I was in school, I had trouble learning. Very few metaphors were used to explain anything difficult. Nothing made sense to me when it was all numbers, formulas or concepts that were just words. They didn't seem to equate to anything in real life so I had nothing to mentally hang this stuff on to. The Professor for our basic electronics class didn't like teaching. Ninety-nine percent of the class failed. I mean literally failed. He gave us a make-up exam to get out of extra work. I remember doing that exam, going to him and saying, "Did I pass?" He looked at me and said, "What are you going to do if you pass?" I said, "I'm going to work for my Dad." He said, "Okay, you pass." I said, "Can I see my mark?" He said, "No." Three quarters of the class went through that. One of the things that stands out in my memory was that he just could not explain to us how electrons would flow in a circuit. We were students specializing in electronics, yet most of us were unable to get a grasp on that fundamental understanding of how current and voltage operate—how they flow. It was just, "There's some here, some there. This component does this, and this one does that." I'd say, "But how?" And he just said more of the same. So most of us never understood it.

Years later I was at a seminar for power supplies for some big manufacturer. The company rep started speaking, then stopped part way into his lecture and said, "You guys aren't getting this." Nobody said anything. He said, "Look, I'm going to back right up to the fundamentals because I've found that most people really don't understand how electricity flows. And then he said something profound. "Just think of it as water. Like water flowing through a hose. And all you've got is various valves—valves like you have to turn the water on for your garden hose. The water (or electricity) is there. We just need to turn on the valve or, in the case of electricity, the transistor, to allow it to flow." And suddenly it opened up everything else for me. Everything made sense. "Oh, that's how electrons flow. Think of it as water." Every kind of circuit suddenly made sense along with what the various components did. Because I could picture in my mind, where these electrons were coming from and how they were either heated or sped up or whatever. It was now a real thing to me. It wasn't just, "Oh, there's this here and that there and this thing does something."

I can relate to your statement about metaphors having a kind of magic. The metaphor using water to explain electricity opened doors that, a moment before, seemed locked shut, impossible to understand. I could completely understand and apply the principles from there on.

WRITE IN THIS BOOK. *As you read through this book, come back to this space and gradually list six of metaphors. As you list each one, think of (and record) how it could have real-world application for you.*

"Metaphors have a way of holding the most truth in the least space."
—Orson Scott Card, author

"The time has come," the Walrus said,
"To talk of many things.
Of shoes-and ships-and sealing wax –
Of cabbages and kings –
And why the sea is boiling hot –
And whether pigs have wings."
—The Walrus and the Carpenter,Through the Looking Glass,
Lewis Carroll

5b: The Power of Novelty

"One of your most powerful inner resources is your own creativity. Be willing to try on something new and play the game full-out." —Marcia Wieder, founder, Dream University

The ability to stretch and think in novel ways is a second high-level exercise for developing I.M.Possible Muscle superpower. Novelty is like reverse metaphor. Metaphor helps us see something new in a familiar way; novelty lets us see the familiar in a new way. Research shows that out-of-the-ordinary events and experiences stimulate the *memory* areas of the brain, so we remember them for longer periods of time than we would more familiar experiences. Metaphors then, especially when highly visual and novel, can serve as doubly powerful memory and thinking exercise partner for reshaping counterproductive behavior that is emotional, deeply ingrained or habitual. These problem areas create weak spots in I.M.Possible Muscle that must be re-trained and strengthened. (See Interview Files "Flexing to Happiness" in Chapter 9.)

Novelty also acts as a superpower exercise for creativity and discovering new relationships between things that formerly seemed to have no apparent connection with one another.[1]

Furthermore, when we see something familiar presented in an unusually original way (that is, from an entirely different perspective), there is an increase in our brain activity and connectivity in regions affecting learning and memory. Not only does it stay longer in memory, but our view of common situations can be transformed!

> Everything that is new or uncommon raises a pleasure in the imagination, because it fills the soul with an agreeable surprise, gratifies its curiosity, and gives it an idea of which it was not before possessed. –
> *William Makepeace Thackeray*

---

[1] http://consc.net/papers/highlevel.pdf

51

"Psychologists have known for some time that if we experience a novel situation within a familiar context, we will more easily store this event in memory. But only recently have studies of the brain begun to explain how this process happens and to suggest new ways of teaching that could improve learning and memory."[2]

Many writers travel to other countries. Why? Differences combine with similarities in new ways, and provide fresh insights. Novelty breeds new ideas. Reading is another all too neglected way of travelling in our techno-lazy world. With turn of the page, the *Wonderland* characters and scenes stimulated both imagination and thought processes. I was able to make connections to new insights during times of muddled mental darkness and tired cliché. There is a place in life for routine. But recognize the difference between the routine and the rut. Practice finding various ways to incorporate metaphor and novelty superpower exercises into your life.

Novelty and Boxing: Inside, Outside and Without

In order to overcome 'impossible' thinking in daily life, it is critical that we develop the range of mental flexibility that allows us to imagine other perspectives (stretch) and challenge our own perceptions (bend). The more skillful we become at identifying unsound or dysfunctional thoughts and beliefs that accompany self-defeating emotions and behaviors, the more we increase our ability to replace them with ones that are sounder and more productive. By extending our access to new insights, we can also expand our knowledge, our options and our future.

Novel thinking, using the box metaphor, happens on three levels: Inside the Box, Outside the Box and Without the Box. 'Think outside the box' is a metaphoric expression used to prod us to expand or re-think what is possible and come up with fresh, new ideas. But when you have a situation in which, no matter how hard you try to think outside the box, the obstacle keeps resurfacing, then what? How can we expand our understanding or creative potentials even further? The problem could be that our thinking is clouded because the box is obscuring the full view. Perhaps it's time to try thinking *without* the box! What does this mean? Find and eliminate the concept of impossible altogether. Instead of thinking outside the box, imagine there is no box at all. Bring in all the 'impossibilities'. Explore every scenario using 'What if' thinking. This fun exercise will help you get the idea:

---

[2] Daniela Fenker and Hartmut Schütze, "Learning By Surprise," *Scientific American*, 17 Dec. 2008, http://www.scientificamerican.com/article.cfm?id=learning-by-surprise.

Imagine you are caught in a traffic jam. What is causing the congestion? What types of traffic, traffic signs, vehicles, drivers, pedestrians and passengers do you see around you? What is the scenery like? How are you feeling? Can you visualize the person who is honking impatiently? (Is it you?) The semi that pushes up close behind you? The kids waving from the car in front of you? What are your reactions? As you imagine the situation, you are likely drawing on past experience and knowledge. I call this thinking "Inside the Box."

What would it be like to be caught in a traffic jam under the sea? What is causing the congestion? Visualize the various kinds of traffic, traffic rules, the drivers, passengers, the scenery you find around and beside you. Who or what is doing the lane splitting? Who would be most likely to drive a vehicle with the bumper sticker, "As a Matter of Fact I Do Own the Road", and what does that vehicle look like? Who is relaxed? Imagine and create your thoughts and actions as you make your way along to your destination.

To imagine this undersea situation requires you think *"outside* the box" when it comes to traffic, road conditions, drivers and everything else related to travel. You will probably get some very creative ideas.

Now imagine a traffic jam in a Wonderland/Through the Looking Glass kind of world. Imagine yourself in the midst of the traffic jam. What is causing the jam? What are the traffic rules and who is policing them? Visualize the kinds of traffic, drivers, passengers, scenery, pedestrians and whatever else you can see around you. Who or what is doing the lane splitting? Are there bumper stickers? Who is nasty? Who or what is relaxed? You can even re-think the whole concept of traffic jam. It could involve a crazy kind of jam fed to sweeten the travelers during rush hour! In this scenario, you can begin to think without the box, where you are far more able to exercise your powers of imagination and creativity.

Outside-the-Box Thinking vs. Without-the-Box Thinking

The laws of focus (more on this in Chapter 13) indicate that, as long as we're thinking outside *a box*, the box is still very much in the picture. You may be thinking outside, but very likely your thought processes are affected by the inclusion of the box. To illustrate:
I say to you, "Let's find a great new place to have dinner, somewhere outside the city." Think about it carefully and honestly. What suggestions might you make?

If it were my city, I'd start researching and suggest various restaurants or wayside eateries in towns within comfortable driving distance. We could discuss the possibilities of each. As ideas flowed one of us may even go farther afield and re-think 'outside the city.' Rethink possible. "Why don't we drive out to the mountains (or park, or seaside, etc.)?" We are thinking outside the box—but there is a still a limit to where we would look for a new place to eat. It is highly unlikely we would look into restaurants in a cross-country state or province. Because proximity to the city still dominates our thinking and decision-making processes.

And that's okay. There are practical reasons for boxes, just like there may be practical reasons for staying within a certain proximity to the city. But the purpose of this exercise is to allow you to experience the difference in activation of brain networking and thinking processes when we take a particular box out of the picture altogether.

What if I were to say to you instead, "Let's meet for dinner. We can go anywhere you want. No limits."? Now what are you thinking? Probably the first thing you do is clarify what I mean in terms of distance from your town or city. Because it's a completely different animal when you get rid of that particular box altogether. Once you are assured there is no box, how does your imagination open up? You are no longer mentally measuring the distance from your choice to the city. You can now travel around the world, so you begin to research and consider all sorts of exotic destinations. Because all mental barriers are removed, you think and research differently. You talk to people you may otherwise never have consulted. New worlds are opened for exploration!

Even the concept of dining can take on a different aspect.[3] Be a kid again in a tree house restaurant in New Zealand, or eat with the sea creatures in a transparent, undersea restaurant in the Indian Ocean! How about dinner in a bank vault or on a floating island? Would you dine just on cheese, or while swaying in the breeze? Cook it by yourself or be served by an elf? Could you eat up in the air, or inside a dragon's lair? Share a table with a cat. catch your dinner in a hat? (Apologies to readers and Dr. Seuss—couldn't resist.)

At any rate, you've got the picture, right? And what a picture it is. Yes, the city still exists. You may still choose to dine close by. But when it no longer dominates your direction, you are free to open doors to discovery you would not even have looked through before.

---

[3] See *The Most Unusual Restaurants in the World*, http://restoran.us/trivia/unusual.htm.

And that's the point: When we choose to limit our thinking to *outside* the box, we are keeping it in our mental viewfinder where it still influences our focus. However, when we choose to think *without* the box, we each still make the ultimate decisions on what to keep and what to reject—but our criteria for choosing will not be overshadowed by some aspect of our personal reality that is keeping us in no-win (impossible) territory. This applies to the outlook you bring to career, creative, personal, spiritual, family, social or any other goal.

> "Think left and think right and think low and think high. Oh the thinks you can think up if you try!" – Dr. Suess, To Think I Saw it On Mulberry Street

Think of the box as a container full of traditionally used *means* to accomplish a purpose you want to achieve. When you think without the box, you take the box away to make room for even the impossibilities to appear and be clearly considered. It doesn't mean you are committing. It just means you are stretching and flexing to your full I.M.Possible range. When you can freely explore the world of *"What if?"*, even the impossibilities are on the table. If they are truly impossible, we can take them off. Even so, I have found that, more often than not, this exercise pushes us through to new I.M.Possible territory. The following presented one of my most difficult thinking-without-the-box challenges:

When I was first faced with fallout of the events that robbed my husband and me of the life and future we had built, I realized I had to rethink everything that had once been possible. The bridges we had built had been destroyed and we were plunged into damage control measures on a scale we could never have envisioned. The situation required that I rethink 'impossible' on several levels in order to do what had to be done. I could not now afford the scope and caliber of professional expertise and guidance necessary, so through much heartache and trial and error, I retrained my thinking and re-shaped my perspectives to overcome one impossible hurdle after another. For every hurdle I overcame in my battle for justice, there were powers working against me to erect new obstacles. I searched in the box and out of the box to find ways to surmount each obstacle, only to find, like the heads of Hydra[4], another in its place. But I was determined to keep fighting. To me, there was really only one impossible thing: it was impossible that the main perpetrators should not be exposed and forced to pay the consequences. There came a time, however, when I had to summon the strength in myself to consider the unthinkable. What if...I declared an

---

[4] From Greek mythology, Hydra was a poison-breathing, death-dealing ancient serpent with reptilian traits and possessing many heads. For each head cut off, Hydra grew two more back.

optimal victory (discussed in Chapter 17) in what I had accomplished thus far, even though the outcome was what I had hoped? What if…I moved on with my life, instead of continually fragmenting my focus between the present, the future and the past? What if…I focused on the good things I still had in my life, the new blessings we'd experienced and on rebuilding with the new knowledge and skills I had gained during this time? Wait. To come so far, with all the evidence amassed and the sacrifices made, and just walk away now? Impossible! Never, never, never! But there it was. That was my box. Everything else I chose to do, every other advantage I had or could gain, was restricted by existence of 'the box'. I could not let it go. Getting justice. Alerting the community. Exacting retribution. All of my 'thinking outside the box' was really about finding new ways to work the box and make it into something that couldn't be made on my terms.

Then little by little, the I.M.Possible Muscle exercises began to shift the boundaries in my mind. One thing led to another. Eventually, I began to rethink not the possible…but the impossible. As I did, each small effort led to another. I began to see as well as feel the effects of all I was learning and practicing about my own I.M.Possible Muscle processes. As my book grew through fiber-by-fiber and moment by moment I.M.Possible exercise, so did my ability to break through other boundaries. Including those that had formerly entrapped me in a life-limiting box of hatred, anger and pain. Had I not been willing to think without the box, I could never have moved far enough beyond to make the writing of 'I.M.Possible Muscle For The Mind' an I.M.Possible reality. How thankful I am to be free of the box! Had I not disposed of it altogether, I could never have built this other structure, made of bigger and better, stronger materials.

It is important at this point to emphasize that the I.M.Possible exercises referred to herein are always aligned to socially, mentally, environmentally and morally responsible behaviors. I.M.Possible blends fantasy thinking with real-world assessment of long-term outcomes and consequences. In allowing full reign to our imagination, it is constructive solutions, thoughts and positive emotions we are seeking to create.

Regardless of who we are, we all have a box (or boxes) that limit our ability to realize our full potential. There is a time and place for boxes, definitely. There is a time to focus within the box and a time to think outside the box. However, I.M.Possible Muscle superpower lies in the ability to consider: Could the thing I am sure is impossible be the very thing I need to rethink?

"The difficulty lies not so much in developing new ideas as in escaping from old ones." —
John Maynard Keynes, economist

In-the-Box Thinking – *This is what I've got, what I am. These are facts I know to be true. Here are conditions or values that are not negotiable. This is the way it is.*

Outside-the-Box Thinking - *I'm going to re-think the possibilities to achieve this end. What if I could step outside the box of tools I've been using? What if I could bring something new to the box of possibilities I've been using so far? What could I do differently to improve on conditions that exist right now?*

Without-the-Box Thinking - *I'm going in the direction of the impossibilities. What if there was no box? What if B was my ultimate purpose in life and we lifted away all the rules now in place for getting from A to B? What if I could just walk away from the box, begin from where I am now and start from scratch? What is that box? What could I discover if there were no walls in my mind obscuring the view? In getting 'there' from 'here', in how many ways could I change 'here'? What if I changed the direction of 'there' and went in the another direction altogether?*

Albert Einstein was a visionary whose I.M.Possible Muscle would likely feature among the most highly developed in human history. Known for his concept of thinking like a child, his respect for the power of imagination allowed him to look at even physics and the universe in profoundly different ways. He understood that his imagination would help him see the I.M.Possible instead of confining his vision to what everyone else thought or assumed to be true at the time. By conducting *thought experiments* Einstein was able to see the world from new and different perspectives. Even this great physicist encountered formidable opposition when he refused to allow the accepted theories and beliefs of the day to define the boundaries of impossible. Einstein observed, "Great spirits often encounter violent opposition from mediocre minds." In fact, it was through exercising his great imagination that Einstein challenged and revolutionized scientific theory and reshaped human understanding of the nature of our universe.

In another spectrum, Theodor Seuss Geisel, whom the world knows as Dr. Seuss, author of the beloved *Cat In The Hat* series, revolutionized children's primers by infusing educational material with unique visual characters, humor, whimsy and imagination. His first book, *To Think I saw it on Mulberry Street*, was rejected by 27 publishers as 'too different from other juvenile books on the market'. Dr. Seuss book sales now top 300 million and he is the 9th best-selling fiction author of all time.

Step away from the realms of possible and impossible. I.M.Possible materializes for those who dare to challenge popularly perceived boundaries.

CREATING REALITY: GETTING THERE FROM HERE   SCOTT

SCOTT: One of your key thoughts was, *"Impossible things, are they really impossible or are they possible in a way you hadn't yet dreamed?"* That's something I run into at work all the time. We design covert custom surveillance equipment for law enforcement, government and industry. The reason this is so challenging for me is because they need to solve problems and gather information in completely new ways, often in ways no one has done before, so I need to figure out how to do that. Often I run into the phrase, "You can't get there from here." That concept materializes over and over again in my work. There may be some technological reason why I can't solve a certain problem. And I'm up against a brick wall trying to figure out what to do. So, I have to start thinking, *"Really, I just can't get there from right here. Am I giving up too soon, or is it really just not possible to do what the client wants?"* Sometimes I reach a point where I just push my chair back, look at the mess on my bench and go, *"You just can't get there from here."* Then I think, *"Ha, but that implies that you can get there from somewhere else."* So, I just stop trying from this place where I am and [start trying] to get *there* from a different direction, from somewhere else.

JDN: By just changing *here* [your present position].

SCOTT: Just take a step sideways. Go somewhere else. First, stop trying to get there from *here*. Go somewhere else, to a new *here* and try again to get there.

JDN: That's a key point. You go from thinking outside the box to thinking without the box.

SCOTT: In my technology approach, sometimes I have to go back, talk to the customer and get more information. Do I really need to capture what they said they had to get, in the way they thought they had to get it? Often it's difficult to get the information I really need because of the dynamics and sensitivity involved in this field. They don't want to tell me about all the bad stuff that's happening, so it takes an effort to really get the data I need. Sometimes you have to really dig to get the required insight. Often I find out, *'I didn't have to get there from here. I can start from another route and still get the end result—data for a conviction.'* Whether it's a different technology approach, gathering the data in a different way, it involves finding out from the customer that some other type of data will accomplish what they want. Often the reality is very different from what the customer initially said. The point is, I no longer try to get *there* from *here*. Instead, I've moved off from being stuck where *here* was. If I couldn't move where *there* was, data that would help prosecute or whatever, I moved where *here* is. I can move here. I can go somewhere else first. And then try and get to the result or destination. Usually I can. If not the first time, the second time, the third time... Eventually you find the way. Just change *here* if

58

you can't change *there*. And then you can get to wherever your particular *there* is. It still allows you to achieve the results you want, but sometimes it takes longer. Now, you've got extra steps, or there's more effort, more work. Or maybe, you have to learn new things, adapt in new ways, but still you *can* get *there*.

JDN: And the greater the value to your end purpose, the more you're going to have to reconsider moving off your starting point when *here* isn't working.

SCOTT: Yeah. Sometimes it's a step sideways, sometimes it's a step back and you can get a little bit depressed. You have to be careful not to get married to your approach. *"No, this is the only way,"* or, *"No, this is what I have to do."* And then you get stuck. You haven't changed *here* at all, when where you are starting from is the whole problem. You're just beating your head on a wall, hanging on to some ideal, circumstance or concept that needs to change. You've got to be willing to let go. The trick is figuring out if you're letting go of something that is creating a losing situation, in order to move forward. Or are you just giving up? You don't want to just give up, because maybe it *is* the only way. But the point is, change where you are or figure out if it's worth it to keep at it some more.

CREATING REALITY: IMAGINE IT REAL   RYAN

RYAN: I've studied some areas of neuro-linguistic programming. I use that on actors a lot, where, when you're talking to them, you say things like, *"Listen. Get this very clear in your mind."* You're sort of hypnotizing them with those words. It connects with something in their brain. They're glued to what you're saying. And then you say something like, *"Imagine. Imagine being very happy, and imagine…"* and you say the word *imagine* about ten times. Now their mind is clear and it's full of imagination. It doesn't even matter what you're telling them. You just tell them that their mind is *clear*, that they're using their *imagination*, about ten times in a row and sure enough they go into a place where they're very clear and very imaginative. And that's all I want. What you're saying doesn't even matter as much as some of the words you're using to program them.

JDN: So what does the word *imagine* elicit, what is the mental state, that you may not otherwise have been able to get?

RYAN: The words *clear* and *imagine* literally just kick-start their imagination. And that's what you want from an actor. You want them to be in make-believe. It's really basic and child-like what actors do. But a lot of them get real caught up in, *"Well, I don't want to look fat,"* or *"I don't want people to notice I have a receding hairline,"* or *"I don't want people to see my double chin,"* or *"I have pock marks,"* or *"Is my make-up good today?"* You know all these different things that are in an actor's head. You want to get them out of that and just sit there and be comfortable and play. *Imagine* puts them in the zone where they can do that.

Write In This Book: *You are trying to get from point A to point B. From here to there.*

Where is here?

Where is there?

Practice thinking 'without the box.' (The first thing to do is define the box) Suggestion: Ask yourself, "If I were to start by thinking outside the box in solving this problem, how would I identify the box?" Perhaps it may help to ask: "What is the unchangeable condition (or conditions) attached to the end goal (purpose) that I would like to achieve?"

What is in the box? How does this impact your ability to move toward your goal?

Now what happens if you take away the box altogether?

What happens if you change the identity of the box in any way you want? What would the new box look like? Use your imagination and allow yourself to be creative, to play with ideas.

What is in the box?

What are the tools and/or other means you could take away or use (resources, knowledge, experience, etc.) from inside the current box to achieve your end goal (purpose) and create a new box?

"Only the flexibly creative person can really manage the future, only the one who can face novelty with confidence and without fear. I have learned the novice can often see things the expert overlooks. All that is necessary is not to be afraid of making mistakes, or appearing naïve." – Abraham Maslov, psychologist, conceptualized a 'hierarchy of human needs', considered the father of humanistic psychology

"When I used to read fairy tales,
I fancied that kind of thing never happened,
And now here I am in the middle of one."
—Alice, Alice in Wonderland, Lewis Carroll

6. Impossible Dreams to I.M.Possible Realities

"It is better to believe than to disbelieve; in doing so you bring everything to the realm of possibility." —Albert Einstein, theoretical physicist, Nobel Prize laureate

Do you find it hard to believe that you personally have the intellect, or natural ability, to achieve an I.M.Possible success? At some point in time, you may have been given one or more of the impossible messages: *"There is no hope," "It's too late," "You don't have the brains," "You have no talent,"* or *"You won't succeed where others failed."* If so, this chapter is dedicated to you. Here you will meet people who have been told the above, not once, but many times. As you build your own I.M.Possible muscle, you, too, will come to realize the absolute unreliability of such sweeping statements.

Some people are born with resources that make life easier for them in many ways. It would be wonderful if we could all have the same starting-point advantages, but the present day reality is, quite simply, life is not fair. And it's getting less fair every day as the world grows more unpredictable, the justice system is replaced by a legal system, and consumer pockets are mined ever deeper to refill a bottomless pit of corporate greed. Most people are left with no option but to find a new way to cope—or to make one. This requires building our own powers of self-reinvention and making the most of whatever means and materials we can access.

I was not one of those lucky children born into a doting family. Nor did I have money to pave the way or patch over rough spots. It was a long and difficult process to triumph over those disadvantages. I didn't always appreciate it at the time, but this intense struggle actually helped me develop an inner 'something' that I now think of as I.M.Possible muscle.

What does that inner 'something' involve, and how can you develop it in yourself? The quiz that follows should give you some clues.

Who Am I?

The following people did not let discouragement, past failures, background or unfavorable odds define what they had the potential to become. They kept going where other people would have given up. Can you identify the I.M.Possible Muscle-builders described below?

Q: Her father died before she was four and her mother worked several jobs, so she and her younger brother were raised by their grandparents. As a teen, she was fired from working at an ice cream store because she kept forgetting to put bananas in banana splits. She entered the American Academy of Dramatic Arts but was sent home after a month, having been told she had no talent and that she should find another career. The school sent her mother a letter that said, "Don't put any more money into this. This girl will never make it." Who was she?

A: *Lucille Ball, of "I Love Lucy" fame. One of the most popular and influential stars in the United States during her lifetime, Ball was nominated for an Emmy Award thirteen times, and won four times. She was among the first recipients of the Women in Film Crystal Award, won a Golden Globe Award in 1979, the Lifetime Achievement Award from the Kennedy Center Honors in 1986 and the Governor's Award from the Academy of Television Arts & Sciences in 1989. She was the first woman to own a major film studio.*

Q: His teachers wrote him off as being too stupid to learn anything. He received only three months of formal basic schooling, suffered from poor hearing and was fired from his first two jobs for being unproductive. At age twenty-one, he was faced with trying to save his family from wretched poverty and foreclosure on their home. Who was he?

A: *Thomas Edison. Edison held 1,093 patents. Among his inventions were the household light bulb, an electricity system, the phonograph, a moving picture projector and the stock ticker.*

Q: She was nearly penniless, on welfare, severely depressed, divorced, and trying to raise a child on her own while attending school and writing a book. Who is she?

A: *J.K. Rowling. Author of the Harry Potter fantasy series of books, which has sold over 400 million copies and counting, won multiple awards, and is the basis of a blockbuster film series.*

Q: He didn't talk until he was four years old or read until he was seven. His teachers and even his parents thought he might have a learning disability. At age fifteen he dropped out of school. To get into technical college he had to write a special exam, which he failed the first time. He graduated with so-so grades and for years could only find odd jobs. Who was he?

A: Albert Einstein, the physicist who changed the future with his research and theories on space and time, light and energy. His theory of relativity led to the development of atomic energy, something he later regretted because of its misuse for destructive purposes.

Q: She was a self-taught artist who didn't begin painting scenes of her rural life until she was in her seventies. Who was she?

A: Grandma Moses. She became one of the most renowned artists of the 20th century.

Q: He had a difficult start in life and retired at age sixty-five with just a $105-a-month pension and an old car to his name. Setting out to sell the one thing he knew people would love, he slept in his car, knocked on doors, endured mocking because of his clothes, and was rejected over 1000 times before he found someone to back him. Who was he?

A: Colonel Sanders of Kentucky Fried Chicken fame.

How did each of these I.M.Possibilists overcome impossible?

- They were working towards something about which they felt true passion. They were true to their own I.M.Possible dream—their own dream—not somebody else's.

- They made a plan and followed through on it, making adjustments where necessary.

- All were determined to do their utmost to achieve their vision or die trying. (See Chapter 18, Collaring Evil.) Each had to deal with setbacks and detours along the way in the form of career changes, rejection, health crises, personal tragedies, etc., but each rallied and brought all they had back into the game.

You're probably thinking right now, "Oh sure, those people are famous. They had something special going for them. Talent and money sooner or later get all the breaks. You've either got it or you don't." *Wrong.*

> *"Miracles become manifest to the person who continues to look after everyone else has concluded there is nothing to see." —The Author*

Wrong. Wrong. Think about it. They *became* famous. The people whose names you recognize above became widely known for one reason or another, but money and fame came later, as a result of something much simpler: personal motivation and follow-through. *Their outcomes were created through a deliberate choice of thoughts and actions.* Each had progressively developed strong

I.M.Possible Muscle fibers. They had a passion for what they were doing and a determination to make something meaningful of their lives. They were able to fight and eventually overcome mammoth obstacles because their motivational force was stronger than the forces exerted by fear.

You are no different than they. Where you are at this moment of your life course does not determine where you will finish. Consider Winston Churchill, widely regarded as one of the most influential people in the history of Britain. Of his earlier days, Churchill said, *"I was, on the whole, considerably discouraged by my school days. It was not pleasant to feel oneself so completely outclassed and left behind at the beginning of the race."*

Do you know anybody in school who was 'the kid everybody laughed at?' Think about Thomas Edison, who said, *"My teachers say I'm addled . . . my father thought I was stupid, and I almost decided I must be a dunce."*

> **"To make our way, we must have firm resolve, persistence, tenacity. We must gear ourselves to work hard all the way. We can never let up."**
> —George Bernard Shaw, playwright

Have you ever been written off by others (or even by yourself) as someone who's the loser, who just doesn't seem to get it? Albert Einstein faced this challenge from his early years. His father, Hans Albert Einstein was ready to write off young Albert at the age of six, saying, *"He told me that his teachers reported that . . . he was mentally slow, unsociable, and adrift forever in his foolish dreams."*

Do you know somebody who has lost their job, is performing menial labor or trying to do anything they can to make a living? Look at Colonel Sanders who, at the age of sixty-five, began again from the bottom to create a new reality for himself.

If you think you need a certain social status in life to be successful, remember this: Before they achieved a certain level of success, these people's contemporaries saw them as nobodies. Their social circles weren't full of rich or famous high flyers. People thought, "What are they ever going to accomplish? They'll never amount to anything."

Do you believe success is impossible for you? Remember, before they achieved recognition these people were just like you and me. They had an I.M.Possible destination but no ticket to ride. Each had to make a way or find one, starting from ground zero. They had to wait and endure. They had to try again and again. And again. And again.

I am another in the long list of people who had to hew out a new pathway, beginning within; by trial and error doing whatever had to be done get to the next level…and the next. I know how it feels to begin at ground zero, fighting to recover from life-altering effects of horrific physical, mental, emotional and financial devastation—all at the same time. But had discouragement or circumstance been allowed the final say, you would not be reading this book right now.

How bad did it get? Let's just say if you'd been at the bottom of the barrel, you'd have had to look through a hole in the base to find me. My self-concept underwent a brutal period of breakdown, to the point where I could hardly recognize the person that had been *me*. It's easy to tell someone else what you would do if you were in their shoes, but when *you* are actually faced with your worst nightmare, you realize you knew nothing at all. You may *think* you know exactly what and who you are, but it is during those impossible times, in facing the unthinkable, that we are introduced to our real self. When nothing is left but the core, you find out what the core is made of. *What means more to you than this thing that has happened, or is happening?* To my surprise, I discovered that my commitment to live a meaningful life was stronger than the opposing forces that would hold me down and destroy what was left. And there was much more left than I could believe at the time. So if you feel hopeless at any time, take a page from my book. This is for you.

> *"What a [human being] actually needs is not a tensionless state but rather the striving and struggling for some goal worthy of him. What he needs is not the discharge of tension at any cost, but the call of a potential meaning waiting to be fulfilled by him."* — Viktor Frankl, psychiatrist, Austrian

If you really want to defeat impossible things and find your own personal success, or make a real and valuable contribution in this world, you don't need to be a scientist or a top athlete. You don't have to write a classic novel or invent something that will, as a by-product, make you rich or famous. You don't need official titles or formal approval to accomplish the most important things you will ever accomplish with your life. In fact, if you depend on those things, if you seek inner fulfillment through them, the most important things in life will surely pass you by. Neither great wealth nor fame is evidence of true worth. As goals in and of themselves, these are bottomless pits that breed only chronic dissatisfaction, self-centeredness and superficiality.

Moving forward you will come to understand how your true self-concept creates the driving force behind your goals and the decisions you make each moment in your life. You will learn how to change your self-concept to align with the purpose you want most to fulfill.

You do possess the ability to learn to navigate through I.M.Possible territory. *Tiny steps will eventually lead to great strides. It is within your power to change the way you drive your thoughts. It is within your power to readjust your course and manage adverse conditions along the way so they don't carry you in the wrong direction.* Each of us is ultimately in the driver's seat of our own mind and it is left to us—and no one else—to take control of the steering wheel.

The I.M.Possible Spirit

"Do not go where the path may lead, go instead where there is no path and leave a trail." —*Ralph Waldo Emerson*

I read the above quote when I was about twelve years old. The words seemed to have been penned for me. I knew I would not only make my own pathway, I would *have* to do it. Innovative as I was, even at a young age, there was no one else to get me started, no one to point the way. Self-determining success in spite of the nature of the challenges (which I now refer to as I.M.Possible success) was going to have to be a largely inside job. And as I discovered, it's always an ongoing learning process. As long as we live, we are, and need to be, a work-in-progress.

My way of looking at the world has often differed from the common or conventional. When in junior and senior high school, I found it increasingly difficult to relate to the other students. In the tiny farming community where I lived, the high school population was only about two hundred students. There was no support system or understanding of gifted children (for which I met the criteria). It was an incredibly lonely time in many ways and I couldn't leave it behind fast enough.

The road we must forge for ourselves is not an easy one. I.M.Possible is not for the faint of heart. By following the I.M.Possible Muscle-building formula, even unconsciously, I *did* accomplish the seemingly I.M.Possible—not once, but time and again throughout my life. I know from experience; my own and that of others who use this blueprint; it will hold up even under tragic circumstances and extreme challenge - when the dream changes and other I.M.Possible achievements have seemingly been laid to waste. There is still a way to transcend and thrive.

"Whatever you do, you need courage. Whatever course you decide upon, there is always someone to tell you that you are wrong. There are always difficulties arising that tempt you to believe your critics are right." —Ralph Waldo Emerson, essayist, lecturer, poet

I.M.Possible? What if I Just Don't Have the Muscle?

Were your grades in school terrible? Have you ever been told you don't have a low IQ? In his book, *How to Think Like Leonardo da Vinci*, Michael Gelb reveals important findings concerning the ongoing and diverse potentials of our brains. In each individual, intelligence emerges at different times, and with such a range of varieties and shades that it is impossible for any IQ test to quantify our true capabilities.

> *"Only the curious will learn and only the resolute will overcome the obstacles to learning. The quest quotient has always excited me more than the intellect quotient."* —Eugene S. Wilson. Dean of Admission. Amherst College

According to Gelb, *"The theory of multiple intelligences is now accepted widely and when combined with the realization that intelligence can be developed throughout life, offers a powerful inspiration for aspiring men and women."*[1]

This means *you*. Yes, you. You have incredible internal capabilities. Your I.M.Possible Muscle:

- Is more flexible and multi-dimensional than any supercomputer;
- Can learn seven facts per second, every second, for the rest of your life and still have plenty of room left to learn more;
- Will improve, not decline, with age, if you use it properly;
- Is *not* just in your head as it networks throughout your body and external world;
- Is capable of making a virtually unlimited number of synaptic connections with infinite potential thought patterns.

> **"Deep within the individual is a vast reservoir of untapped power awaiting to be used. ...The trouble with many people is that they got through life thinking and writing themselves off as ordinary commonplace persons. Having no proper belief in themselves, they live aimless and erratic lives largely because they never realize what their lives really can be or what they can become."** —Norman Vincent Peale, minister, author

What Does This Mean for You?

When asked what he hoped was the most valuable lesson people would learn from his autobiography, Sir Edmund Hillary said, *"I would like to think*

---

[1] Michael Gelb, *How to Think Like Leonardo da Vinci* (New York: Bantam Dell, 1998) 4-5.

that it would indicate to people that you don't have to be a genius or an exceptional person to take part in interesting activities and to ultimately be successful in them."

Never believe you can't accomplish a goal, or succeed against the odds, just because you scored low on IQ, SAT or other tests designed to quantify your potential. These cannot possibly take all the variables into account. *No other person can define what you are capable of doing, being, and what you will ultimately become.* There are many ways and time frames in which individual abilities and outcomes develop and appear.

For those who dare to think outside of, or without, a traditional box, there is, unfortunately, never a lack of people or circumstances to discourage and push you back in. At times it may seem like you are viewing the world from a completely different window than others around you. Opposing viewpoints may become uncomfortable for us in personal situations. Keep this in mind: The bold souls who are willing and able to forge ahead, despite opposition or majority disbelief, are the lifeblood of inspiration and progress. If everyone thought and perceived in exactly the same way, human originality and novel creativity would most certainly, by definition, be impossible. *Just as physical muscle training endows us with increasingly ability to perform feats requiring flexibility or strength, I.M.Possible thoughts and actions can make possible the strength and resilience you need to ably respond when anyone tries to influence you through demeaning talk about your value or abilities.* As with building physical muscle, becoming all we can be in a personal sense requires a willingness to go beyond present boundaries. Time and again, jeerers and naysayers have been proven wrong in a big way. The list of *impossible* underdogs, past and present, who went on to become I.M.Possible achievers, goes on and on. Many had been written off by others as hopeless or lacking in talent. The road along the way was often difficult, presenting twists, dangers, and detours. They suffered emotional upheaval, including great fear, moments of self-doubt, and confusion. But in the end each defied the odds and found success. Perhaps you are one of these people, and are moving on to your next I.M.Possible goal. If not yet, you can *certainly* join their ranks.

"Trust that little voice in your head that says 'Wouldn't it be interesting if...'; And then do it." —Duane Michals, photographer

---

Leonardo da Vinci once observed, "It had long since come to my attention that people of accomplishment rarely sat back and let things happen to them. They went out and happened to things." Although likely not familiar with da Vinci's observation, Cliff Young, a 61-year-old sheepherder, 'happened' to world-class athletes of the marathon world when he entered their ranks. His example should inspire anyone and everyone to fight their fears and rethink *impossible*.

Every year, Australia hosts a 543.7-mile (875-kilometer) endurance race from Sydney to Melbourne. Considered among the world's most grueling ultra-marathons, the race takes at least five days to complete. It is normally only attempted by world-class athletes, typically aged thirty or younger, who train specially for the event. Sponsored by big names such as Nike, entrants are equipped with the most expensive specialty clothing and footwear.

In 1983, a 61-year-old sheep farmer by the name of Cliff Young showed up at this race. He was wearing baggy, old overalls and had galoshes pulled over his work boots. People thought he was just another spectator until he walked over to the table to pick up his race number. Everyone, including those at the registration table, thought it was a publicity stunt. But, despite laughter and jeers, toothless Cliff went to join the other runners. The press and other athletes questioned him.

"Who are you and what are you doing here?"

"I'm Cliff Young. I'm from a large ranch where we run sheep outside of Melbourne."

They said, *"You're really going to run in this race?"*

"Yeah," Cliff nodded.

"Got any backers?"

"No."

"Have you ever run a marathon before?"

"No."

"Then what makes you think you can finish this race?"

Cliff replied, "See, I grew up on a farm where we couldn't afford horses or tractors, and the whole time I was growing up, whenever the storms would roll in, I'd have to go out and round up the sheep. We had 2,000 sheep on 2,000 acres. Sometimes I would have to run those sheep for two or three days. It took a long time, but I'd always catch them. I believe I can run this race."

When the race started, the pros quickly left Cliff behind. The crowds and television audience were entertained because Cliff didn't even run properly; he appeared to shuffle. Many even feared for the old farmer's safety. The professional athletes all knew that it took about five days to finish the race. In order to compete, one had to run about eighteen hours a day and sleep the remaining six hours. The thing is, Cliff Young didn't know that!

When the morning of the second day came, everyone was in for another surprise. Not only was Cliff still in the race, he had continued jogging all night. Eventually Cliff was asked about his tactics for the rest of the race. To everyone's disbelief, he claimed he would run straight through to the finish without sleeping. Cliff kept running. Each night he got a little closer to the leading pack. By the final night, he had surpassed all of the young, world-class athletes. He was the first competitor to cross the finish line and he set a new course record. When Cliff was awarded the winning prize of $10,000, he said he didn't even know there was a prize. He said that he did not enter for the money, and divided his winnings among five other runners who Cliff said had it tougher than he did. This act endeared him to all of Australia. And that crazy shuffle that everyone laughed at? Today, the "Young-shuffle" has been adopted by ultra-marathon runners because it is considered more energy-efficient. At least three champions of the Sydney-to-Melbourne race have used the shuffle to win the race. Furthermore, during this race, today's competitors do not sleep. Winning the race requires runners to go all night as well as all day, just as Cliff Young did. Cliff was a humble, elderly man who undertook an extraordinary feat and became a national sensation.

The people you meet throughout this book didn't wait for someone to create a pathway for them, or even to point the way. Most didn't just think outside the box; they didn't even see a box. (See, Outside-the-Box Thinking vs. Without-the-Box Thinking, Chapter 5b.) They just knew what they wanted to accomplish at the end of the day and persevered despite opposition, failure, learning curves, setbacks, and starting over again. I hope their stories and the knowledge you gain will convince you to do the same. Let nothing hold you back. *You can begin now. This moment.*

> *"At first people refuse to believe that a strange new thing can be done, then they begin to hope it can be done, then they see it can be done—then it is done and all the world wonders why it was not done centuries ago."* —Frances Hodgson Burnett, author

CREATING REALITY: I.M.POSSIBLE THINKING   TIM

TIM: People that have changed something in the world or their lives, changed anything—changed business, changed their approach, changed something—they've done something different. The herd is going that way. They go, "Hmm, I wonder what happens if I go this way instead?"

JDN: That's the common factor - deviating from norms that people blindly accept because it's always been done that way, or because the majority must be right. The ability to change, to let go and work forward in spite of our fear, is a component of a strong I.M.Possible Muscle. You never break new ground without leaving familiar territory.

TIM: That's not to say everybody needs to be a world leader, a corporate leader, or anything else except what is meaningful to you.

JDN: Heavens, no. Athletic achievements, the ascent of Mount Everest and so on are just analogies. We each have our own Mount Everest, and our own lesser mountains, to conquer first.

TIM: Yes, each of those examples is a simile to everyday living. You choose the application to your own life. Try doing it differently. I.M.Possible involves having the courage and a mindset to keep trying something differently until you get a different result, a productive result. The first place to start in order to deviate from the habitual or the crowd norm is within yourself.

WRITE IN THIS BOOK: *What does inspiration mean to you?*

When you think of your I.M.Possible dream, what is your fear in moving forward?

How do you imagine courage?

List three things that inspire you and explain why:
1.

2.

3.

Which of the above are available to you in some form now?

Write down one thing you would like to do that you would normally be too fearful to try. Start small. Note: Come back after you have read about the One-Sock Process in Chapter 11 and list the steps you would take to achieve this one thing.

"Security is mostly a superstition. It does not exist in nature, nor do the children of men as a whole experience it. Avoiding danger is no safer in the long run than outright exposure. Life is either a daring adventure, or nothing." —Helen Keller

"Oh, how I wish I could shut up like a telescope!
I think I could, if only I knew how to begin."
For you see, so many out-of-the-way things had happened lately, that
Alice had begun to think that very few things indeed were really impossible.
—*Alice in Wonderland, Lewis Carroll*

7. I.M.Possible: Is It Really Like a Muscle?

"Great ideas originate in the muscles." —Thomas Edison, inventor

Picture a time in your life when you were at your peak power physically. Maybe you are at a peak fitness level now. How much more can or could you accomplish compared to a time when you were not as strong or fit? Think carefully. How many areas of your life are affected for the good or ill by your level of physical strength and fitness? Not just physically, but mentally, emotionally, professionally and socially?

Your personal I.M.Possible capacity grows in a similar way to muscle power. How so? The more you mindfully work it, the stronger it becomes. The more you train it to stretch and bend, flexibility range increases, fibers lengthen, and so does your reach. The more you practice the more these changes become instilled in muscle memory. As your skill and discomfort endurance increase, so does your ability to manage weighty - or subtle - challenges that would otherwise pin you down or bar the way to greater long term outcomes.

Impossible to I.M.Possible - Why Get With the Muscle Program?

In this chapter, the parallels between physical and I.M.Possible Muscle are intended to provide a strong visual technique for working your way through challenges. Why devote an entire chapter to this correlation? If you don't know, review the information on the power of metaphors! Using the tangible form and familiar framework of muscle development, you will be able to visualize how the accumulation of small, even minute efforts grow, and increasingly transform, your ability to change Impossible to I.M.Possible.

To our brain, there is no real separation between these two types of muscle. Our thought and behavioral patterns determine how each develops. There are many similarities in their respective processes. Understanding this muscle transformation process can help you lift past the impossible time and again.

It is easy to see (and gratifying to demonstrate) when we have well-developed physical muscle, isn't it? Flexing our arm muscle is the simplest way to command a muscle to appear so we can see it. The first thing any small boy does when he wants to show off his strength is to proudly flex his arm to make a muscle. We may not be a small boy, but in a similar way, we all want our muscles to respond well when we call upon them to do so. Unfortunately, we often don't realize how out of shape we are until we find ourselves in a situation where we need to use strength we *thought* we had. Have you ever had to move a piece of heavy furniture or other object, and with all your heaving and straining, it just won't budge? Then you know how frustrating it can be to call on muscles that simply don't have the strength to get the job done.

Similarly, we can take for granted that we have the ability to deal with life's myriad challenges right until the time we come up against a roadblock to happiness or success that simply will not move despite all our efforts. When faced with challenges involving physical muscle, we know that, in order to be better equipped to meet those challenges, we have to exercise to get stronger. However, when confronted with mental, emotional or other life-related obstacles, we're completely baffled in terms of what we need to do. Why is this?

Well, would you expect to build the muscle required to lift two hundred pounds simply by walking over to a 200-pound weight every day and making an attempt to lift it? Probably not. This is true of impossible obstacles in any area of

> Just as we develop our physical muscles through overcoming opposition - such as lifting weights - we develop our character muscles by overcoming challenges and adversity. - Stephen Covey

life. They are not overcome head on. The truth is, impossible situations are seldom only about an elusive goal or the obvious obstacle. Impossible to I.M.Possible breakthroughs are achieved first and foremost as a by-product of building, training or refining particular internal qualities or characteristics. By learning how to do this, and then practicing in the right way, we can work our way through, over, around, and in the face of enormous obstacles—not just one, but many. Let's examine the following as a purely hypothetical example:

You find it impossible to join in physical activities such as biking or hiking because you know you would never be able to keep up with everyone else. You tell yourself, "It's impossible. I'd have to work out and change my diet. I can't do it. Not possible. I try to get motivated by reading up on hiking and biking. I've bought the workout equipment. But I'm still sitting at home alone, feeling more impossible than ever."

In this situation, it is easy to feel overwhelmed. When we get entrenched in impossible mode, we have to work our way out moment by moment, building the necessary muscle fibres through deliberate exercise.

So How Do I Flex to I.M.Possible?

In our example, you have *to give up* some relaxation time in order *to get* time to work out physically. Now the obstacle isn't that you aren't fit. The obstacle is your comfort zone; relaxation mode. In relaxation mode you meet with another obstacle; high-fat and/or low-nutrition drinks and snacks. It's likely you are addicted to salt, chemical and sugar-laced unhealthy foods. To knock down these obstacles, you need more than advice and work out equipment. Why is it so hard to do what you need to do? The more you repeat any action, the more deeply you become invested. Your brain is trained to justify and rationalize your position; your body has maladjusts. If you can't change the action at this level, you're stuck at the gate. Think about it. Riding or hiking with physically fit friends may have been your impossible goal, but is your fitness level the first and biggest barrier? No. It's the fact that you feel helpless to fight your way through many obstacles keeping you in an impossible state.

> If you plan on being anything less than you are capable of being, you will probably be unhappy all the days of your life. -Abraham Maslow, psychologist who developed Hierarchy of Needs

I.M.Possible exercises build fibers that intertwine to form the underlying structure (the traits) necessary to lift you out of a state of paralysis. You will increasingly be able to break away from comfort zones and tolerate the discomfort that actually acts as a transformation process, making way for I.M.Possible goal achievement. Your I.M.Possible workout is underway even as you flex your mind through these chapters.

Consider just how many areas of your life are affected by your level of physical fitness. As you improve your overall I.M.Possible fitness level, you will also discover unforeseen advantages in your greater I.M.Possible Muscle strength and flexibility. Many other challenges will no longer seem as daunting as they once were!

Why 'Use It or Lose It' Isn't the Whole Story

Putting our muscles to work is the very reason for their existence. If we don't use them, they waste away. The better conditioned and trained our muscles are, the more useful they will be when we need them to take on extra challenges. Now imagine. What would happen if you flexed your arm and got a very poor or painful response? You would not be able to depend on your arm for anything but the most minimal of tasks. You would not be able to lift a bag of groceries or push a vacuum. Would that concern you? It should.

Our brain learns not to activate muscle areas that are never called on to perform. This is true for both physical and mental muscle. If we fail to regularly exercise our I.M.Possible Muscle or neglect it in certain areas, we (1) won't develop vital skills, and (2) can become lazy and ineffectual. As this process continues, we increasingly feel unable to overcome challenges or achieve goals that could, in fact, be well within our power to reach. The best way to improve any muscle, is to begin small and work our way to progressive gains. You will be shown many ways to do this.

> "Character cannot be developed in ease and quiet. Only through experiences of trial and suffering can the soul be strengthened, vision cleared, ambition inspired and success achieved." - Helen Keller

Every barrier you encounter presents an opportunity for you to build I.M.Possible Muscle. As you hurdle small barriers, you build new fibers and strengthen your powers of accomplishment. The more we strengthen and train our I.M.Possible Muscle for full use by practicing the right way, the better condition it will be in to tackle bigger and even impossible-appearing obstacles as they present themselves. What is involved in practicing 'in the right way?

Exactly How Does I.M.Possible Muscle Grow?

I.M.Possible Muscle does not develop by repeating the same old exercise routine day in and day out any more than physical muscle could be trained to perform Cirque du Soleil feats through such means.

How do muscles become stronger? When you exercise physically, muscle fibers strengthen, grow and become denser. The myofibrils inside the fibers increase in size and number; capillaries develop in order to bring more blood to the muscle. All these actions increase the size and usefulness of our muscles.

We don't at first grow new muscle fiber but we begin to access more of the muscle we already have and use it more effectively. Each muscle's many working parts are coordinated more efficiently. Once this initial reaction is complete, further gains come from actual new muscle growth and development. I.M.Possible Muscle growth works in a similar way. We gain an increased ability to make more mental connections to various types of possible solutions, to increase the strength of those connections, and to follow through with actions as necessary to accomplish important goals. As we build, we can also increase our access to networks and possibilities that exist outside of ourselves.

Why We Need to Break It Down to Build It Up

The stress we direct at our muscles (for example, by lifting weights) breaks them down at microscopic levels. Our body's natural response mechanism to this stress is to adapt by rebuilding the specific breakage with stronger materials, better suited to meet the new demands.

Just as the actual breakdown of our physical muscle precedes its remodeling, growth of our I.M.Possible capabilities requires breaking down old patterns and responses so it can be rebuilt and strengthened. A refusal to bend blocks our ability to grow. We will continue to feel pain until we allow ourselves to be broken down, so we can be reshaped.

At first, there is likely to be some very real discomfort. Most of you have experienced this in a literal way after starting a new exercise program. However, in both cases, new improved muscle tissue materials gradually develop and are ready to use in more strenuous situations, providing greater strength, flexibility and resiliency.

As we build muscle, we soon learn we have a wealth of untapped potential that needs only to be switched on. *By simply choosing to not take the easy or familiar path, to ask something new of oneself, is to begin the process of awakening and exercising that potential.* Yes, there will be discomfort and the going can be tough at first. We create momentum as we persevere. Gains become more rapid and transformation occurs on levels that would not otherwise have been attained.

"The only way to be a champion is by going through these forced reps and the torture and pain.... The last three or four reps is what makes the muscle grow. This area of pain divides the champion from someone else who is not a champion. That's what most people lack, having the guts to go on and just say they'll go through the pain no matter what happens." —Arnold Schwarzenegger, bodybuilder

Impossible Muscle Fibers: What Do They Do?

Physical muscles are composed of bundles of individual muscle fibers. Each individual fiber is made up of thousands of thread-like myofibrils. In I.M.Possible Muscle, these threads are formed through the individual thoughts and actions we make in every moment of our lives. The dynamics taking place at these micro-levels determine the degree to which the bigger fibers ultimately grow and develop. Myofibrils weave together moment by moment to form the bigger I.M.Possible Muscle fibers. These, in turn, make up bundles of experiences, abilities, skills, qualities, beliefs, accomplishments and resources.

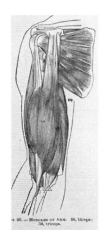

4. 58. — Muscles of Arm. 58, biceps; 59, triceps.

The connective tissue that binds these fiber bundles together is our belief system and values. There is an interconnected relationship between the tissues and fibers of both physical and I.M.Possible Muscle. The qualities of one directly affect the characteristics of the other. It is this combination of tissue and fiber that defines and gives our I.M.Possible Muscle its capacity and strength. Combined, these fibers are the foundation for our overall I.M.Possible power and potential.

The extent to which we work and develop the *quality* of our I.M.Possible fibers will determine the extent to which our lives ultimately have meaning and purpose. For example, we can choose to actively pursue personal fulfillment, perhaps in a specific profession or by developing supportive, healthy friendships and relationships (= high quality). Conversely, we can choose to waste innumerable hours aimlessly internet surfing, playing video games or sitting in front of a TV screen (= low quality). In order to reach I.M.Possible goals, there is no remote control or wishful thinking shortcut to build and strengthen or detoxify those fibers in the areas that cause us to remain in impossible mode.

"Nothing good comes in life or athletics unless a lot of hard work has preceded the effort. Only temporary success is achieved by taking shortcuts." —Roger Staubach, football player

---

How Do We Build Our I.M.Possible Muscle Fibers?

The secret to I.M.Possible success lies in becoming more and more effective at building the individual fibers, starting with those directly in front of you. Each I.M.Possible Muscle fiber we build represents a support component required to attain our big-picture goal. Every moment in which you choose an action that leads you to a healthy, rational goal or productive direction helps to create stronger goal-oriented neural connections. Like tiny myofibrils, each of the moments of choice builds upon the others to form the quality and number of fibers that give underlying strength to your I.M.Possible Muscle. The fibers in front of you may include (but are not limited to) the following:

1. Any productive, positive action that pushes you away from negative influencers or counterproductive activities (resistance and defense training)
2. Every consecutive thought or action that leads you one step closer toward a specific goal (interval and endurance training)
3. Every step toward a supportive or interim goal, the accomplishment of which is necessary to the achievement of a greater goal (cross-training and flexibility training)

Consider this very simple example. Your I.M.Possible goal may be to travel to Spain for a week's vacation but this seems impossible because you have a tendency to buy impulsively and your credit card is maxed out. For your I.M.Possible Muscle to help you overcome the obstacles between you and this goal you will have to build the three types of fibers:

- Awareness/Cognition Skills: focus, realignment, error correction;
- Abilities/Qualities: patience, self-discipline, and focus on the genuine goal (not the decoy provided by impulsive shopping);
- Anticipation/Association: platforms leading to, or supporting future goal achievement (milestone accomplishments and outcomes).

Examples of fiber-building exercises to reach your goal might include:

1. A productive action that lifts us away from negative activities or influencers: **Instead of going to the mall, you take your travel guide and head to the park. (Bonus fibers: Walking to the park also feeds oxygen to your brain and body, and saves on transportation costs.)**
2. A positive, productive action that takes us one step closer to a specific goal: **You make lunch at home instead of eating out, thereby saving money to help pay off your credit card bill.**

3. The achievement of an interim goal, the accomplishment of which is necessary to the achievement of a greater goal: **You pay off your credit card bill so you can take your dream trip to Spain**.

Direct your attention on each achievement, feel it, and generate an awareness of 'internal reward'. To help strengthen this awareness, ask yourself the following: *What does this accomplishment say about me? What part of me allowed this achievement? What is now increasingly possible for me?*

If you get stuck in chaos mode and don't know where to start, or feel unable to start, the following chapters will give you a variety of powerful aids, including a micro-formula, for getting to and through the mental blocks and on to fiber building.

How I.M.Possible Threads and Fibers Network and Cross-Train

Enter a single word or phrase into the search engine of your computer. How many different connections will your computer make using that single entry? When my editor performed a Google search for the word *happy,* the computer delivered more than 3.2B (yes, billion) responses relating to the word *happy*. Now, imagine feeding that same word into a super-computer, one with [at least] a million times more information-networking capability. In the case of the word *happy,* the results would be 3,200,000,000,000,000 (six more zeros!)—a number we cannot even begin to put into perspective. Does such an uber-computer exist? It absolutely does. *It is your brain.* The brain doesn't simply take in information on one level. Everything we do and think processes through multi-level, multi-layer super computer-like networks—often affecting us powerfully in ways we do not even realize. This comparison—which is in fact, quite valid—gives you some idea of the complex interactions that take place between our bodies and our minds.

There is, thankfully, a critical difference between your brain and the computer. Often technology engineering providers know that the functioning and interoperability of their software and applications are hugely constrained by corporate agendas and other external realities over which we, the end user, have no control. Each of us, however, has a personal ability to build, expand, debug, direct and reprogram much of our own personal internal systems and networks.

Productive moment by moment choices leading towards a positive end goal build a strong foundation for our brain to become solution-oriented. Remember, *the key to success in physical or mental muscle building is a willingness to practice with intent to improve, movement by movement.* The more I.M.Possible networks and pathways are strengthened, the more we are able to override ingrained, counterproductive thinking with productive actions and more powerful solution-oriented thought processes.

Learning to repeatedly make I.M.Possible choices moment by moment results in brain behaviors and transformations from which you can build up, step by step, to the next I.M.Possible phase. Phase by phase, your brain will become more powerful and more resourceful in helping you search out, recognize and develop new ways to navigate sudden changes or crisis situations. And then—one day—you will find you can lift the final barrier between you and your I.M.Possible goal.

CREATING REALITY: I.M.POSSIBLE NETWORKS   DR. KOLB

DR. KOLB: I want to debunk the idea that specific functions are isolated in a specific place in the brain; there are networks involved in everything we do.

JDN: So, different areas of the brain may be likened to an engine for specific mental or physical functions, but every time I create an action or thought, it's not just the motor but entire networks that are involved and interact..

DR. KOLB: Yes. Thoughts and actions—anything influencing our mind and body—don't affect just one brain area. The connections that we build are very powerful because you are affecting entire networks. The connections and interconnections that take place are numerous.

JDN: Sort of like when I lift something. It feels like I'm using one particular muscle, but in reality many others are being used or changed.

DR. KOLB: Exactly. Your body posture, the way you hold your head, everything is being changed as you make a movement. The movement is a dance. *Any* movement is a dance. Everything we do integrates with everything else.

JDN: There is much more to a single thought or action than we realize. Compounded over time, it can change the course of our whole life.

How Fast Does I.M.Possible Muscle Build?

No one develops a strong, muscular frame from a single workout. That will likely just leave us sore. When we first begin a new exercise program, our muscles and their nervous system counterparts are just getting dusted off and creaking to life, full of potential we simply haven't been taking advantage of. In fact, most of the loss of physical strength and muscle that people experience as they age is due, quite simply, to inactivity, not to lack of ability or the aging process. Exercise must be regular, appropriate and sustained in order to maintain physical stamina and strength.

In the same way, I.M.Possible Muscle is built slowly, especially at first. Even in the initial stages, changes are happening. The threads are forming. Fiber-by-fiber, the results build, even though they may not be apparent to us as quickly as we'd like at first. As with physical muscle development, we may notice little to no visible change or progress in the early days of a new exercise routine. But change *is* happening and suddenly, one day our progress is clearly seen.

When I was in school, there were always kids who naturally had bigger muscles (most of them) or who were able to perform certain exercises better than most. In the end life is a great equalizer. Sooner or later even those with exceptionally favorable circumstances or advantages come face to face with a wall that does not give way. Each must go through the same types of I.M.Possible exercises (processes) in order to break through this wall and reach the next level. Otherwise progress will stop at that point.

Remember the story of the hare and the tortoise? The rate at which we personally increase or impair our I.M.Possible Muscle strength depends, not on natural ability or material possessions, but on the choices we make in each moment. The more intentional and productive our moments, the sooner we will see results, and the clearer it will become that our life holds potentials well beyond the familiar and the obvious.

Keep in mind as well that other factors come into play. Performing the *right* kind of exercise relative to the goal is critical. If you want to develop upper arm strength but will only work out on a treadmill, don't be surprised when progress isn't all you'd expected. In this case, the exercise you choose to perform is not appropriate for the objective you wish to attain. If we continue to repeat exactly the same physical exercises, never increase the frequency or intensity of them, or check to make sure they are appropriate to the goal, how could we possibly expect to increase in strength or ability? The same principles hold true with respect to achieving any I.M.Possible goal. You've got to work toward it strategically and *in the right way*. If along the way your progress seems to have stopped, it is necessary to identify the area that has become your plodding treadmill. You must continually review your outcomes and adjust as needed in order to make progress.

Results of I.M.Possible Muscle Building

Anyone who works out in a gym or religiously adheres to some kind of physical fitness program knows how exciting it is to finally begin to see rewards in the form of bodily transformation. In addition to the benefits of looking better and feeling stronger and healthier, we find we also begin to engage in activities that were formerly not possible.

We often receive rewards we hadn't expected when we first started. For example, when I began working out and getting regular exercise, the benefits went far beyond my body shape. My energy levels increased, my temperament was sunnier, I was able to think more clearly, my PMS was less severe and I slept better! Furthermore, I was able to complete tasks that would previously have had me looking for assistance. I was able to do more for others as well. Because I felt better, I radiated more self-assuredness and positivity. Other people responded in kind and I found myself widening my circle of acquaintances and opportunities.

You can reap similar crossover benefits as you continue working at the I.M.Possible fiber-building process. A truly amazing thing about our I.M.Possible Muscle is this: The good that can be accomplished through its conscientious exercise is unlimited. You see, *our brain processes are so powerful they can alter every*

> *"If I set for myself a task, be it so trifling, I shall see it through. How else shall I have confidence in myself to do important things?"* - George Clason, author

other process in our bodies! With every new stage of development, we are changed physically, mentally, intellectually and emotionally. Such changes can equip us to accomplish goals and break through personal barriers that once seemed impossible. As you will find, they can even change the way other people view and respond to you!

Best of all, I.M.Possible Muscle does not present the natural plateaus that physical training and diets do. As long as you keep practicing with intent to improve, you will see results. One thing leads to another. As you achieve small victories, you will start believing. You will see the impossible becoming I.M.Possible. Your mindset will change from: *"One can't believe impossible things"* to *"With practice, I'll can do six I.M.Possible things before breakfast!"*

Compete with You—Not with Anyone Else

In starting your own muscle-building regime, it is essential not to let age or circumstances deter you. *Julia Child didn't learn how to cook until she was almost forty and didn't launch her popular show until she was fifty.* Don't compare your rate of I.M.Possible Muscle development with anyone else's. *Andrea Bocelli didn't start singing opera seriously until the age of thirty-four. Some 'experts' told him it was too late to begin.* Many prodigies don't achieve early greatness in their field (remember Lucille Ball…) while top performers in all fields include many who showed no special early aptitude.

I.M.Possible Muscle development and the speed at which formerly impossible obstacles are removed will be unique to you. The secret is to focus on where you want to go, identifying and working the fiber in front of you, not worrying about, or contrasting yourself with another's assets or abilities. I.M.Possible victories are about proving what you, not they, are truly capable of doing.

"It takes courage to grow up and become who you really are." —e. e. Cummings, poet

---

The Building Program: Impossible to Possible to I.M.Possible

At this point you may be thinking, "That sounds great. It makes sense in theory. It gives me hope. But I'm still not clear on what I really need to *do* in my situation." Stick with me. It was mental fatigue and confusion about *what to do next* that kept short-circuiting my ability to make any lasting or meaningful progress during my own impossible times. I'm not going to leave you to muddle through on your own as you try to bridge the gap that separates your access to equipment from your ability to make productive use of it. It is one thing to identify what we need to do, but another to understand *how* to do it. Not to worry, we'll get there. One step will open the way for the next.

I'd Rather Just Do It – Why Would I Want to Know this Stuff?

When I started working out at the gym, I was impatient for the trainer to quit explaining and let me get started. It wasn't long before I came to appreciate the value of the extra knowledge to my progress and to my ability to maximize gain and minimize pain.

Fitness facilities provide differing work out tools and training exercises because people must use a variety of weights, equipment and methods to rehabilitate and/or strengthen different muscle areas. If you don't have the knowledge or experience in using them properly, however, chances are you won't get the full benefit. Likely, you won't know how to start, or, you *will* start, become discouraged and give up. Worse, you may even injure yourself.

While professional trainers do not, nor should they attempt to, fill the role of a doctor or therapist, they provide you with a basic support system for effectively working through those gaps between 'wanting to do' and 'doing.'

In a similar way, each chapter throughout the remainder of this book has been designed to provide support beyond I.M.Possible Muscle-building exercises alone. Obviously, neither I nor Dr. Kolb can be there in person to coach you through every step, so, in the pages that follow you will find a very carefully designed series of guidelines and insights. These are meant to give you a variety of means to coach yourself (and others, too) through some of the toughest gaps between knowing and doing.

To ensure accuracy in using physical muscle comparisons, I consulted Carl Macdonald, an elite performance enhancement and physical rehabilitation specialist. Carl helps his clients achieve seeming miracles with their own impossible seeming physical muscle challenges: injuries, muscle disorders and chronic muscle and joint-related problems. He was intrigued by the parallels between physical muscle training and building I.M.Possible muscle.

CREATING REALITY: I.M.POSSIBLE MUSCLE AT WORK   CARL MACDONALD

CARL: One of the most powerful concepts in your book is that you don't have to believe at first to get results. You can still get there. I've always used that process in my profession to help people to get physical results but didn't consciously realize it. If you are practicing in the right way to match your goals, you will start to see results. Belief, when it comes, will definitely help speed the process but you're still going to get the results you need to *start* believing—if you practice in the right way.

When I first discussed the concept of practice coming before belief with you, I immediately realized how many times this proved to be the case in my field. I've often worked with people who, for one reason or another, either didn't really believe much could be done to help them or they'd get to a certain point and be sure they couldn't do anything more, which is rarely the case. *When these people find they can now move physically in ways they hadn't believed possible anymore, they also gain confidence to do more. They realize how much they'd have missed out on had they stuck with their old life routine or concluded they were a hopeless case."*

For instance, in 2001 I was training the two directors of the heart transplant program at the Calgary Foothills Hospital, who were pioneering a new approach with exercise for heart failure patients to enhance survival while waiting for heart transplants. Normal protocol for these patients, in the meantime, was essentially: Do nothing, no exertion or they could very well die.

So, they sent me a young police officer who was on the highest priority list for a heart transplant. He'd lost 60% of his heart muscle after suffering a heart attack in his vehicle. He was physically wasted from the necessary bed rest and was devastated, depressed and frustrated. He'd just become engaged to be married when this happened and his whole world had come crashing down.

The surgeon, of course, tried to explain that getting a heart transplant isn't like getting a new part put in your car where you make an appointment, get it replaced and away you go. She wanted him to improve mentally as well as physically as much as possible before such a critical surgery but he wasn't buying into that. The guy just wanted to get a new heart now. Although not really wanting to, he enrolled in personal training with me to get what improvements his diminished state would allow. He thought the exercises would be a waste of precious time but agreed to just 'try' it. He met with me three times a week. I told him, "You made a commitment, just keep practicing the exercises and give it a chance." Gradually, as was inevitable, the improvements began manifesting themselves. Practice lead to results, which lead to belief.

Despite the fact that he was still in a crisis position, he no longer saw his situation as impossible. He could see for himself that he was making progress. As the days and weeks passed his enthusiasm grew. Even the expected angina he was told to expect during his workouts didn't discourage him. By this point, he no longer wanted the transplant until it became absolutely necessary.

The development of his I.M.Possible Muscle was as significant as that of his literal muscles. He went on to set a new I.M.Possible goal: passing the police force physical activity test. Against all odds, he actually went on to improve his remaining 40% heart muscle to the point where he was able to perform at a level where he could pass a test intended to be applied to people who are 100% healthy. He was then able to return to full-time desk duty in the profession he loves.

In the context of this book, that was a prime example of the fiber-building process and of *impossible* giving way to I.M.Possible Muscle on multiple levels.

"If you don't go after what you want, you'll never have it. If you don't ask, the answer is always no. If you don't step forward, you're always in the same place." —Nora Roberts

---

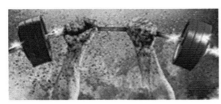

I.M.Possible - Muscle for Your Mind
Rethink Impossible
Redefine Possible

WRITE IN THIS BOOK: (As your coach, I urge you to mindfully complete these critical impossible to I.M.Possible exercises).

Name one impossible goal as well as the obstacle you feel stands in the way of its achievement.
List up to six I.M.Possible Muscle fibers you would like to build to help you overcome those obstacles. If you're unsure what fibers you need to build, come back to this exercise as you read through the book.

1.   GOAL:

2.   OBSTACLE(S):

3.   MUSCLE FIBERS TO BUILD:

The discipline of writing something down is the first step toward making it happen.
Lee Iacocca, businessman, former Ford Corp. engineer, ret chairman Chrysler Corp.

"Let me see—how IS it to be managed?
I suppose I ought to eat or drink something or other;
but the great question is, what?"
—*Alice, Alice in Wonderland, Lewis Carroll*

8. I.M.Possible Fibers:
Six Basic Essentials

"First say to yourself what you would be; and then do what you have to do." —Epictetus

Within you, right now, is the power to do things you never dreamed possible thanks to your I.M.Possible Muscle. The extent to which you can tap all that potential depends on how well your brain is able to function. The physical condition of this vital organ will crucially impact your effectiveness in recruiting all of your I.M.Possible Muscle fibers.

The fibers of any muscle are only as strong as the underlying tissues allow them to become. Poor diet, nutrient deficiency, and lack of other physical basic necessities can prevent or inhibit muscle growth in both I.M.Possible and physical muscle. If you don't supply those tissues (made up of cells) with the nutrients, rest, water, and oxygen they need to support growth, daily function, wear and tear, and regeneration, your outward performance will suffer as well. In fact, it is possible to reach a point where all progress stops until you address the problem. *To maximize both your physical and I.M.Possible Muscle capabilities, make the following six key fiber essentials a regular part of your daily routine.*

1. Aerobic Exercise: An I.M.Possible Powerhouse

The word *exercise* is of Latin origin, meaning 'to ward off or prevent'. Before technology changed our modern world, resulting in people minimizing physical movement beyond pushing a TV remote or typing on a keyboard, physical exercise had been a natural part of daily living. It was recognized to be necessary to health and survival. Today, if we think of exercise at all, we think of it more in terms of training or weight loss. Scientific research now indicates that we should view daily physical exercise the same way today as it was viewed years ago, *as an essential component to I.M.Possible living.*

When I attended the Brain Week Neuroscience Conference with Dr. Kolb at the Hotchkiss Brain Institute in Calgary I found that, regardless of the speaker's area of research—stroke, Alzheimer's, emotional instability, incontinence, etc.—there was a common thread. Aerobic exercise was included in every list of research findings as a key factor in warding off brain disease and aging effects, for optimal healing and maintaining sharp, healthy, long-lasting brain cells. [Frontiers In Science, Mar 16-18, 2011]

Yes, *evidence clearly shows that exercise helps to slow or reverse the brain's physical decay, much as it does with muscles.* Why is this? Because the sustained movement of aerobic exercise increases heart rate and breathing requirements, causing more blood and oxygen to flow through your brain. This not only helps you think better, it is energizing and aids the removal of toxins and body wastes. Regular aerobic exercise also lowers your resting blood pressure and heart rate, slows your breathing, provides more oxygen for your body cells and improves blood circulation.

Weight control and overall fitness are the obvious benefits of regular exercise. Did you know, however, the health and quality of life benefits go much further? Aerobic exercise for thirty minutes to an hour at least three to four times a week helps prevent obesity-related disease and illness, reduces stress and re-channels energy constructively by metabolizing elements that would otherwise become toxic.

Why Exercise Is Better than Medication for Depression

Have you ever battled with severe feelings of depression? According to research statistics, at least 50% of the North American population suffers some form of depressive disorder in their lifetime.[1] Other studies show that 8 out of 10 Americans are affected in some way by depression.[2]

There are many different causes and types of depression, and though we may not be able to wave a wand to make them disappear, there is something we can do that can greatly help in the battle.

A ground-breaking study done by the Duke University Medical Center proved regular aerobic exercise to be as successful as medication in treating Major Depressive Disorder (MDD). In fact, a 10-month follow-up revealed the exercise-only group was actually experiencing better results than those with medication only. The research conclusion:

---

[1] Bryan Kolb and Ian Whishaw, *An Introduction to Brain and Behavior, Third Edition* (New York: Worth Publishers, 2011) 592.

[2] http://www.nimh.nih.gov/news/media/audio/elizabeth-lin-on-diabetes-and-depression.shtml

"Among individuals with MDD, exercise therapy is feasible, and is associated with significant therapeutic benefit, especially if exercise is continued over time."[3]

There are vast amounts of research evidence in addition to the above, but I became a believer through first-hand experience. When I don't exercise regularly, my husband notices the difference within a week. I am far more subject to stress and feelings of depression. It is often very difficult to fit exercise into my days. But the sacrifice more than repays the time it takes. I can think more clearly and am far more energetic and productive than I am if I don't exercise.

A friend with whom I'd discussed this book related this experience:

My brother Guy suffered for many years with depression. He was always sleeping. Even when he was awake he was tired. I told him about the I.M.Possible Muscle essential fibers. He bought an exercise gym and a treadmill and committed to exercising for an hour a day. After four months Guy was a completely different person. He had so much energy. He was always reserved and now he actually wanted to be around people. He believes it's all because of the exercise.

FEED THE FIBERS: *Aerobic Exercise!* **Ideally, you should exercise three times a week to the point where your heart rate is significantly elevated above your normal level for at least twenty minutes. Make sure whatever you do is sustainable, and becomes a natural part of your life. Consistency will make it easier each time. You will very quickly experience the benefits. Regular practice will result in making exercise a permanent part of your personal routine. When you just do it, fit happens.**

---

2. Take a Hike

Fresh air, sunshine, oxygen and movement! The simple act of going for a walk provides this multitude of I.M.Possible essentials. More than just a body exercise, walking is vital for brain mental balance and health. Why?

- Walking is not strenuous. Your leg muscles don't take up extra oxygen and glucose as they would during other forms of exercise.

---

[3] M. Babyak, T.T. Baldewicz, J.A. Blumenthal, W.E. Craighead, M. Doraiswamy, S. Herman, P. Khatri, K.R. Krishnan, K. Moore, "Exercise treatment for major depression: maintenance of therapeutic benefit at 10 months," *Psychosom Med.* 62, no. 5 (Sep.-Oct. 2000), www.ncbi.nlm.nih.gov/pubmed/11020092.

- As you walk, blood circulation is increased and you effectively oxygenate your brain. (*This is one of the reasons why walking can literally clear your head and help you to think better.*)

FEED THE FIBERS: *Walk!* **Go for a walk. Even a 10-minute walk will make a difference. Walk every opportunity you get.**

---

3. Just Breathe It Out

Have you ever been stuck in a long line at the supermarket or caught in traffic and found your temper and blood pressure rising as everything around you slows to a standstill? Were you aware that any situations that cause you to feel stressed out, worried or anxious produce associated changes in your body, such as shallow breathing, sweating, heart palpitations and even dizziness? This quickly becomes a cycle of stress increasing stress. You are increasingly unable to think clearly. Your I.M.Possible Muscle weakens, making it more difficult to conquer the situation. Overwhelming feelings of anxiety can even lead to panic attacks, whereby you feel you have lost all control of your situation. During such stressful moments, has anyone ever advised you to just breathe it out, or to stop, take a deep breath and count to ten?

There is sound reason to follow this advice and make it an I.M.Possible practice. Leading psychiatrists, martial arts experts and Navy SEALs all place breathing techniques at the top of their training essentials list. Why? Because learning how to control our breathing is key to regulating other body processes and to having clear, focused thinking. It is a vital factor in controlling extreme emotions. Learning to control your breathing is crucial to I.M.Possible victories. It is a huge component in controlling high emotion, allowing a calm, logical mind to work its magic. Taking in full breaths, slowly, long and deeply:

- Carries more oxygen to your brain, strengthening your I.M.Possible capabilities. You can think faster, better and at higher levels.
- Causes more oxygen to flow through your bloodstream, which carries it to various parts of your body, delivering vital components needed to keep your health stable.
- Relaxes and eases muscular tension, lowers blood pressure and heart rate, and lessens other physical symptoms of anxiety.

FEED THE FIBERS: *Breathe it out!* To help get you started, try this I.M.Possible breathing exercise called the **Rule of Four.** Breathe in to the count of four, then out to the count of four. Do this for four minutes, at least four times a day. Practice is essential. In four, out four, four minutes, four times a day. The more you do it, the more deep breathing will become second nature.[4]

"Tension is who you think you should be. Relaxation is who you are." —Chinese Proverb

4. Drink or Your Brain Will Shrink

Have you ever heard anyone say, "I've got to take a break. I'm running out of steam"? When a person 'runs out of steam', we understand they are, at that point, tired and unable to function well. The expression originated in earlier times when locomotive steam engines depended on water in boilers to produce the steam to power the train. If the water in the boiler became low, the amount of steam being produced would drop, causing the train to slow down or even stop. What does it literally mean, then, to run out of steam? To be deficient in water, of course! This same principle holds true for humans. Deficiency in water leads to symptoms of mental and physical burn-out.

Your brain is 70 % water—and absolutely greedy for it. Water is essential for sending the signals from your brain to the rest of your body. Often when we get busy, we don't realize the first symptoms of dehydration are mental confusion and sleepiness.

Research shows that dehydration not only affects the size of the brain but also how it works. Just 90 minutes of steady sweating can shrink the brain as much as a year of aging [would], researchers believe. Starved of water, the grey matter is also forced to work harder. —Institute of Psychiatry, King's College, London, UK

The next time you start to lose concentration and focus, try drinking a glass of water. Your hydration level is linked to your mental clarity and your physical energy level. When you feel you are running out of steam, the next fiber-building action you need to take could well be to drink water. Keep yourself hydrated all day long.

---

[4] Aileen Milne, Christine Wilding, *Cognitive Behavioural Therapy: Teach Yourself,* (London: Hodder Education, 2010) 166-167.

FEED THE FIBERS: *Drink water!* Drink four (recommended minimum) to eight glasses of pure water a day. Add a tablespoon of lemon juice if you can—it is commonly believed to be an excellent blood cleanser.

5. Fuel the I.M.Possible Muscle

Scientific research finds that the brain responds to nutrition in a very powerful way. What you eat affects your mood as well as how fast and how well you think. I recommend you make it an I.M.Possible task to do some research on nutrition. Blueberries, raw walnuts and fish (or fish oil supplements) are fabulous brain food. Your I.M.Possible Muscle needs sufficient vitamins, especially vitamin B, and amino acids in order to function at full capacity. Green super-foods such as green tea, spirulina and wheatgrass can give you many of the nutrients you need to blast through your day.

Due to the difficulty of getting all the nutrition we need from even a balanced diet, almost everyone needs to take some form of supplements. A qualified doctor or nutritionist is a valuable aid in helping you identify any deficiencies in your nutrition.

FEED THE FIBERS: *Fuel your I.M.Possible Muscle!* Decide how, in your circumstances, you can best nourish your I.M.Possible Muscle. Money spent on a small amount of healthy food will give you far greater value than the same amount spent on junk food.

6. Sleep to Remember

Adequate sleep an absolute building and maintaining a sharp mind and emotional stability. The body performs most of its maintenance work, including balancing your emotions, while you sleep. When deprived of the needed rest period, your body and mind don't have the opportunity to properly recover from daily wear and tear.

Lack of sleep also lowers your overall brain functioning. Researchers in a 2002 Harvard Medical School sleep study found that adequate sleep has a direct relationship to learning new actions as well as to skillful performance.[5] If you remain too long in a sleep-deprived state, you will find it increasingly

---

[5] Matthew P. Walker, Tiffany Brakefield, Alexandra Morgan, J. Allan Hobson, Robert Stickgold, "Practice with Sleep Makes Perfect: Sleep-Dependent Motor Skill Learning," *Neuron* 35, no. 1 (2002), 205-211.

difficult to concentrate, co-ordination and reaction time will slow down, and you will become moody, irritable, quick-tempered and depressed. If you want to increase I.M.Possible muscle strength, here are some additional reasons to consider your sleep habits:

- Sleep involves several distinct stages with special functions at work. Slow Wave sleep (meaning, brain waves are slow) is a time for tissue growth and repair.
- Key immune system chemicals increase during Slow Wave sleep. Losing Slow Wave sleep means decreased immune system function.
- Rapid eye movement sleep (REM) helps us to keep our sense of direction: mentally, emotionally and physically.
- During REM sleep, our memory circuits are strengthened. Neurons in this area are stimulated in a process that has an effect comparable to that which weightlifting has upon muscles.

FEED THE FIBERS: *Get adequate sleep!* **You'll think and perform better on seven to eight hours of sleep each night. If you find yourself short on sleep midday, refresh yourself by taking a 20-minute catnap.**

How to Build the Fiber In Front of You

Every moment in which you choose actions that: 1) feed into the physical health of your brain, 2) move you in a healthy, rational way towards positive goals, or 3) change the way you would normally respond or act in order to move in a more positive direction, you create new sets of connections in your brain that weave themselves into the transformation of your I.M.Possible Muscle.

Different people face different challenges and demands, so there is no one-size-fits-all fiber-building program; everyone's needs are different. Whatever your own personal program may be, fiber-building choices in front of you may include, but are not limited to, the following:

- *Any positive, I.M.Possible-essential fiber-building action that lifts you away from a choice that contributes to impossible weakness. For example, instead of letting your temper boil, you breathe deeply and slowly, and say a silent prayer for patience and wisdom to deal with the situation.*

93

- *Each consecutive thought or action that takes you one step closer to a specific I.M.Possible goal. For instance, you get your running shoes (use the One-Sock Process in Chapter 11) as a step in motivating you to work out or go for a walk.*
- *An action that feeds your fiber's basic physical essentials. You drink a glass of lemon water or have a cup of green tea.*

Below is an exercise you can use in the moment, to strengthen your I.M.Possible fibers, if you are feeling stressed, emotional or confused:

Change your breathing: Regulate, deepen and slow it down. Compose yourself, close your eyes and think about what you could or would be doing right now if you were to listen to the soft inner voice, in the back of your mind: "The best I.M.Possible thing I could be doing with this moment would be, if I weren't so ___ (Fill in the blank: tired, busy, afraid, angry, stressed, bored...) is _____. " Now keep breathing slowly, deeply and take the next step toward the above.

To build the fiber in front of you means, depending on your circumstances, to advance your next action or thought one notch from where you are now towards an action that will take you closer to what you want to accomplish. Any big I.M.Possible victory is really only an accumulation of tiny I.M.Possible victories. Even if it is something as apparently simple as drinking a glass of water instead of soda pop, one notch up from feeling or feeding into impossible is progress. You are becoming more than you were the moment before. Each step changes your brain in a good way. Each change releases chemicals and initiates new mental connections that set the platform for building the next fiber and so on.

Go back to the basic essential I.M.Possible fibers in this chapter when you aren't sure where to start at any given moment. Other questions you can ask yourself to build the fiber in front of you are:

1. Is there some essential task you have been putting off that you know must be done and that you could or should be doing right now? No matter how small, if it is weighing on your mind, do it now. (See the One-Sock Process, described in Chapter 11 of this book.)

2. How can I communicate with someone positive? If there's no one in your home with whom you can do this, seek out a different resource. For example, if you can't turn to your parents or your spouse, ask yourself, "Is there a teacher, counselor, friend, acquaintance, doctor, organization or agency that might be a source of new insight or support?" Do some research. Learn something—even if just one new thing—about your I.M.Possible goal.

3. Do something kind or share kind words with someone. Go outside, take a walk and say something kind to the first person you see.

Identify the Value in Your Thoughts and Actions

Value is the worth we place on anything. Gain can only be achieved when you are willing to give something up in return. Physical, mental, emotional and spiritual health come at a cost of some kind. The cost can take on many forms. If you have the option to feed and build these underlying fiber qualities, but choose not to exchange the time and effort to do so, the cost might well be personal, family, financial, social, professional, spiritual, emotional, mental, physical or all of the aforementioned. It might well spill over to encompass others, whether those close to us or anyone else whose life our choices impact. Human perception is subject to unforeseen circumstances, faulty knowledge, manipulation and blinding emotion and so on. If we aren't diligent in doing reality check exercises the cost could continue to climb out of proportion to the value of the gain. You can maximize the quality of your outcomes if you honestly evaluate the cost vs value of the choices you make. The moments count. What is being exchanged for what? Here are some questions to help you begin:

*   Is what I am doing the absolute best thing I could be doing right now to help me achieve my I.M.Possible goal?
*   Is what I am doing right now contributing to impossible (making excuses, frozen with fear, performing negative activities, procrastinating) or: Is it a forward-moving activity that advances me in some way toward the I.M.Possible? (For example, if you hate the thought of riding an exercise bike for forty-five minutes, find an exercise routine that works for you, one you enjoy doing on a consistent basis—but get your exercise.)
*   Are my thoughts and actions right now aligned with healthy core values? Do they show respect for lives that depend on my health and integrity?
*   Just because I did it this way yesterday, do I have to do it this way today?
*   If I knew I was going to die tomorrow, what would I change about the way I've lived my life? What would I do this moment?

Now is not too late. As long as you are alive, change for the better is absolutely I.M.Possible. Make use of your new-found knowledge. Try - and experienced the difference reality-based deliberate practice can make to your outcomes. If you should, for some reason, happen to fall into a rut, pick up this book and read it again. Practice using the information and One Sock Process to build upward and press onward. *Per ardua ad astra* is my signature expression. "Through hardship to the stars". Whatever that those stars represent to you personally; you have the means available to reignite your thinking and get back on your journey toward a new reality and I.M.Possible outcomes.

Do not ever again miss the opportunities that might have been in store for you because you've let your I.M.Possible Muscle go into impossible mode. Don't lose another moment. Instead lose 'impossible'!

CREATING REALITY: DON'T DIET—LIVE IT   **NIC**

When I asked my seven-year-old grandson, Nicolas, if he wanted cookies or cake, he replied, *"No, thanks"* and asked for fruit instead. I said, "Wow, fruit instead of junk food. Good for you. Are you on a diet?" Nic answered, *"No, I'm on a live-it!"* He thought a moment, then added, *"They should call eating junk food a diet because it makes you die."* Out of the mouths of babes. What a fantastic I.M.Possible attitude! Instead of feeling deprived, healthy choices are live-it choices that help us to make the best of our bodies and our lives! (Nic credits his teacher, Miss Roy, for the live-it concept. You're an I.M.Possible hero, Miss Roy!)

LEGAL DISCLAIMER: The information in this book is not meant to be used as a replacement for medical advice, intervention or other therapies. Obtain medical clearance from your medical practitioner before embarking on any new fitness, nutritional, dietary or exercise activity.

WRITE IN THIS BOOK. *Make a list of fiber-building essentials that are already part of your routine.*

Now list those you are going to add to your I.M.Possible essential routine.

"Everyone should be his own physician. We ought to assist and not force nature. Eat with moderation what agrees with your constitution. Nothing is good for the body but what we can digest. What medicine can produce digestion? Exercise. What will recruit strength? Sleep. What will alleviate incurable ills? Patience." —Voltaire, writer, philosopher

Alice had gotten so much into the way of
Expecting nothing but out-of-the-way things to happen,
That it seemed quite dull and stupid for life to go on in the
common way.
—Alice in Wonderland, Lewis Carroll

9. I.M.Possible Warm-Ups: Antidote to Self-Sabotage

"Become an impossibilitarian. No matter how dark things seem to be or actually are, raise your sights and see possibilities—always see them, for if you are willing to really look, they're always there." —Norman Vincent Peal, minister, author

Do you recall the light saber from the *Star Wars movies*? When activated, the device emitted an energy beam strong enough to knock down opponents, and transform or cut through obstacles within its radius. The power could be focused for good or evil, to harm or help - thus the famous phrase, "May the force be *with* you." Originally intended for upholding the good, light sabers required a great deal of skill and dexterity to wield, as well as attunement to the force.

Imagine such a light saber really exists, and you own one. Wouldn't you want to make sure you knew how to use it before you switched it on, instead of just waving it about and hoping for the best? Think of the trouble Luke Skywalker would have caused had he unknowingly walked around packing a light saber that had a faulty switch, emitting power at random? Farfetched as it might seem, the scenario aptly illustrates what many of us are unconsciously doing in every day in our real world. In what way?

Did you know that, every day from the time you wake up, you begin to generate mental energy that impacts many of the outcomes in your personal world? The nature of this influence acts something like a switch on the Star Wars light saber, triggering a chain reaction of cause and effect responses and outcomes.

The personal internal force discussed here is not based any mystical woo-woo or you-can-attract-anything-you-want theorists. It refers to neurological, physiological and psychological interactions and to principles governing cause and effect. You see, thoughts and actions direct and transform brain activity and create a flow of chemical and electrical signals

97

via neural synapsis. Included in this processes is the activation of various types of emotional energy, commonly summarized as positive or negative. The nature of this energy is picked up or sensed by others, often on an unconscious level. There are many theories put forth as to exactly how this occurs, especially in humans, who are extremely complex.

Cognitive neuroscientists offer one explanation, known as *'theory of mind'*,[1] which basically says we make assumptions about the minds of other people by observing their behaviors and by listening to their words.

We pick up many cues without being consciously aware, such as body language, facial expressions as well as social and environmental interactions. In doing so, we develop a 'theory of mind' about their mental state. Regardless of the underlying dynamics involved, the fact remains that we *are* affected, often quite significantly.

For example, if Mom wakes up in a good mood, her husband and kids are likely to respond in a similar way. If one of her family has a problem, she's able to remain upbeat and provide helpful input. We might say the atmosphere is one of good energy. However, if Mom is in a bad mood, worried or sad, she doesn't have to say anything. Others pick up on it. Life slows down in more ways than one. They ask, "What's wrong?" (or avoid asking). Energy levels are lower. Moods are less cheery; family may try to tiptoe around her—but all have to work harder to maintain a positive atmosphere in the house, even with each other.

Can you think of specific examples in your life, perhaps at work, school or recreation, where the mood or attitude of one person has an impact on the attitudes and behaviors of others? You've no doubt heard the term *energy signals* when referring to the metaphorical flow of energy from one to another person. Have you ever heard someone described as having a 'magnetic personality'? Or, as 'lighting up the room'? On the other hand, the opposite influence has been likened to 'a wet blanket'. Think of a time when someone you met gave you 'good vibes' or 'bad vibes'. How did you respond? If you take time for reflection, you will probably acknowledge that your reaction was influenced, not just by the observable interaction between the two of you, but by an associated emotional 'atmosphere'.

> **"The energy of mind is the essence of life"** – Arisotle, from The Philosophy of Aristotle

---

[1] Bryan Kolb and Ian Whishaw, *An Introduction to Brain and Behavior*, 4th ed. (New York: Worth Publishers, 2012), 541

What It Means to Go with the Flow

When others meet us, they too—consciously or not— pick up sensations and cues regarding our state of mind. We can cause the likelihood of a positive or negative outcome to increase depending on our internal energy flow. Let's take a look at a few ways in which this force can generate a snowball-like progression of cause and effect.

Have you ever heard someone say, *"This day is just going from bad to worse"*? What may seem like bad luck on days like this is far more likely to be the cumulative effects of negative energy. The worse we feel, the more negative energy we create and project. When our thoughts center on doom and gloom, sure enough, nothing seems to go right. The more negativity we portray, the more the world outside, and inside of us, respond accordingly. It's a phenomenon is often referred to as self-fulfilling prophecy. Axioms such as *'you reap what you sow'* or *'what goes around comes around'* are more expressions of the cause and affect cycle. Fortunately, these principles apply equally to our ability to positively influence our own daily direction, as well as the state of mind of others—including those we personally don't know or who don't know us. We simply can't foresee the powerful effect our own positivity may have on others, or how the effects might 'grow as they flow.'

There is a saying; *"The world makes way for those who know where they are going."* Ironically, the world will also often make way for those who simply look and act as though they know where they're going. Why is that? Because their inner energy flow radiates; it is evident in their facial expressions, their posture, their speech and actions. Those around them pick up on this and respond in ways that harmonize with the message relayed by these non-verbal cues. Again, there are many theories as to how this happens; energy flow does not have to imply a literal physical force transmitted to others, it also involves our influence over others, knowingly or not, through the generation of 'theory of mind'.

Here is one simple example: A number of years ago, during a busy downtown lunch hour, I was walking up the steps to a lunch date, when a man and woman, both of whom looked like fashion models, came dashing past me down the stairs. The young man suddenly stopped, turned, and ran back up a couple steps to my side. "You look like such a happy person. I felt like I'd just passed through a ray of sunshine," he said. "I just had to tell you." "Why thank you," I responded. "What a lovely thing to say." With a broad smile and wave of his hand, he rushed on down to his waiting companion.

I've never seen him again, but we exchanged gifts that day—gifts that cost nothing, but spread warmth and goodwill. That reminder, of the power within to generate good-will and happiness, motivated me to be more aware of opportunities to do so. Whether through sincere compliments, expressions of appreciation, or showing compassion to someone in need, it is ours to switch on if only we choose. Who knows how many people might benefit from a chain reaction that begins with a kind, smiling countenance? Such is the mental flow of positive energy.

Impossible vs. I.M.Possible: Managing the Flow

Do you find it hard to believe that the way you pronounce a word can make any real difference to your life? Can words, even those you say to yourself, actually prompt brain regions to release chemicals and produce a chain of reactions so powerful, they change your entire day—even your life? In this section, you will experience for yourself just how the I.M.Possible self-talk formula acts as a warm-up activity for taking on any kind of challenge.

While researching the power of self-talk and words, I conducted an experiment, first on myself, then on Dr. Kolb, and then on twenty friends and random acquaintances of widely differing cultures and backgrounds. Before I reveal the results of the experiment, would you like to experience here and now, as they did, the power behind the formula that can transform Impossible blues to I.M.Possible energy?

Try the experiment right now, as outlined below. Answer the questions posed before reading the interview responses.

1. Take a deep breath and close your eyes. Focus completely on what is taking place inside of you.
2. First, think of the word *IMPOSSIBLE*. It is a powerful word. Listen to your internal response. Say it out loud. Say it again. And again.
3. Now, say the following aloud, "This is an IMPOSSIBLE time in my life. Today, I approach life from an IMPOSSIBLE point of view."

How do you feel? Write down the negative sensations—physical, mental, emotional—you get when you hear yourself say those words.

Did you feel a mental barrier go up as you said IMPOSSIBLE? The responses I heard from my test group participants were unanimous in tone:

100

- "I felt negative, hopeless, felt like I didn't even want to try."
- "Felt almost lethargic, what's the point, don't even want to get up."
- "I don't even feel like starting..."
- "Feel like I'm up against a wall"

Do their answers sound a lot like yours? Of course they do. And no wonder. You've pronounced it "IMPOSSIBLE". Therefore, it is!!

*Now, repeat the same procedure above but change the way you pronounce the key word Impossible to **I.M.Possible**. Really* allow yourself to feel the difference. (Remember of the two-part message in this word: "I AM Possible because I *make* possible." This isn't just a pie-in-the-sky mantra—*it means you resolve to do whatever is necessary, including any learning and change and adjustments this entails, to allow constructive results to occur.)*

1. Take a deep breath, close your eyes and focus internally.
2. Pronounce out loud "I AM POSSIBLE." Say it 3 times more.
3. Say aloud, clearly, "This is an I.M.Possible time in my life. Today I will approach life from an I.M.Possible point of view."

Now how do you feel? List the physical, mental and emotional sensations that come with your words.

My guess is that your response aligns with those of my test subjects, some of whose responses are recorded below:

- "Energized, motivated, time to get up and go do."
- "Feel excited, feel like anything is possible."
- "Elated, a feeling of anticipation."
- "Very up, confident, powerful... positive, hopeful—empowered."

Interestingly, all those on whom I used this experiment described similar emotional responses to *Impossible,* and to *I.M.Possible.* In both cases, we are generating internal energy feedback from our I.M.Possible Muscle, telling us whether it is being strengthened or weakened by what we are doing or thinking. How and why do words have such power?

Impossible is a strong word. It carries strong messages to our psyche, which has a profound impact on our thinking, and on our belief system. When you pronounce your objective as impossible, you lock onto a no hope mindset. You set restrictive boundaries. *Where we focus is where we go.* Thoughts

101

feed our focus, which impacts how our brain perceives and processes information. To support attainment of your focus goal, it fires neuro-chemical signals triggering emotions and behaviors. That is why impossible messages leave you feeling paralyzed, helpless or uninspired. You are actually telling your brain to create this outcome. Focusing on *Impossible* inhibits your ability to access areas of your brain that exercise your capabilities and potentials. Does this help you better understand how we can create a vicious cycle of self-defeat that is hard to break?

But we can break it! When we think and pronounce the word "*I.M.Possible*", we are not only changing the pronunciation. We are setting up a chain of chemistry and connections in our brain and body that propel us forward. We move away from negativity, the fuel for hopelessness and failure. *Don't allow your thoughts to lodge in an Impossible place.* I.M.Possible energy is uplifting energy. Whatever is truly impossible at this moment is irrelevant to your next step forward. Your focus is aligned to the step directly ahead that *is* achievable.

Start using this warm-up formula today. Practice. Automatically re-visualize the word *IMPOSSIBLE,* every time you see it, to the sound and thought "***I.M.POSSIBLE*** (I MAKE POSSIBLE). I WILL MAKE WAY FOR IMPOSSIBLE TO BECOME A NEW POSSIBLE."

"What this power is I cannot say; all I know is that it exists and it becomes available only when a man is in that state of mind in which he knows exactly what he wants and is fully determined not to quit until he finds it." —Alexander Graham Bell, inventor

The Power Players

Negative thinking literally weakens your I.M.Possible Muscle. How? By creating significant changes in brain activity. So what effect can these changes have on our productivity, performance and outcomes?

- It is harder to think and process information quickly.
- Your ability to reason and make decisions slows down.
- Problems develop with mood, memory and temper control.
- Feelings of depression, violent acts and difficulty remembering
- Sleep becomes disturbed.
- The above can easily lead to a pattern of negative thinking.

In comparison, gratitude and positive thinking also incite brain activities. I.M.Possible thoughts can result in:

- Endorphin release within the brain. A relaxed state of mind.
- An ability to think more clearly, to learn and make error correction.
- A greater ability to make rational decisions.
- An increased or stabilized healthy self-confidence.
- Good posture (which has many physical and psychological benefits).

When you change your self-talk, you change the transmission of neural signals that activate emotion-producing brain circuits. As you change your emotions, you change the nature of your brain activity. Words are one of the simplest but most powerful tools for building your I.M.Possible Muscle. *The words we feed into our brain can provide a formula for rising above obstacles and achieving goals one word and one moment at a time.*

Turn to the Belief Chart on pages 128 and 129 and examine it closely. You will be better equipped to battle impossible thinking when you are able to follow, step by step, the process of how we create our own Impossible versus I.M.Possible outcomes. This chart will help you to see just what the words you feed yourself do to your brain. Say the words aloud as you follow the progression of cause and effect. Feel how the thoughts, mental pictures, or words each activate particular areas in our brain that produce a corresponding emotion. Can you understand that the nature of such thoughts is not going to activate opposing emotional circuits out of the blue? For instance, we can't think violent thoughts and expect to feel calm and peaceful inside. Our decision-making process will be networked towards conflict, and away from healthy, productive outcomes. If we

> *"Shallow men believe in luck. Strong men believe in cause and effect."* - Ralph Waldo Emerson

speak discouraging, degrading words to others we should expect these are going to trigger circuits linked to an angry, resentful or disheartened response. We must deliberately choose words, thoughts and actions that will signal or trigger the facilitators in the brain area for the particular emotion we would like to feel or that we would like to bring out in someone else.

Impossible to I.M.Possible? How Do We Hit Reset?

When we gain greater control over what goes into our head, we gain greater power to direct our thinking along productive lines. The first thoughts of our day can set the tone for the rest of the day. Once the energy starts flowing, we have initiated momentum, and it is then easier to go with the flow. A positive attitude is like a magnet for positive results. The more

103

you create a positive energy flow in and around yourself, the more you create opportunities for I.M.Possible outcomes.

How Words Connect to Emotions

There is a time-worn phrase used by young children to put on a brave face when the teasing and name calling starts: *Sticks and stones can break my bones but words can never hurt me.* It would be wonderful if it were true. But anyone who has ever felt pain as a result of cruel words, won't be surprised to learn that emotional injury can have a far more severe and lasting impact than physical injury.[2] Words can indeed be likened to an energy force. Words can make us feel powerful or powerless, joyful or sad, energetic or lazy, tense or relaxed. Yes, someone's words can even change the course of our life. How can mere words wield such immense force?

Words matter big time. Neuroscience has shown that different words cause different effects in our brain, as you found when you did the experiment using the words *impossible* and *I.M.Possible.* Using modern imaging technology, scientists have been able to observe that regions of our brain are affected by different types of words. They discovered that the words fed into our brain actually activate different regions of the brain, causing us to respond according to the meaning we give to them.

Yes, whether spoken, heard, written, read or thought; words produce images in our mind. Based on the emotional networks these images activate, correspondingly signals are transmitted, causing the release of hormones into the bloodstream, which in turn affect the chemical firing of neurons in your brain. What does this do? It creates emotions that trigger other responses in us physically and mentally. Our emotions then network further to produce corresponding thoughts that affect actions and ultimately our outcomes. Those outcomes form the big picture that creates and determines our personal reality.

---

[3]After two years   interviewing fourth- to twelfth-graders around the country, the center's researchers found that name-calling and cursing were among the most frequent triggers of violent behaviors...police records found that homicides frequently began with verbal provocation. – *Ronald D. Stephens, executive director, National School Safety Center Los Angeles*

---

[2]   Bryan Kolb and Ian Q. Whishaw, *Introduction to Brain and Behavior, Third Edition* (New York: Worth Publishers, 2011), p 396.

[3] *Source: The Benevolence of Manners,* Linda Lichter, *(New York Harper Collins, 1998)p 108*

CREATING REALITY: ACTION REACTION	RYAN

JDN: I learned from Bryan that every word we say or hear activates entire networks and areas of our brain. And, you are your brain. So the concepts we attach to words set us up for different directions—different ways of creating reality related to the meaning we give them and how we choose to act on them.

RYAN: As a movie director, I don't automatically yell out the word "Action!" when we start a new scene. I think *action* is kind of a loaded word. It makes the actors get really amped up unnecessarily. I usually just say, "Okay, whenever you guys are ready start saying some stuff..." Saying *action* makes the actors get really tense, like something's happening. But I don't want 'em that way. So I don't say it anymore, at least not very often. Unless it works into the scene...

JDN: A scene where you want them revved up at the start. That's how powerful words are.

Are you starting to get the picture? Here it is again: Words trigger emotional responses in the brain. (The words in music do this, too.)Whatever is heard produces mental pictures, causing the activation of emotion-producing circuits to correspond with those images. These visual images make us feel happy, sad, angry, motivated, defeated and so on. Emotions, in turn, draw us toward related thoughts and actions. The momentum builds as corresponding regions in our brain are further activated and reinforced. Words encourage us to be our best or they rip away our self-worth and our abilities to reach goals and life's ambitions. Battles are won and lost; lives are saved or ruined because of words spoken aloud or in the mind.

Throughout this book I remind you that our thoughts are ultimately under our control and can be changed. After all, thoughts are made up of the words and pictures *we* feed into our brain. Change your thoughts, and you

> *"If you have lost confidence in yourself, make believe you are somebody else, somebody that's got brains, and act like him."* - Sol Hess, comic writer

will change your brain and your actions. Change your actions, change your outcome. Change your outcomes, change your life. By becoming aware of the unconscious chain of processes that predispose us for success or for failure, you are further along in developing a default I.M.Possible mindset. How? As soon as you re-sculpt your self-talk and become aware of the affects of external mental input, you re-construct the platform for your thinking. *In a world where much of life is beyond our control, the strongest force we can exert to control the outcome of our lives—for good or for ill—is our thoughts.* Because thoughts power every choice we make, including our reaction to circumstances that test us to our limits. The very act of realigning our thoughts to an I.M.Possible perspective is immediately empowering. We think in terms of not only what can be done, but of possibilities above and beyond. Use all your efforts to move towards the light. Think in terms of what *is* possible for you right now that is one step in the direction of your positive goal. Think in terms of developing your greatest potentials in all the ways that could happen.

"In each of us are places where we have never gone. Only by pressing the limits do we ever find them." –Dr. Joyce Brothers

---

The Formula: Your I.M.Possible Warm-Up Exercise

Have you ever exercised or started a rigorous physical activity without first warming up? I have. What happens? It's much harder to get started, it takes longer to really get into the activity, and the chances are fifty-fifty you'll strain something and not feel it until later. By then, the damage will be done. Warming up makes a huge difference to the outcome of any exercise routine. How?

If we go into our workout cold, we are more prone to injury and will have lowered endurance and exertion levels. Warming up physically before a workout gives the body opportunity to optimally prepare itself for physical exertion. It increases the blood flow to the muscles and increases the elasticity of the fibers and connective tissues. Joints and muscles increase in their range of motion. Hormonal and enzymatic changes occur to provide better access to energy. The body physically warms up. Too, we psychologically prepare for the activities ahead, and the muscle-mind link is enhanced.

Your I.M.Possible Muscle works in much the same way. The I.M.Possible self-talk exercise prepares your I.M.Possible Muscle to meet challenges similar to the way in which warm-ups do to prepare your body for a physical workout. To overcome obstacles of any kind in the course of your day, having mentally warmed up in advance will make a big difference in your problem solving ability.

Warming up with the I.M.Possible formula is important for a number of reasons. Benefits include, but are not limited to:

- Activating our mental muscles, improving energy and alertness

- Increasing the ability to be flexible, learn and make error corrections (instead of refusing to bend)
- Helping prepare the body and the mind for more strenuous activity
- Reducing risk of mental as well as physical stress, strain and injury
- Enabling an increase in our overall performance
- Increasing the flexibility of our mental networks, allowing them to network with more stretch or expansiveness

A well-conditioned body or mind is always in a greater state of readiness to address unexpected demands. The warm-up exercises will take your mind to an even higher performance level, and prepare it for exertion more quickly. For instance, when you first wake up in the morning, does it sometimes take you a while to just get your day going? Does it seem as though half the day is gone before you really get into the swing of things? Even though being *physically* warmed up all day is not possible, if you are prepared *mentally* you will be able to get from zero to one hundred much more efficiently.

The fitter we are, the more quickly we are also able to return to baseline after an episode of increased exertion, whether mental or physical. For example, if you become angry because a driver cuts you off on the highway, or a phone call exasperates you, or if your computer has you boiling with frustration (again!), do these feelings ever continue to affect your mood for some time afterward? An I.M.Possible mindset makes it easier for us to cope with the strain in volatile situations, and will help us more rapidly bring ourselves to a calmer baseline level, so events such as these don't grow out of proportion or ruin our day.

The first line of defense? Go into I.M.Possible warm-up mode. Make it your default mode. Immediately flex "This is impossible" self-talk to *"I.M.Possible."* Get your muscle working with I.M.Possible self-talk such as, *"I will make a way for this to become possible. There is always at least one other choice of thought or action I can make in any situation. I AM Possible. This is where I want to go. Here is what I can do that is possible for me, right now, at this very moment."* With practice you will progressively become more able to do this.

Don't overthink it. The strain involved in taking too big a leap is lessened as each step leads us—by degrees—to the next. You will train yourself, and in so doing, change your relationships with others. By changing your response, you change the experience, because the behavior of others is often dependent on yours. For example, if a conversation I'm having with someone takes a turn into trash talk or gossip, I've learned to be calm, have a sense of humor (absolutely vital) and say (either directly or indirectly), *"This is spamming my mind. I'm going to flip it into the junk filter because it really doesn't do anything good for either of us."* There are many ways in which we can retrain the negative circuits in our mind. The processes outlined in this book will help you to begin and give you tools you can use with everything else you read, learn and do in life.

In the 1960s, Dr. Robert Rosenthal of Harvard University conducted a famous experiment called The Pygmalion Effect. This experiment proved the impact our expectations can have on actual results. The experiment went as follows:

At the beginning of the school year the principal called three teachers into his office. The principal told these teachers, "We feel that you're the best teachers in this school. And, as a reward, we're going to give you the best, highest-IQ students in the school for the coming year. Don't tell the students anything about this. Don't tell the parents. This is just a reward for you because you're the best teachers. Just teach them the way you normally would." So that's what the teachers did. At the end of the school year, these students' grades were 20-30% above those of the rest of the school. Not only that, but they led the whole school district in academic accomplishment!

The teachers were called in to see the principal again. He told them, "You did an excellent job with these students." The teachers said, "It was easy. You gave us the best students in the school." The principal then told the teachers, "Well, no, that was just an experiment. Those children were chosen at random. They weren't gifted at all." You can imagine what the teachers thought. They said, "It must be us, after all. You told us we're the best teachers in the school." They were then informed, "No, that was part of the experiment, too. Your names were chosen out of a hat."

Think about that: average class, average teachers, but way above-average results. How do you explain it? The only thing exceptional was the teachers' expectations. And interestingly, the expectations were based on totally false information. Yet, the students excelled—they got what they expected to get. Positive expectations produced positive results.

It is no fairytale; it is hard fact: No matter who you are or what your situation in life, you have the power to change your life for the better immediately. If you are focused on I.M.Possible—warmed up for it—you are far more likely to be in a position to recognize possibilities and to create and act on opportunity when it presents itself. In fact, in the very act of reading this book you have already begun to warm up and exercise your I.M.Possible Muscle.

CREATING REALITY: FLEXING TO HAPPINESS	SCOTT

JDN: You do battle with the impossible every day on many levels. It's part of your profession and the pressure is tremendous. Plus you deal with all the regular stresses of balancing home, family and other responsibilities. No one has complete control of their negative emotions. At least I don't, as you know. So how do you deal with that so well?

SCOTT: For the last year, I've been working with the I.M.Possible Muscle visual and working the happiness area. At first, it was very hard because you're just trying to figure out how to do it. What to do. It's this thing that's conceptual and it's going to be different for everybody. I just keep visualizing and working at it. When I feel sad or down or bad, there's a lot of things that happen, but I flex towards happiness in my head.

At first, it didn't seem to work at all. We read about athletes who are able to do feats that seem superhuman, but it actually takes incredible repetition and skills practice. So I kept doing it just like going to the gym. I kept doing it, kept trying and it began to work. You showed me pictures of what these synapses are supposed to look like and how they work with chemicals passing in between and causing different emotions and physical responses. I just thought of those synapses in our brain, how neurons wire together when they've been fired together over and over so you have to keep repeating thoughts and activities before new ones get built in. It helped when I put that knowledge together with visualization of the I.M.Possible Muscle. Instead of synapses, I visualize fibers that form a connection to my I.M.Possible Muscle and as it gets stronger, it can pull happiness to me.

When negative emotion hits for whatever reason, if I don't do anything, I end up like anyone else who loses control of their emotions. I'm either furious or upset or worried, but I'm non-functional. All I can think about is bad things. But then I started trying to visualize an actual muscle, and the stronger it got the more it could close the gap between where I was and where I wanted to be. I know it's just an imaginary visual and not literal, but it works for me. I picture this muscle as contracting like a bicep. It lays flat and when you curl your arm it goes into a ball. It contracts and it pulls your arm towards you. So I think about this I.M.Possible Muscle flexing in my head, pulling my brain on one side and happiness on the other. I use the techniques you discuss to do the same kind of thing when it comes to any counterproductive emotions.

Happiness is really important for me. *But it's equally important that happiness isn't equated with anything.* And, that sounds pretty weird, because people think, "Well, happiness is security and having enough money and having my dream job or mate or whatever," but no, it's not. Because that stuff can all be taken away and it can all change and it just doesn't matter. And a lot of people have all that, the things that should define happiness, but they're not happy.

So happiness, instead, just has to be happiness in itself. I.M.Possible, for me, involves being a happy person, just being happy. And anybody could argue and say, "That's stupid. You have to be happy for a reason." But my reply is, *"Listen, this is what I feel. This is what gives me peace so I can be productive and help other people be productive. It doesn't matter if you think that's wrong or not; this is what I feel."* I've got to be really careful that happiness or peace of mind isn't equated with a certain thing because that certain thing will never *be* happiness. Happiness is a state by itself. I can be a happy person *despite* other things, instead of *depending* on other things. And I understand that some things can contribute to happiness, just like others can contribute to sadness and depression. But I'm talking about an attitude you choose to make your default mode as a matter of course, in spite of what life throws at you.

When You Just Can't Handle "Think Positive!"

"Good thinkers do not necessarily think harder, longer, or more exactly; they have simply learned to think in directions that are more likely to be productive." —Unknown

You are in the middle of a crisis. Your world is falling apart. You are hanging on for dear life and don't know how to cope. You turn to family, professionals, friends, associates, and what do you hear? *"Start thinking positive instead of negative. You've just got to think positive!"* How does that advice make you feel? *"Wow, that's the solution. Thank you so much."*? I don't know about you, but I react with the mental equivalent of a boxing glove, and it's *POW!* to the advisor—right to the moon!

Regardless of good intentions, the words *think positive* unfortunately often elicit just the opposite reaction. When I posed the scenario above to a random cross section of people, each person could identify a time when the admonition to "think positive" made them feel worse rather than better. Some of their comments:

Lynette: *When I am very upset and someone tells me to just think positive, it makes me angry. It is minimizing my problem.*
Richard: *The phrase is so overused, it's meaningless.*
Ryan: *Going through a crisis situation, think positive just sounds patronizing and insensitive. It can actually make you more defensive of your negative feelings.*

Yes, when we are suffering deeply, we seldom appreciate 'Be happy!' advice from others. Why is that? This may be partially because when we are overtaken by emotions of misery and sadness, the word *positive* is associated with the pleasure or the reward region of our brain. Our brain processes resist linking feelings of pleasure or satisfaction with conditions of misery and unhappiness.

Switching emotional gears is even more challenging when the underlying issues are deep and unresolved. Our thoughts and emotions have no way to make the transition to the conflicting concept *positive*. Not surprisingly, we feel defensive instead of encouraged. The real-world truth is, no one wins the battle 100% of the time. We can, however, minimize the casualties. If the underlying trigger is hormonal, chemical or hidden, and it's building and ready to snap, you can't just stop it from coming on. And if there's a very stressful event or a physiological problem underlying our emotions, something will act as an emotional trigger sooner or later.

> "Emotional competence is the single most important personal quality that each of us must develop and access to experience a breakthrough."
> —Doug Lennick, American Express Brokerage

We don't leave vacant space around our emotions. Emotions activate the networks that are the doorways to thoughts, so when the *emotion* comes (sadness, frustration, depression), immediately on its heels are *thoughts* that come spilling into our heads. As emotions bring thoughts, thoughts amplify emotions. They feed off each other and grow.

How often do we make ourselves unable to function because we are overwhelmed by feelings of anger or fear? Anger at what? Fear of what? Some hypothetical situation that hasn't even occurred or some real situation that is occurring? When we feel somebody has wronged us or upset us at work, home, or anywhere else, we begin to get worked up, don't we? Something happens and our minds take it, work it, twist it, and we start thinking further on down the road. We create scenarios in our mind: *"In a confrontation I would do this…";* *"Well, now I've lost this, and I'll never be able to do that";* *"Bad guys always win and nothing will ever change."* Whatever the cause, we feel increasingly depressed, stressful, antagonistic or confrontational. The point is, with the emotion comes thoughts. And the emotions and the thoughts keep each other going. We have unleashed a negative energy flow and the more it flows, the more it grows.

Once we have a certain momentum or intensity established, it can be nearly impossible to switch the direction and stem the flood of emotions. But *nearly impossible* is not impossible. In the realm of I.M.Possible there is always a way you can turn the tide.

In developing the I.M.Possible Muscle processes, I discovered that the general advice to think positive, is located on a rung higher up the emotional

111

ladder than we can reach directly from many impossible positions. So what would act as a handhold we *could* reach during times like this? How could we begin to climb upward?

Consider the original attempt at comfort: *"You've got to quit thinking negative. It's bad for you. You need to think positive."* Now try this. Replace the term *positive* with *productive* in the following phrase: *"I don't blame you for feeling the way you do. It's a challenging situation, but negative thoughts will only produce more hurt. How can you move forward from here? What is the most productive thing you can think or do in the situation right now?"* Note: These words do not have to be vocalized by someone else. During dark times, I think-productive self-talk to re-focus my brain away from impossible to I.M.Possible. (In Chapter 12 you will see further how our choice of focus affects our personal perceptions and our external outcomes.)

The idea of productive thinking doesn't minimize our pain or diminish our challenge; it doesn't suggest our problem is merely one of mood. Whatever the cause of our personal suffering, we do generally recognize that we want to, somehow, stop things from getting worse, which would be counterproductive.

Productive thinking is geared towards future positive results, which is a much easier concept to connect with

> *"I merely took the energy it takes to pout and wrote some blues."*
> —Duke Ellington, jazz legend

and act on when we are in a great deal of mental confusion or pain. We can then move onward and *through* the crisis to a more positive mental state. The word *productive* activates action and solution networks. How does it do this? We know our I.M.Possible Muscle is an action muscle, right? During productive thinking our brain switches on motivational as well as reward circuit regions. We now have a means to create an emotional transition. Productive thinking gives us something to do; it gives us hope, which makes us feel better. Our brain is able to change enough to reset our focus and direction. Productive actions take us through each tiny but progressive step, advancing from chaos to coherence to achievement.

Scott relates how he used the One Sock Process in this way:

To get myself to change physical or emotional direction when I don't feel like it, is hard. But I know it's the right thing to be doing and the better thing to be doing. Continued thoughts of "I don't like this. I hate this," will only lead you further down. I have to use the One-Sock Process [discussed later in this book]. Think one fiber, one moment at a time. The productive actions produce positive feelings, which, of course, lead to increasingly positive thoughts. Even if you can't think positive immediately, do the first productive action. Get your brain to help you over the hump. I've found that what your book says is true. Our actions affect our thoughts as much as our thoughts affect our actions."

Remember, our brain works on the basis of processes. When talking — whether to oneself or someone else—the words have to make sense to us on an emotional level or we won't connect with them, regardless of their value. So if you're not in a place where you can switch from dark thoughts to 'think positive,' kick in with your I.M.Possible Muscle. Think 'productive.' Whatever the distress, productive thinking beats counterproductive thinking every time. The natural outcome of healthy, productive thinking is a more positive direction. Your brain will reward and encourage you by activating circuits that create positive feelings.

CREATING REALITY: TAPPING THE POWER OF WORDS   DR. KOLB

JDN: You were telling me something interesting about how words network to different areas of our brain. You used the word *hammer* for an example, an action word. When we start to be aware of all the effects words have in activating different parts of our brain, we can have a new skill to use in driving our own self-talk and managing counter-productive words coming from others. The other day when I was feeling overwhelmed I started saying words like *healing* and *comfort* and *organized*. Just words that were positive, productive words. I did start to feel less stressed, more relaxed. How does that happen?

DR. KOLB: The subtleness of this is easy to demonstrate. If I say to you "What's *fall?*" You'll tell me it's a season. But, if I say to you, "I tripped this morning, I scraped my knee. By the way, what's *fall?*" Now you're biased the other way. Not the season, the drop down. So we can bias our choice of meanings of things by what's happened before, so that events that occur are interpreted based on what's just recently happened—even though it may have nothing to do with what just happened.

JDN: We've created a reality for that word based on something that acted as a context bias. The area of our brain activated by words or phrases is dependent on the meaning of that word to us right now.

DR. KOLB: Yes. Nouns are [points to head] back here. Verbs are up here. We've activated different brain circuits. So *fall*, as in *fall down*, is an action. It makes us feel differently than when we say *fall* as a season, which is a noun. Also, how we feel about the season *fall*, for whatever reason, will also affect what brain regions are activated. If we put people in scanners, we can show the differences in brain regions that are activated based on how we've tricked those brain regions.

JDN: Would this be valid advice: If you want to change your feelings from a counterproductive place and your mind is full of chaos—if you just want to start

113

somewhere—start by pronouncing words to yourself that have a positive, comforting connotation?

DR. KOLB: If you can, yes. Think of Julie Andrews, the song sung in *Mary Poppins*, "My Favorite Things." The kids are sad, so she sings this song to them... "Raindrops on roses and whiskers on kittens..." And it works. They start thinking about pussy willows and kittens and so on. Their emotions follow.

JDN: Warm and snuggly things. Feed and lead yourself to action words that relate to going where you want to go or words that energize or motivate you. But before you can get to that speed, you have to start by changing gears.

Get Off Your "But"

When you are trying to reach your I.M.Possible goal, how often do you find yourself saying, *"I want to do this, but...,"* or, *"I need this, but...,"* or, *"I really shouldn't do this, but..."*? Think about it. Write down one of the *but* sentences you say to yourself when you are in an impossible mode. Remember, words are powerfully linked to emotional and behavioral circuits in our brain. *But* is a brick wall word—it leads to impossible. When we say or think the word *but*, we unconsciously cause the firing of the neurotransmitters that not only inhibit positive actions, they also produce negative emotions to match the roadblock message we have just fed into our mind.

Now say the same sentence again, this time replacing the word *but* with the word *so*. *"I want to achieve this, so...,"* or *"We want to accomplish this outcome, so..."* Do you feel the difference in your mind? The word *so* is a natural bridge; it is not a brick wall. The focus is towards a solution, not a dead end. You signal your brain network to search out ways to create what you want. You become much more receptive to conditions or information that supports a positive outcome.

The next time you find yourself saying, *"I would, but...,"* remember, sitting on a *but* just makes it grow. To make your *but* disappear, move off of it and do something else. Make it *so*.

CREATING REALITY: CHANGING GEARS   **SCOTT**

SCOTT: In my experience, a huge exercise in training your I.M.Possible Muscle to combat negative emotion is to get busy with something productive. Do an essential or productive action or task, even if you don't like it. I like to ride my bike but, in the cold winters here, I can't. So I have to get that exercise some other way or I don't function as well. I don't like going to the gym, going all that way and sweating on the machines. It's cold, its rainy or whatever. So I've got to do what I need to do over what I'd rather be doing. Even the act of doing a productive thing to help yourself, even if you don't like it at the time—at some level inside, it helps. The brain processes do kick in and motivate me to do the next thing; it's easier to keep moving forward.

JDN: That's really building those fibers in your I.M.Possible Muscle so it can flex positive towards you.

SCOTT: I find it's essential to be able to do that. Because I can't control any other person. I can't control many things that happen in life. What I can control is my choice of response; what I.M.Possible fiber I can build to bypass the counterproductive thought and draw happiness closer. And I couldn't do that at first, either. But slowly it started getting better; slowly it became less difficult to switch gears. I still fail sometimes, but somehow I've learned how to stop my brain from imagining negative things, from thinking these things. I found that if I tackled the thought, used my I.M.Possible Muscle to pull happiness into my thoughts instead, it's doing lots of things at once. It's pushing the negative thoughts away. It's pulling happiness as a concept toward me. If that means putting the radio on louder, listening to a song, or thinking back to something in my history, it doesn't matter what it is, as long as it's a good thing.

You've got to say, "No, I'm doing a productive thing to try and help myself— to get better, to a positive place. It's not a thrilling thing, maybe not even a thing I like, but it's a productive thing." And doing that always does lead to a more positive place. [It] gives you a sense of moving toward a greater accomplishment. The I.M.Possible mindset really does make a difference

---

WRITE IN THIS BOOK: *Identify one to six areas that push your hot buttons (or your fear buttons).*

1.

2.

3.

4.

5.

6.

After reading Chapter 11, return to this section and develop visual images or One-Sock Processes that will help you to regain emotional control and think productively for each.

For one day become aware of the words you use and hear. Observe and record the affect they have on you and the people around you.

Use positive words in situations where you would normally have used negative, or given no response at all. Observe how the results differ and record the experience.

"People often become what they believe themselves to be. If I believe I cannot do something, it makes me incapable of doing it. But when I believe I can, then I acquire the ability to do it even if I didn't have it in the beginning." —Mahatma Gandhi, Indian leader

"It's the oldest rule in the book," said the King.
"Then it ought to be Number One," said Alice.
—Alice in Wonderland, Lewis Carroll

10. I.M.Possible Primary Rule: Practice

"No one ever gets far unless he accomplishes the I.M.Possible at least once a day."
—Elbert Hubbard, American industry pioneer (paraphrased by author)

What is the Number One rule for building I.M.Possible Muscle? You know this one. It's the same as for training physical muscle. Practice. Intentional, focused, deliberate practice, with intent to progress. How does this kind of practice differ from other types of practice?

It may surprise you to learn that practice in itself does not make perfect. In fact, bad habits are as much a result of practice as good ones. Everything we do repeatedly is a form of practice. Even a vicious cycle is a form of practice. So while it can be said that practice makes permanent, only a certain calibre of practice makes perfect. *This involves humility, the willingness to make appropriate adjustments, a determination to persevere toward the end goal despite discomfort—and your dedication to doing whatever is required.*

Use for example, a set of weights at the weight station in the gym. Two people, call them Kelly and Sean, approach the weight station. They are identical in stature, physical condition and muscular potential. Neither has ever lifted more than 15-pound dumbbells before. Unsurprisingly, lifting a set of 30-pound dumbbells represents an impossible feat for both. Each makes various attempts but is soon overwhelmed by the effort. The weight remains *impossible* for either to lift. The two men, however, have differing reactions. Here's what each thinks to himself:

Kelly: *It's impossible for me to lift that weight. It's much too heavy. I don't know why I even tried. I must look ridiculous to all these other people. Look what they're doing. I'm so weak. It's impossible for me ever to lift so much weight. I'll stick to what I'm comfortable doing already.*

Sean: *That's the weight I'm going to lift. I'll make it possible. I'll get trainer guidance and set goals. I can picture the moment of triumph! I can do fifteen pounds now. Practice will take me to 20 and eventually I will build the strength necessary to lift those 30-pound weights.*

117

Six months later, the two are at the gym again. Kelly timidly tries to lift the 30-pound weight, with the same negative results as before. Sean grasps a 30-pound dumbbell in each hand and lifts them in turn. Impossible had given way for him. What changed for Sean but not for Kelly? Not the 30 pound weight. What changed was this: Sean had developed the necessary power to lift the weight. He was able to transform the impossible to I.M.Possible because his internal directing force was I.M.Possible. Sean:

- Did not let the present impossible moment block his vision of an I.M.Possible future;
- Defined what he wanted to achieve and didn't allow anyone else to discourage him;
- Exercised his power of imagination and vision so he was able to view the weight in terms of I.M.Possible—a challenge to be achieved;
- Visualized himself in accordance with his goal, mentally seeing himself in the future actually lifting that weight;
- Was prepared to pay the price for reaching his goal; he committed the time and effort necessary to practice, movement by movement, to acquire the necessary technique and muscle strength.

In contrast, Kelly was practicing on a mental treadmill so was unable to make any progress. His energies were directed at Impossible. "If my problem can't be solved on these terms, I can't change anything in order to solve it." What does this attitude indicate about Kelly?

- Impossible was the start and finish point for him; thoughts had practiced, and developed a pattern, in creating barriers to progress;
- Previously, Kelly had practiced in a way that enabled him to progress to a certain point—but no further;
- He allowed himself to be controlled by fear of what others might think of him;
- Kelly saw himself only in terms of his present limitations and did not visualize his dream in terms of a definite goal he would attain;
- Kelly was unwilling to practice forward and tough it out through discomfort zones to create a new comfort zone; He was not willing to re-form old practices to find out who he could become.

Is it surprising that Kelly was, after six months, still unable to lift the weight? Sean and Kelly are fictional characters, but each represents very real perspectives that play a key role in failure or success. When faced with significant challenges, are you a Sean or a Kelly?

I.M.Possible: The Little Things Are the Big Things

How can small, day-by-day changes in behavior help you to counteract discouragement and move through wall-like barriers in front of you right now? When you make small changes in behavior, you will begin to see results. Even if the results are small, they will begin to create a change in your attitude. The opposite holds true, too. If you do nothing, tomorrow's memories will look pretty much the same as today's. All you will have to look back on will be more of the same. Without a change in behavior, the weights you were unable to move today aren't going to move tomorrow. When you make day-by-day changes, you will lead yourself out of your deep mental rut. It is by doing one little thing, and then another, and another, progressively building on each one, that we create new realities. Each step counts. It can't *not* create a change.

The world is full of people, everyday people you never read or hear about, who transform the impossible into the I.M.Possible. This book introduces you to just a few. And they all do it the same way—preparation and intentional practice (including the failures and learning curves) until their goal has been achieved. Each time we practice, our brain lays a deeper foundation upon which we can build. A simple example can be found in learning to type on a computer keyboard. Once you have spent enough time typing at a keyboard, you will have developed sufficient muscle memory so you will

> **"Great things are a series of small things brought together."**
> —*Vincent van Gogh, artist*

no longer need to think about each keystroke. If you practiced typing without looking at the keys, this memory even allows for accurate typing without looking at what keys are struck. The more you practice, the greater your increase in speed and accuracy. Have you ever watched a professional drummer play a solo bit during a musical performance? Learning to play that well has got to be worlds more difficult than learning to type. It is hard to believe anyone can master such incredible speed, dexterity and rhythm. These musicians actually move faster than human thought. In fact, drummers require more coordination than any other musician. They have many different functions going on *at the same time*. So how do they learn? I asked Duane Egan, who has played drums for many years, to explain how he taught his young son to gain such coordination. The simplicity of the learning example he provided me is fascinating. This excerpt is taken from: www.tigerbill.com/drumlessons/secrettofourwaycoordination1.htm.

119

I.M.POSSIBLE MUSCLE FOR THE MIND

1. Practice playing snare drum with right hand only (all sixteenth notes).
2. Practice playing cymbal ride with left hand only (all eight-note triplets).
3. Practice playing bass drum with right foot only (all quarter notes).
4. Practice playing hi-hats with left hand only (all eighth notes).
5. Practice playing the right hand and left hand parts together.
6. Practice playing the left hand and left foot parts together.
7. Practice playing the right hand and left foot parts together.
8. Practice playing the left hand and right foot parts together.
9. Practice playing the left hand and left foot parts together.
10. Practice playing the right foot and left foot parts together.
11. Practice playing the right hand, left hand, and right foot parts together.
12. Practice playing the right hand, left hand, and left foot parts together.

You've got the picture. "You practice each step over and over and over," said Duane "until you can do it in your sleep. Then you go on to the next step. If the basics aren't second nature before you step it up, you have to go back to the basics again. Eventually some guys have two tom toms, some have twelve. It can vary, but no matter what, each one has had to step their way up..."

Regardless of the nature of the goal, we build our ability to create new outcomes and new skills in the same way. By regularly and progressively building the right muscle for the task, movement by movement, moment by moment, fiber-by-fiber. As it grows and develops, this composite muscle, controlled by our brain, gives us the ability to transform seemingly impossible challenges into I.M.Possible victories.

Depending on how serious you are about your goal and the level to which you want to take it, keep this in mind: Patience and perseverance are key. All good things take time; great things take even longer. Greatness isn't handed to just anyone. On the other hand, with a lot of initiative and hard work, anyone—including you—can achieve great victories against incredible odds.

"If a man is called to be a street sweeper, he should sweep streets even as Michelangelo painted or Beethoven composed music or Shakespeare wrote poetry. He should sweep streets so well that all the hosts of heaven and earth will pause to say, 'Here lived a great street sweeper who did his job well.'" —Martin Luther King Jr.

120

How Practice Gets You through Your Discomfort Zone

With practice, you will gain increased I.M.Possible power to balance and quickly change a negative, draining response into one that is proactive and creative. In order to create new I.M.Possible networks to help you achieve a formerly impossible goal, you must make choices that do more than just substitute one behavior choice for another. The choice must be goal-supportive. You can't make just any old switch and expect you are going to build your I.M.Possible Muscle and move closer to achieving your goal. A gambler hoping to overcome his addiction to gambling would not gain anything by simply switching from poker to blackjack. A switch from chocolate to French fries would not help a person trying to lose weight. The choice you make must serve to advance your progress towards your I.M.Possible goal.

Are you beginning to see how conditions that make something impossible are often more a matter of choice, not concrete fact? Practice the I.M.Possible fiber-building techniques on a regular basis. The more you use the processes, the easier it becomes for you to bypass or prevent these impossible thoughts, actions and reactions before they begin. If you do find you're starting down that road, you'll know how to shift and free yourself mentally. You can then channel your energy in the best *I.M.Possible* way given the circumstances you are in.

CREATING REALITY: THINGS TAKE TIME   DR. KOLB

JDN: One of the huge reasons people get frustrated is because we are trying to jump straight to the top of the mountain. And we're becoming depressed because we've already made this huge mental leap to where we want to be without making the connection to the little steps in between.

DR. KOLB: Very true. I remember when I was learning how to ride horses, I would get very frustrated because I couldn't do it. Well, how long did it take to learn how to walk? Quite a long time. Or when people say to me, *"Grandma had this stroke and is in rehab and she's not doing well."* And I say, *"How much rehab has she had?"* and they say, *"Well, she's gone twenty times."* Do you know how long it takes to become an expert at something? A million times. It doesn't happen in twenty times. But we have this expectation...

JDN: We get frustrated because our ultimate goal is postponed or it still looks a long way off. What we aren't realizing is that it's only going to appear by continuing to take one more step towards it and one more and then the next. *Every move takes you closer, but it takes every move.*

121

I.M.Possible Above and Beyond: To Be a Champion

To become an expert at anything, practice and repetition for at least 10,000 hours or 1,000,000 times is needed; far more to become a master. Still, practice alone isn't enough. Many people work hard for decades without approaching greatness or even making significant improvement. So what's missing? Personal trainer Carl Macdonald explains, *"Many people cite the phrase 'Practice makes perfect.' I like to quote Vincent Lombardi: 'Only perfect practice makes perfect.' Practice on its own won't get you to that level. Practicing poorly will hold you back."*

The top performers in any field are among those who devote the most hours to *targeted, intentional practice*. This is activity that is explicitly intended to improve performance. All learning and improvement takes place when we reach for objectives that are just beyond our level of competence or comfort—one step at a time. Using the feedback we get from our results, we try again. This involves high levels of repetition until we have finally reached the new target. We then raise the bar and repeat the procedure.

"As human beings, our greatness lies not so much in our ability to remake the world... as in our ability to remake ourselves." —Mahatma Gandhi, father of India's independence

Creating Reality: The I.M.Possible Muscle-Building Process

All progress occurs in accordance with the outline below. *Progress is an outcome of repeatedly working with focus and concentration to achieve something that we have not yet achieved.* When we make progress, we achieve new skills, abilities and knowledge. Failure, mistakes and error correction are also an inevitable part of the learn-change-grow process.

Generate knowledge (thoughts). See in your mind's eye a problem or challenge, the first one that comes to mind. Now generate an I.M.Possible question or procedure. Imagine a spectrum, a horizontal line, here on the page. Write it down (or chart it) to stimulate brain networks for clarity and mental imprint:

> ➤ **Here is where I am (Point A).**

> ➤ **Here is where I want to be (Point B).**

1. What steps are necessary to get from A to B?
2. What is making this appear impossible right now?

Produce behaviors (actions).

1. What do I need right now to get started? List your resources (e.g., helpful people, internet, books) that could help with the steps, or be of assistance with moving through potential barriers.

2. Imagine and list (or actually do) a single action (e.g., makes a phone call for input, or completes a step toward the solution).

Create reality.

1. What happens?
2. What outcome should result?
3. What outcome does result?

Generate more knowledge.

1. Observe results.
2. Evaluate: What happened? Why?
3. How does that impact my goal?
4. What new information does this give me?
5. Who or what could help me to be more effective?

Produce behavior.

1. Choose your response, given the outcome and evaluation.
2. Plan your next step.

Here are six I.M.Possible elements of deliberate practice that you can apply to maximize your I.M.Possible processes in any aspect of life:

1. *Determine your goals before you start work.*
2. *Practice with conscious intent to improve performance.*
3. *Repeat to establish pathways.*
4. *Focus and concentrate during performance.*
5. *Evaluate and obtain qualified feedback.*
6. *Be willing to correct errors and make adjustments.*

"You play the way you practice." – Pop Warner, football coach

---

It's Never Too Late to Build I.M.Possible Muscle

So for those of you who are worried (as I was) that you may have missed your opportunity to be great at something—even a great mom, dad, teacher, or friend—because you didn't start when you were young or because you lack an in-born gift, stop worrying and begin practicing for something you would like to achieve.

Even those few lucky people who are born prodigies understand that natural ability will only go a limited distance on its own. Those who are born with inherent genetic aptitudes or gifts still practice intensely with deliberate focus and intent to continually broaden and stretch their abilities. Superior performers have developed concentration and dedication and deliberately practice in ways that will lead to improvement, knowledge and proficiency.

What motivates I.M.Possible achievers? Passion, vision and purpose. You must have a passion for what you are doing and be willing to sacrifice your present comfort zone for a future vision with a higher purpose. To conquer the impossible you must fully commit to the journey and be

> *"Never let the word 'impossible' stop you from pursuing what your heart and spirit urge you to do. I.M.Possible things come true every day."* —adapted from Robert K. Cooper, neuroscience expert

willing to adapt to the discomforts and uncertainties of exploring new territory. Einstein spent ten years thinking about special relativity before he was able to publish his breakthrough paper. He spent another ten years before completing general relativity.[1]

Thomas Edison, a master of perseverance, urged, *"Nearly every man who develops an idea works at it up to the point where it looks impossible, and then gets discouraged. That's not the place to become discouraged."* Professional football player and all-time great receiver Jerry Rice is a modern athletic version of Edison. No fewer than fifteen teams passed him up because they considered him too slow. What did he do? Did he let the barriers of the present separate him from his I.M.Possible goal of playing football? No. He practiced so hard, the other players got sick trying to keep up with him.

The fiber-by-fiber processes that have been used by all great achievers throughout history have been proven effective time and time again. Science and research have provided ample evidence to this effect. The only difference between your level of ability in a particular area and that of the person you would like to become is practice—a lot of practice—with concentrated effort and intent to learn and improve.

Many people think Tiger Woods became a world champion golfer because he was born with the gift. A look at his pre-championship days tells the real story: Tiger's father introduced him to golf when he was just

---

[1] Greg Satell, www.digitaltonto.com/2011/what-makes-you-so-smart/

eighteen months old! Dad Woods encouraged him to practice intensively. Tiger had racked up at least fifteen years of practice by the time he became the youngest-ever winner of the U.S. Amateur Championship, at age eighteen. Tiger Woods makes it clear that he never takes his abilities for granted. He continually tries to improve, devoting many hours a day to conditioning and

> *"Research now shows that the lack of natural talent is irrelevant to great success. The secret? Painful and demanding practice and hard work."*
> —Geoffrey Colvin, Fortune Magazine, Oct., 2006

practice. In the spirit of great achievers, Tiger remained willing to learn and change in this area of his life, remaking his swing twice. He did not allow ego to blind him to the fact that a willingness to readjust established ideas is an essential element in growth and advancement in order to excel.

When scientists specializing in the field of human achievement used psychometric tests to measure a variety of experts from different professions on their powers of speed, memory, and intelligence, they found that these individuals had no particular gift in these areas. Their demonstrated superiority was domain specific, meaning these people obtained their skills by practicing long and hard and with a focus on what they wanted to achieve.[2] Once again, this is confirmation that, regardless of how you define personal success or fulfillment, the biggest factor in your own level of achievement is determined by *you.*

Dr. K. Anders Ericsson, professor of psychology at Florida State University, coined the term deliberate practice. For nearly twenty-five years he has studied geniuses, prodigies and superior performers. He concluded:

For the superior performer the goal isn't just repeating the same thing again and again, but achieving higher levels of control over every aspect of their performance. That's why they don't find practice boring. Each practice session they are working on doing something better than they did the last time.

Most people think of practice as something you do to get better at technical skills. I know I did. So we miss the key point. Would you like to become a better parent? A better teacher? A kinder person? A happier person? Do you ever find yourself repeating any of these phrases:

> *"I want to become a better…"*
> *"I want to discover…."*
> *"I want to be a more [you define the quality] person."*

---

[2] K. Anders Ericsson, Ralf T. Krampe, and Clemens Tesch-Römer, "The Role of Deliberate Practice in the Acquisition of Expert Performance," *Psychological Review* 100, no. 3 (July 1993): 363-406.

"I want to find a solution to..."
"I want to become the kind of person who..."

Any area of personal challenge that is truly important to you can be broken down into tasks where you can make continual and progressive steps forward. Practice every day by making deliberate changes in your routine thoughts and actions. As you experience regular, positive outcomes you will be creating and establishing new pathways in your brain. Step by step you will gain more knowledge, ability and confidence. Remember, the more we practice, the more we gain knowledge. The more we gain knowledge, the more we can change. It is only by such conscious efforts that we gain the necessary material to make the next tough decision or adjustments on the journey to an I.M.Possible goal.

CREATING REALITY: INTENTIONAL PROGRESS   TIM

TIM: I've had people who want to work for our company say to me, "I've got thirty years' experience." And I say, "No, you haven't. What you've got is one year's experience thirty times. Because you never progressed. You've done the same thing constantly for the last thirty years and when you look at some of the guys that are out there - highly specialized, highly skilled, really sought-after within their fields. Those are the guys that have progressively changed, taken some risks. Not the guy that shuttled a car around for thirty years. There's a place for everybody, absolutely. However, those specialist skills require a different approach altogether.

"There is no such thing as a natural touch. Touch is something you get by hitting a million golf balls." – Lee Travino, championship golfer, with unusual 'golf-course' characteristics

WRITE IN THIS BOOK: *Even if you cannot believe right now, get started testing the processes <u>and choose to deliberately practice using something you have learned from this book.</u>*

Record your progress here here. Approach your efforts as a daily work-out. Assume the attitude, "It will be interesting to see what happens."

"Put up in a place where it's easy to see, this cryptic admonishment T.T.T. When you feel how depressingly slowly you climb, it's well to remember, THINGS TAKE TIME."
—Piet Hein, Danish scientist, mathematician, poet

CHART 1A: IMPOSSIBLE BELIEF-TO-OUTCOME FLOW ©

"There's no use trying. One can't believe impossible things."

Your focus: *This is impossible!*

Your emotional neuro-circuits activated: Depression, stress, helplessness.

Your energy signal: Give up. Give in. It's always going to be the same.

Your brain circuits activated: Inhibitory, depression, avoidance, fatigue.

No Victories = Stronger Disbelief=Stronger Resistance to Trying =
Few I.M.Possible Things Can Be Achieved

Impossible is a dead end—a graveyard of hope.

CHART 1B: I.M.POSSIBLE BELIEF-TO-OUTCOME FLOW©

"Why sometimes I've believed as many as six i.m.possible things before breakfast..."

Your focus: *This is I.M.Possible!*

Your emotional neuro-circuits activated: Hope, motivation, determination.

Your energy signal: Let's go! There's a way and I'm going to find it!

Your brain circuits activated: Excitatory, anticipation, creativity, alertness.

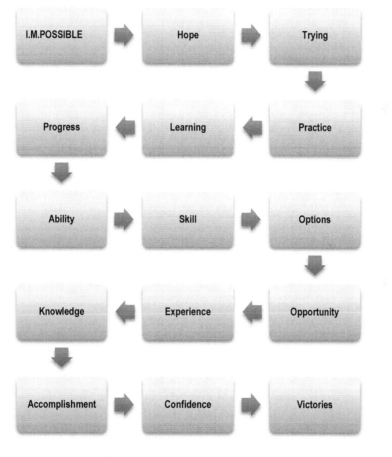

Victories = Stronger Belief =
More Impossible Things Can Be Accomplished

I.M.Possible is alive with endless possibilities—
a wonderland, a birthplace of miracles.

"Why, the best way to explain it is to do it."
—*The Dodo, Through the Looking Glass*

11. Impossible to I.M.Possible:
A One-Sock Process

"Start by doing what's necessary; then do what's possible; and suddenly you are doing the Impossible." —St. Francis of Assisi

Have you ever been overwhelmed by circumstances or deadlines? Despite our best efforts, there are times when the demands of life just become too much for us. We can then become increasingly stressed or frazzled. Our thoughts start wandering all over the map. Or we feel incapacitated and freeze into complete inaction. The to-do list becomes a blur and we accomplish little to nothing.

The demands of today's world bombard us with deadlines stack up and everything requires attention yesterday. At such times, we need a process we can use to get or stay on track even when life is chaotic and we just can't think where to start next. It was during one of these *impossible* times that I developed the One-Sock Process, a blueprint for achievement, broken down to the most basic level. It happened like this:

> There are risks and costs to a program of action. But they are far less than the long-range risks and costs of fearful or comfortable inaction.

As I my understanding of how we can become more like architects in creating and re-creating our own reality increased, I mindfully looked for ways to use put that knowledge into practice. Acting as my own coach, I began to make small moment-by-moment changes that would each spark changes in my brain. Repetition, I knew, would lead to changes in network circuitry. The outcome would be a change in me and in my reality. I worked with these three basic neuroscience principles:

1. By changing our thoughts, we can change our actions.
2. By changing our actions, we can change our thoughts.
3. By changing our thoughts and actions, we can change our outcomes.

These are facts of life. They are universal principles that are true for every situation in life.[1] To anyone who now feels stuck in a hopeless place because of past mistakes, it is critical you really get what this means: *Your past does not have to define your future. You can change your outcomes, starting now.*

How Memories Create Our Future

"It's a poor sort of memory that only works backwards." —The Queen, Through the Looking Glass

Working memory is the means by which past experiences are combined with present events to produce future effects. This is how we create and re-create our reality every day. These past experiences include not only accurate memories of events, but also inaccurate memories, and both accurate knowledge and faulty or partial knowledge. If we keep doing the same things in the same way, our experiences never change, and our memories and knowledge base will stay the same. We don't learn anything new. Flexing into new territory gives us the opportunity to correct past errors, find solutions, or create wonderful new outcomes.

The One-Sock Process: How It Came into Being

"In a year from now you'll wish you had started today." —Unknown

One of my I.M.Possible goals is to keep my brain and body as fit as possible by doing regular aerobic workouts. One morning I decided to mindfully put the above principles to work in a very basic way. I was so impressed with the results that I recorded the experience immediately afterward exactly as I remembered it. You may find yourself relating similar types of thoughts and behaviors to situations in your own life.

To make myself work out four to five times a week was very hard. I would start out well and then phase out slowly until three weeks had gone by and I was back to square one. One morning, I got up and went straight over to the big, easy chair and picked up a novel. I battle with a sleep disorder, so was very tired and depressed and didn't feel like I could move, let alone work out. Here are some of the "impossible" excuses I gave myself:

I don't want to work out;
I'm not even dressed yet;
I'm so tired. I couldn't possibly take two steps; I'd give up;
I don't have time; I'm already behind in my day (but honestly, I was going to spend the same amount of time sitting in an easy chair with a novel);

---
[1] I call this *The Law of The Way It Is (DeNovo's Law)*. It states, "An outcome that occurs or will occur regardless of disbelief, arguments or efforts to the contrary."

I feel miserable and this is so comforting;
I hate looking at myself in shorts;
I don't feel well; I need this rest;
I'm waiting for a phone call; The phone will ring just when I get started; What good will it do? And so on…Excuses— I'm a master.

So I said to myself, "I always do this. I don't want my tomorrows to look like this." I remembered the Wonderland scene where the Queen said to Alice, "It's a poor sort of memory that only works backwards."

I realized my brain had developed a pattern of thoughts that kept relying on yesterday's behavior—I was thinking backwards. Such thinking kept me on the path of least resistance, instead of taking action that I knew would make me healthier and happier.

This scared me.

I told myself, "If I don't take control, that old pathway will never change and my outcome will never change." I decided, "Today, now, I will begin. This moment. I.M.Possible. Anything at all I do in the next moment that takes me away from the old thinking and towards what I know I should be doing is building and strengthening I.M.Possible Muscle fiber. Eventually, I will be able to push past the obstacle. So what is the nearest fiber in front of me this moment?"

"Can I put on one sock?" *(You see, I was all snuggled in a blanket because I was cold. If I put on a sock, I knew I would be warmer.)*

✓ *So I got my ankle socks and put on one sock. Of course, I then put on the other one.*

No pressure. No thinking past that moment; only, "Can I just build this one fiber—the one in front of me—a fiber I have access to right now?"

I then asked myself, **"Can I just put on my work-out shorts? I don't have to work out, but can I just get them on?"**

✓ *I put on my workout shorts.*

"Can I put on my top?"

✓ *I put on my top.*

Next fiber: **"Can I put on my running shoes? I don't have to work out but if I put my shoes on, I'm more likely to work out."**

✓ *So I put on my running shoes.*

"Can I go get my water bottle? Just go get it, nothing else."

✓ *Got it.*

"Can I fill it up?"

✓ *I filled it up.*

"Can I get my iPod and put it on the treadmill?"

✓ *I got my iPod and my water bottle and put both on the treadmill.*

My thoughts were changing as a result of my actions.

"Okay, here we are…doing much better already—building one fiber at a time. I'm still tired but feeling better."

And my actions were changing as a result of my thoughts.

"Can I turn on the TV?"

✓ *Yeah, I can do that.*

"Can I get on the treadmill? Yes!"

✓ *I got on the treadmill. I was taking ownership of my goal.*

"Can I start walking? I don't have to walk any longer than I want, I don't have to run today. Can I just start?"

✓ *And so I started. Thinking positive all the time, not letting my mind drift to anything negative. Thinking about how much easier this was than I thought, instead of how much harder. It's incredible what feeding yourself those positive self-messages does.*

✓ *Fifty minutes later I had completed my workout. Energized mentally and physically, and ready to build the next fiber in front of me.*

By first changing one thought, I could change an action, then a thought, then an action. *One thing leads to another.* Baby steps though they were, I changed the outcome. It worked. In becoming aware of the power I had to change my own reality, I had regained control of my brain instead of allowing myself to go into default mode and be led unthinkingly down old pathways to old results. The chaos in my mind had given way to the focus on what was truly possible in the very next moment.

My I.M.Possible Muscle responded immediately by releasing minute amounts of dopamine and making connections to a little more ownership of my bigger goal, which was to work out. Every moment, every step we take toward any of our goals, causes chemical changes that propel us a little more toward achieving or owning that goal. I used my written account to demonstrate to my husband and friends how I was successfully adapting the techniques I was writing about to my own life on a daily basis. Although I didn't tell them, "Now you go home and try this," throughout the months that followed, a number of people told me about challenges they had overcome by using what they referred to as 'that *One-Sock Process*'. They rated this as a top tool for making progress through chaos. Both Dr. Kolb and David Coleman have made use of the One-Sock Process in their professions.

Why Is All Achievement a One-Sock Process?

One-Sock Process seemed to me to be a very appropriate name to represent the basic formula for building I.M.Possible Muscle. After all, when athletes or bodybuilders are about to train or work out, where do they start? What is the first thing they do? If you're thinking *stretch* or
warm up, you're starting too far along in the process. Before they get as far as warming up, they have to dress for what they are going to do. *What is the*

133

most basic action required when getting dressed for a workout? Put on one sock, of course. And then the other.

An athlete has to start with the most basic step in the process, just like the everyday Joe who is trying to get down to his treadmill or across town to the gym. *The difference is that trained athletes have also trained their brain to immediately override or redirect thoughts or feelings that would discourage them from 'just doing it'.* They go straight past thinking about every little action they must do between putting on one sock and warming up for participation in their chosen sport, but they complete every step regardless. We all start at the same basic place when it comes to getting from Point A to Point B in anything we do in life—the beginning.

Once we have established a routine or when we feel really pumped to do something, we don't consciously go through every mental step, each thought and action to be completed. This is because, just like putting on that first sock, the real starting point now seems too insignificant to connect with its importance in reaching the end goal. However, *it is this failure to respect the power in these moment-by-moment steps that causes so many people to give up before they even start. Or, if they do start, they give up shortly afterwards.* They decide that, if the journey to their destination cannot be made in one huge leap or a couple of leaps at most, it can't be made at all. The truth is, all those tiny movements and actions lead us to the next action and the next. In fact, it is all those tiny movements that determine whether we eventually become the master of our intention.

In my case, I was no longer in a place where I could take the mental leap from, "Here I am in this chair, snuggled in and warm and sleepy," to, "Yes, I'm going to go over to that treadmill and start warming up for a workout." It was just not possible. The reasoning, of course, was that, all I had to work with was what was *impossible*, so there was no use trying. I certainly wasn't going to get to I.M.Possible if I were to attempt to follow that line of reasoning, at least not from where I had set the starting point. You see, it's not that I couldn't get to where I really wanted to go; rather, *I had made it impossible to get there when my mind was using my ultimate destination as the starting point.* In actuality, what I needed was to start at a different place, at a place I would be able to reach at that very moment, and go on step by step from there.

If you think, do or say something that takes you in the direction of where you want to ultimately be (and one further step away from some destructive or unproductive place), you've just changed your position for the

134

better. You've just increased your I.M.Possible progress. That step becomes a reality. You can start in the next moment. Every moment is all we've got. *Every moment has power.* Each choice we make of thought or action in that moment either draws right over the same lines of our old reality or creates a new picture in the pages of our life book.

Remember: *If nothing changes, nothing changes.* Thought, behavior and outcome patterns are processes of your brain. The impossible obstacles in your life will continue to appear in ongoing scenarios that repeat over and over and over again until your brain's thought process is changed. This, in turn, will establish different beliefs. In turn, you will have a far greater ability to attract the resources or conditions required to create productive and positive outcomes.

> *All changes, even positive ones, are scary. Attempts to reach goals through radical means often fail because they heighten fear. But the small steps disarm the brain's fear response, stimulating rational thought and creative play.* - Robert Maurer, physicist

If you want to get to your I.M.Possible goal and you are having a hard time, take it back to the present moment. Start with a basic step. If you can't think positive, think productive. Use the One-Sock Process. Micro-step yourself through productive thoughts and actions in order to achieve your goals, and also to navigate sudden changes or crises that may arise. *Don't pressure yourself with anxiety about what you will or won't do in the moment after this.* Let it unroll. The small-rewards processes that take place in your brain along the way will create a new set of dynamics. When feeling stuck, remember these three facts of progress:

1. *Achievement is a moment-by-moment process.*
2. *You don't have to believe at first, just start to practice.*
3. *There is always a way to lift I.M.Possible out of impossible.*

With each stage of I.M.Possible success are new challenges. Remember, setbacks are part of life and learning. These do not take away from the value of your prior achievements and efforts. However, you must continue to consciously practice in order to successively develop the fiber mass necessary to reach your I.M.Possible goals. Train and strengthen I.M.Possible Muscle fibers at least half an hour every day. The more you practice and the more you look after the fiber essentials, the faster you will develop.

What if it Really Is Impossible for Me to Do?

The answer to the above question is simple: *If something is impossible, then it's irrelevant, even if the condition is temporary.* If you have tried every means at your disposal, recognize that fact and move on. Don't focus on the impossible because, if it truly is impossible, there is no sense in dwelling on it. Go back to I.M.Possible. Think in terms of: *How can I move forward in some way? What do I have left? What is the fiber in front of me I can build right now? Is it a thought? An action? Should I go back to fiber essentials? How can I see this in terms of a solution? How can I move forward in some way? Is there someone I can talk to?*

You will be surprised at what you can accomplish if you keep your focus off the impossible, and direct it toward building an I.M.Possible fiber in front of you at the moment. The next chapter will reveal just how your mental focus changes your brain—and your outcomes.

How You Can Use the One-Sock Process Every Day

When there is chaos everywhere, use the One-Sock Process. Take it one choice or one action at a time. Look only at the moment in front of you and ask, "What can I do right now, *independent of feeling or future,* that will make me feel like I have accomplished something towards my I.M.Possible Muscle development?" Only you know what needs to be done for you to reach a goal, to create new ones, or to revive and re-create your life in some essential way. The important thing is to begin. Do something that feeds into a productive mode in some way. Pick something—*any*thing—that changes the situation for the better in one single way, but just get started. As long as it moves you one moment closer to a productive goal, you are in I.M.Possible Muscle mode.

Get a drink of water, go for a walk, eat something healthy, breathe deeply, smile, laugh, and get to a mental place where you can refocus. Begin to check items off your to-do list one by one. Ask yourself, "What *am I able* to do in the next moment?" The One-Sock Process reward mechanism that takes place in the brain (through the release of neurotransmitters and the change in brain area activity) delivers small rewards that lead to the bigger reward in the form of achievement of your stimulus target—all of which eventually lead to I.M.POSSIBLE goal achievement and permanent neurological change.

Understanding the brain's reward and motivation role in coaxing us onward to success has made a huge difference in my ability to apply the One-Sock Process in any situation. As you put your newfound knowledge to

136

work, you will see how it applies in all areas of life. Why not keep a record so you can see how the micro-steps add up to new successes?

CREATING REALITY: RYAN'S ONE-SOCK PROCESS	RYAN

JDN: Tell me about times you felt it was impossible for you to get to the next level and how you've done it anyway.

RYAN: That feeling happens every morning when I wake up, whether shooting or editing a movie, especially when I'm editing. I'm overwhelmed for at least forty-five minutes with feelings like, "I can't figure this out. I've gotten in over my head. I don't have the answers to these questions people are asking me. Why is my email full? I don't know the answer to any of this. I'm overwhelmed. This is never going to get done. I've just squandered half a million dollars of some investor's money. I need to run away now. I'm going to go to a mental hospital. This is never going to happen."

And then one by one, you start answering those emails. And one by one, you start checking those voice mails, and then you have a couple cups of coffee and you sit down in front of the editing bay or you show up at the set and you start to get in the groove, and you go, "Okay, we'll just do one thing at a time. Alright, let's put the camera over here. There, that looks like a good spot. I don't even know why I'm putting the camera there half the time, but somebody needs to do something, so let's put the camera here. We can move it later if it's not right. Now, let's get us some light. Where are the actors? Get 'em in their make-up. Let me look at the script. Oh my God, the script sucks. What are we gonna do? Well, let's rewrite the scene right now. And then, problem by problem, you start attacking it. Piece by piece. By the end of the day, you sit there and you watch the dailies, or the scene you edited that day that had all kinds of problems as you were going along. You sit back, and you watch it and you go, "All right. That turned out pretty good! We got something there. It's as least as good as most of the other [stuff] that's out there, so let's be happy."

JDN: So, Ryan, you made your own One-Sock Process without realizing it.

RYAN: Absolutely. That's just the way achievement gets done. You really can use it with anything. I don't know how it is where you are, but here, registering your car is a total nightmare. I can honestly say that I've felt like this: "I can direct, edit, and produce, front to back, a full length movie, but if I have to register a car, I'm panic-stricken. I've got to stand in a never-ending line and I don't know if I'm in the right line, and I don't know how to fill out all this paperwork... And just registering your car at the DMV can seem like an impossible thing." Then I think to myself, "Wait a second. Just think of this as a day on a movie set and go into this attacking it like you would attack a challenge on a movie set. And what do I do with that? The DMV is then pretty easy. But if I go in there with, "Oh [crap], I'm in the DMV. I don't know what to do. It's all too much. How am I going to do this?" Then I'm just a miserable idiot like everyone else.

JDN: That's the beauty of the I.M.Possible Muscle-building formula. You can drop it into anything. Once you have the formula, you can use it to apply to any process and create a template that is familiar to you. The process you used in completing your movies is basically the same as was used to finish this book, the same one used by Carl in training people who don't think they can be rehabilitated, by Scott to solve technical issues even the manufacturers haven't been able to resolve, by Dr. Kolb, Tim, Saladin, Richard, Kim, Cara and everyone else I've interviewed in gathering material for this book series.

RYAN: The principles are universal so you can do it that way consciously and save a lot of time and heartache or you can grope around and pretty much spin in the dark.

"Do it now. You become successful the moment you start moving toward a worthwhile goal." —The author

---

WRITE IN THIS BOOK: *Try the One-Sock Process now.*

Pick something that represents a fiber in your I.M.Possible Muscle.

Now identify one task that will help you to build that fiber. It may be a household chore you have been putting off; it may be exercise, a doctor's appointment, an activity with your child, your spouse, etc.

Put on one sock. Feel the mental reward process and see the fiber activate and strengthen. Continue to imagine the one-sock process through the chore, piece by piece, moment by moment, and complete the chore.

Now engage the chore in real time with the One-Sock Process, action by action, and direct attention to each step.

Write down your steps. This will imprint the process on your mind and help you to make it a core strength in your I.M.Possible Muscle. Reward and reinforce your efforts. Celebrate!

Future book series will include reader experiences using the One Sock Process. Visit www.jamiedenovo.com and be a hero. Allow us all to benefit by your story. Whatever your achievement, how did you use the fiber-by-fiber and/or One Sock Processes to turn impossible challenges into I.M.Possible victories?

"Look at a day when you are supremely satisfied at the end. It's not a day when you lounge around doing nothing; it's when you've had everything to do, and you've done it." - Eugene S Wilson, American Educational Administrator

---

She knelt down and looked along the passage
Into the loveliest garden you ever saw.
How she longed to get out of that dark hall, and wander about
Among those beds of bright flowers and those cool fountains...
—*Alice in Wonderland*

12. I.M.Possible Goals, Impossible Obstacles

"The first step to getting the things you want out of life is this: Decide what you want."
—Ben Stein, actor

Regardless of whom we are, or the kind of work we do, everyone needs a vision of what his or her place is, and what it could, be in this world. From childhood on, humans have an inborn need to feel and believe that we have something worthwhile to do. Each of us needs a bigger objective and purpose in life than simply oneself or one's interests alone.

If you have read this far, it is highly likely that a) you have a dream goal in mind that you want to achieve, b) the goal has some pretty heavy odds working against its achievement and, c) at some level in your mind, you would like to fight the battle regardless of those odds.

If you are willing to take on the impossible, it is because you have made a strong connection between your goal and your self-concept.[1] How does your self-concept tie into goal achievement? Self-concept (also called self-construction, self-identity or self-perspective) is about the way you view yourself as a person, who you believe you really are and should be. Ultimately, our brain wants to help us achieve our goals so we can fulfill that sense of who we are.[2] Hardwired into human beings is the need to grow, achieve, create, and connect with the rest of creation.

To break through the toughest discomfort zones, your I.M.Possible muscle must be trained to be strong and flexible enough to bear the weight of, and overcome, the challenges that would hold you down. Otherwise, you will always stop short of what you can actually achieve. The first step in this training is to clearly define and own your goal. Why? This book uses

---

[1] A future book in this series will examine finding our passion and goal-setting.
[2] M. Bong and R. E. Clark, "Comparison Between Self-Concept and Self-Efficacy in Academic Motivation Research," *Educational Psychologist* 34, no. 3 (1999), 139-153.

the word *goal* far more often than it does the word *dream*. That is because goals and dreams are not the same thing. We need both, but I.M.Possible muscle works on a different level with each. The concept of a goal and that of a dream do not trigger the same processes in our brain. A dream is a big picture vision, an outcome or end result upon which we focus inwardly. Dreaming is definitely *part* of the I.M.Possible process. It is a neurological essential that sets up the conditions whereby we can work toward bringing that mental image into being. However, when we structure that dream or vision into a clearly defined goal, we begin the shift into a different state of mind. Read on to discover why a goal is such a powerful thing – and how allowing your focus to drift can shift your goals and sabotage your dreams.

What Changes in Our Brain When We Set Goals?

> *"Would you tell me please, which way I ought to go from here?"* said Alice.
> *"That depends a good deal on where you want to get to,"* said the Cat.
> —Alice in Wonderland

When we set our heart on achieving a goal, much more happens inside us than we are consciously aware of. When our goal becomes clear in our mind, we set off a network of powerful processes and complex connections in our brain.

As you gain a better understanding of some of the basic neuroscience that underlies goal-setting and focus, you can use these insights to help you pull your attention *away* from needless 'decoy' activities that drain energy, time and resources. Of course, as you do this, you will find your progress *toward* the goals that really matter, will begin to grow by leaps and bounds.

According to brain and behavior research, when we set a definite goal, our brain will produce negative feelings in us if we fail to achieve that goal.[3] Again, it's a matter of hardwired processes. The more we focus on an outcome, the more processes in our brain drive us toward the transformation of that goal into actual achievement. Continued focus and failure to make progress in obtaining our focus objective, can generate negative emotions such as depression, defeat, anger or hopelessness. Setting small but achievable goals has the opposite effect. As we focus on small successes, our brain activates networks that generate feelings of hope and support our ability to endure setbacks and detours.

[3] B. M. Byrne, "The General/Academic Self-Concept Nomological Network: A Review of Construct Validation Research," *Review of Educational Research* 54 (1984), 427-456.

The Strength of Desire

According to neuroscience research, many of the same brain processes in the frontal lobe produce both imagination and reality. Such processes allow us to imagine the future and to generate novel ideas and solutions. This area of our brain doesn't make judgment calls as to whether the picture in our mind is healthy or unhealthy, realistic or illusory; it just reflects the picture we feed into it.

When we begin to focus on *wanting* what we visualize, when it is something we do not have, neuro-circuits are activated in our brain that begin to invest us emotionally into the target. The more we think about it, the more we see ourselves as in possession of that outcome, the more invested we become. Our brain takes ownership, and the object of our focus now becomes a goal to obtain. Networks in our brain related to maintaining our self-concept respond with increased activity, releasing chemical neurotransmitters that reward us each time we complete an action that takes us nearer to that goal. Here's an example:

When we were first married, Scott and I were in Mexico, where we were accosted by a timeshare vacation condo salesman. Lured by promises of an authentic Mexican blanket and fancy hotel lunch in exchange for a mere hour of our time, we reluctantly agreed to listen to their pitch. My disgust with the soda cracker "meal" and determination to leave at the earliest possible moment dissolved as I listened to the humorous, engaging salesman describe our paradisiacal lives as part owners of this gorgeous resort property. This paradise villa, and others, were presented on the big screen in glowing color, complete with frolicking, happy timeshare owners—'people just like us.' Visions of inexpensive holidays with family and friends in exotic locales brought a collective gleam to the eyes of this roomful of naïve tourists, my eyes as bright as the rest. Imagine! Those laughing, happy people could be me and my family!

My brain was beginning to take ownership. It began to activate goal acquisition networks connected to my self-concept: *we worked so hard, were deserving, would love to be able to take annual exotic holidays like some of our acquaintances. We would even be able to host family and friends.* These professionals in the art of mental and emotional seduction soon had many of us lined up to sign contracts. Fortunately for me, Scott is made of sturdier stuff. After asking some hard questions of our guy, he dragged me away, confidently asserting the deal would not be gone tomorrow. (No one got Mexican blankets, by the way. The supply had 'just run out.') By the next day, I'd had time to physically and mentally pull away and examine the realities. I realized that my rational train of thought had been derailed by the tropical

141

environment, alluring visuals, and smooth talk designed to stimulate impulsive desire. We hadn't previously wanted or needed to own a vacation timeshare, nor could we afford the several thousand dollars requested on the spur of the moment (plus the annual fees, for years to come). I was even more thankful for Scott's intervention once we got home and had time to do research. At times like this, second thoughts, giving you time to adjust your focus, are generally wisest.

There are other ways in which strong desire can cause us to experience our reality differently than we normally would, until our goal is obtained. You can see this phenomenon at work, for example, in people who are easygoing and fun to be around—until they get into a competitive game. Suddenly, they seem to be out for blood. Winning becomes all-consuming. At times, they may even become vicious, disregarding the effect on other players. The connection between winning the game and personal identity causes the brain to become highly active in some regions and inhibits other regions. Along with many other neurochemicals, the brain releases huge amounts of dopamine, adrenalin and endorphins, so the various regions don't notice pain while competing. This is the goal-attainment process at work.

"Obstacles are those frightening things that become visible when we take our eyes off our goals." —Henry Ford, industrialist

I.M.Possible Achievement:
Not What You Drive, But What Drives You

What do contestants running a marathon have in common with people who are fighting to survive in life and death situations? In both cases, the victors are able to rise above normal limitations and perform superhuman feats. They focus exclusively on the goal. Its achievement is vividly imprinted in their mind, and their brain processes success as part of who they already are! You can do likewise. Whatever your I.M.Possible goal, if you keep your focus steady and your vision clear, your brain will set up the mental, emotional and physical conditions that drive you to work to fulfill your brain's self-image.

Another word about goals: you must clearly determine where the goal you are pursuing ranks on your priority list. Why? Imagine what would happen if you went to the gym and you only had time to do one exercise effectively. But instead, you try to fit in five or six. You could try to lift dumbbells to strengthen your upper arms, while simultaneously running on the treadmill to build strong cardio, while sporadically slowing up to work in sit-ups for great abs; or you could dash from one station to the other. But what would you really accomplish in any of those areas? You would even easily injure yourself, negating any progress. We cannot focus on many goals or on conflicting goals and do well at any of them. We may accomplish bits of each, but I.M.Possible power grows with steady focus.

When two goals conflict, we can be faced with some hard choices. For example, the time and resources necessary to achieve my I.M.Possible goal of writing *Six Impossible Things* required (and continues to require) the sacrifice or postponement of other goals. I have had to shelve, at least for a time, other activities that hold significant value to me. I have had to minimize personal expenditures and distractions as well as manage weighty obligations in the company my husband and I own (which provides our means of living). I also have many family, spiritual, and health responsibilities that cannot be neglected. It was all the challenge I could handle to balance the issues associated with completing this book against other obligations and priorities, which were non-negotiable and had to take precedence.

The choice of what we are willing to give up lies with each of us. Those hard choices may take the form of time, money, resources, ego, things, pet beliefs and tradition—even people. Ask yourself, *"Am I willing to pay the cost to obtain my I.M.Possible dream? What is the trade-off?"*

James Christensen offered his perspective on priorities when working to achieve a dream: *"The balance part has to come into play when you are pursuing any dream. Families are the most important thing. Carol said, 'Come home and help me with the kids. Talk, spend some time.' My plan was that I always had to be there for them, and my dream I did during the cracks."*

I wish I could say I always stayed balanced but it wouldn't be true. Life was, and is, a juggling act. I often dropped the ball, or life threw a dozen new ones into the mix. What I did not do is give up. I used the One-Sock Process to regroup and get back into a healthier rhythm.

I found I had to practice and develop a conscious awareness of how I use my time and resources. Both are limited. I can accomplish some things well or many things poorly. Many times I have to say no to something I would love to do, or be very willing to do, if circumstances were otherwise. I have had to learn to monitor the true cost of each activity I am invited (or tempted) to do, as well as those I'm already engaged in doing. I have to switch track (using the one sock process) if it is causing a non-negotiable priority to suffer. Understanding just how to direct and redirect my focus is an invaluable aid in helping me to do that.

How Do the Small Things Add Up and Eat Away Our Lives?

In a world filled with distractions, do you often find it hard to remember, let alone manage, your priorities? Do you ever look back on the day and say to yourself, "I didn't accomplish what I'd set out to do"? There

> "One reason so few of us achieve what we truly want is that we never direct our focus; we never concentrate our power. Most people dabble their way through life, never deciding to master anything in particular."
> Anthony Robbins, leadership advisor

are times when this is unavoidable but all too often, we simply do not realize how little distractions and time-consuming habits insidiously steal away the quality of our lives. Have you ever made a quick run to the mall intending to pick up just one thing and walked out two hours later with purchases you didn't really need and/or couldn't afford? Or have you ever met a friend for just one drink or other recreation, only to find yourself heading for home hours later, having wasted time and money (or both) that could have been spent on family or building other fibers that were truly aligned with your core values and an I.M.Possible outcome? How do these impulsive diversions happen? If we let them, easily, because:

- *Each distraction we engage in changes our focus.*
- *We can only focus on one thought at a time.*
- *Each time we change our focus we change our brain.*
- *This change sets up a chain of thought processes that lead us away from our original goals, toward new ones, even only temporary in nature.*
- *Unless focus is immediately corrected, sub-goals will obscure the original goal.*

Can you see where impulsive choices that may seem insignificant at the moment take you further away from the accomplishment of your I.M.Possible priorities and goals? Ultimately, the more you fail to move *toward* the truly important goals in your life (the ones your brain has networked into your true internal core values) the more stress symptoms your brain will generate - and the less happy you will feel. Material things or distractions will only make you feel worse after they are obtained if they conflict with your core values or if they take you further away from whatever gives your life a sense of true worth and purpose. Failure in these areas can become part of our self-concept, leading to a cycle of negative thinking and behavior patterns.

The Law of Focus: *Where You Look Is Where You Go*

It's the number one rule in safe driving: look where you want to go, *not* to where you don't want to go. Why? Let's compare our visual focus with a camera. The view finder must be focused on the picture you want to get. If you shift the finder at all, you won't capture your intended picture. (I have difficulty with this, so I have a lot of photos showing only a bit of sky or half a group of people.) As intuitive as today's cameras are, none will produce the picture we *intended* to get, if the viewfinder is not actually focused accordingly. A similar operational principle holds true for the eye of our mind. *The brain is designed to be goal-oriented. It works to create outcomes that image the object of our mental focus.* It cannot process the thoughts on which we set our focus as *non-goals.* Unless we understand this, we can unconsciously lead our brain support network in the wrong direction. If you think, "*I* don't want to be a *failure*," your brain will make the connection from *I* to *failure*, because '*not this goal*' is not recognizable as a goal. 'Not here' and 'not this' are not destinations your brain recognizes, any more than driving your car and staring toward a roadside cliff will ensure the car won't take you over it.

Change Your Focus, Change Your Outcome

When you change your focus, for any reason, the thoughts and images in your mind shift right along with it. To build the fiber in front of you, direct the focus of your thoughts where you want to go. Do not focus on where you don't want to go. When you focus on a negative thought, it is rather like giving your GPS device the coordinates of a location you want to avoid, then expecting the GPS to respond by directing you toward a safer destination.

For another example, imagine this: You are tired of being 'too fat'. You want to achieve a leaner, fitter body. So you type this command into the search engine of your computer: "All articles that are not about being fat." Where is your computer going to focus its networks? My computer responded by searching out 121,000,000 articles related to being fat. Are you surprised it didn't churn out articles related to fitness? Hardly. The search engine is designed to respond to the words we feed it. It won't readily take you to a place for which it doesn't have a clear address. What do you need to do? Enter the command "building a strong, fit body", of course!

Can you see the point now? Your brain, far more wondrous and complex than any camera, computer or GPS, also follows processes that focus on the image of our thoughts. When it comes to input customization, your brain is designed to allow you great freedom of choice. However, once goal-oriented choices have been made, that is, the mental picture established, fixed/hardwired processes take over. The only way to change the processes is to change your focus.

Have a definite picture in your mind of what you do want to achieve. Your brain can then wrap its circuits around that image. When we consistently see—that is, focus—on ourselves as being in possession of our goals, our subconscious mind will move us into actions and emotions that align with the mental image we hold. We give power to the things on which we focus. Our brain will even create new neural pathways as it networks through our experiences, knowledge, imagination, beliefs and environment to support actualizing the image of the future we have created. We will become destination- rather than problem-oriented, allowing a more balanced approach to possible obstacles.

CREATING REALITY: RIGHT GOAL – WRONG FOCUS   DR. KOLB

JDN: We've all seen wreaths in areas where people have died crashing into the pole. It was the last thing they saw. What was their foremost thought before they hit? Almost certainly, *"I don't want to hit that pole. I must avoid the pole."* Is the same true with our thoughts? The more we think we *don't* want something to happen, the more likely it is to happen. Does our brain actually network into some of the same process areas for visual focus as it does for mental focus?

DR. KOLB: After my stroke, I was skiing the first time. I was so concerned about running into something on my left that I ran into a small tree on my right. I thought, *"How could you do that?"* I was so concerned about not running into the branches, I hit the tree. I was so mentally focused on not doing this that I did the equivalent of 'hit the pole', essentially because I was looking in the wrong place. So mentally, the attention processes or the process of directing brain activity for mental events must be the same as for perceptual events. That's quite insightful.

I.M.Possible Power: Moving Past Frustration

Imagine you are watching a child trying to put together Lego building blocks? The child is completely focused on getting each of those bricks to fit into the right slots as it builds toward completing the structure on the box or in its mind. You can almost hear the little gears turning as it tries one way and then the next to put the pieces together. As the minutes pass, the child is unable to fit the pieces together. He becomes more and more frustrated. He loses focus; then even simple pieces won't go together. You can see what's coming next. All joy disappears; the kid hates the project, tears apart the blocks that are already in place and, if might even start throwing them across the room. Once he's told himself that he can't put those blocks together the way he wants, he's quits trying altogether.

Similar scenarios play out every day in the world beyond toddlerhood. There are principles also at play which, unlike Lego blocks, hold true in anything we undertake. The more we allow frustration to take control of our thinking, the more our brain will respond with frustration-oriented emotions and thoughts. One negative thing leads to another. The secret is to identify frustration when it begins and nip it in the bud before it grows out of control, to a point of no return. Techniques available include: immediately using calming thoughts and/or calming actions so that calmer emotions follow; backing up and starting again; taking a break; getting help. How? Use the One-Sock Process. Do more research, analyze where you went off track, get unbiased feedback and determine the adjustments you need to make. Don't let what you *can't* do (impossible) get in the way of what you *can* do (I.M.Possible). Stay focused on "What *can* I do now?"

We've seen how the pronunciation of *I.M.Possible* generates productive energy in our minds, warming us up to produce positive outcomes. This warm up also helps us to set the direction of our focus away from impossible thinking, the anti-destination address. Remember: we give power to whatever we focus on. When you focus on what you can't do, you give it power. I can't say it enough: don't let what you *can't* do (impossible) get in the way of what you *can* do (I.M.Possible).

I.M.Possible vs. Impossible: A Matter of Focus

In *"How to Get What You Want"*, Orison Swett Marden wrote, *"Stop thinking trouble if you want to attract its opposite; stop thinking poverty if you wish to attract plenty. Refuse to have anything to do with the things you fear, the things you do not want."* Although written in 1917, this advice has proven timeless. Our lives will always continue to head in the direction of our actual focus.

I spent many years during my youth running *away* from something I feared rather than *towards* something I wanted. When our focus is on running away from something, we often end up in a place that looks very much like the one we just left. Time and again, in trying to avoid what we fear, we run directly into its arms. During the time spent healing emotionally and creating this book, I found it incredibly challenging to keep realigning my focus away from fear and unfinished business. But, the more I practiced the actions of changing my focus, the better I got at doing it the next time I hit a trigger. My thoughts began to follow. I'm finally beginning to find a new normal. I am able to direct my focus away from the past and negative possibilities, while aligning my sights and energies on the path that takes me toward where I actually want to be.

The mental act of focusing attention activates brain circuitry. Focused attention plays a crucial role in actually altering the structure of the brain. Continual focus on a thing keeps the brain circuits associated with this focus open and active. With repetition, the chemical links in the brain actually become stable changes in the brain's structure. By focusing on what is possible, we create new neural networks and pathways, whereas, if we focus on problems, the already existing circuitry deepens and further etches into our brain. *This explains, at a basic level, why a solution focus is more effective than a problem focus. You are always in the process of becoming what you most think about.* Thoughts shape actions. And actions shape thoughts. These brain connections literally become mind maps that direct the reality we perceive. Accordingly, you become what you think. Again, *here's the key to change: when you change your actions, your thoughts and your brain change.*

It is vital to practice conscious awareness of your inner self-talk. Become sensitive to the relationship between what you are saying to yourself and how it effects your ability to move forward productively.

To build the fiber in front of you, continually direct the focus of your actions toward what you want to become or accomplish. What qualities that match the achievement of your goal? Practice small actions that reflect those qualities. This will motivate your brain to restructure and redirect its internal and external responses. This will eventually become a new pattern in your thinking that will overwrite old, counterproductive brain mapping, taking you from an impossible zone to the I.M.Possible zone.

"I don't like work—no man does—but I like what is in the work—the chance to find yourself. Your own reality—for yourself, not for others—what no other man can ever know." —Joseph Conrad, author

How Qualities Develop

Would you like to become a happier person? Or perhaps, be more patient, humble or generous? Acquiring such traits may be goals in themselves. These kinds of qualities are also of significant in our ability to set and reach meaningful goals. How do we actually achieve a goal that represents a quality or characteristic, rather than something tangible? We need to go back to the basic law of cause and effect. Our thoughts and actions result in outcomes. Practice makes permanent. By mindfully and repeatedly *acting* as though we have patience, endurance, kindness, self-control and so on as we go through the day, our brain will begin to imprint the pattern of responsive behavior. If you repeatedly choose a kind response over a sarcastic or thoughtless one, kindness will eventually become part of our identity. This is a powerful way to override and replace unproductive or undesirable thinking and behaviors.

Have you ever known a selfish person? You can't live in this world and not run into a few. How does selfishness become a behavioral trait? If your focus is on yourself first and foremost, you will choose actions that are selfish and self-serving. Your self-concept, at its most basic level, is that you are more important than anyone else. Life is literally "all about me." Your brain will work to produce outcomes that match this self-concept and give other considerations low or no priority. When other people or events don't make way for you, your brain will produce neurochemicals that activate negative emotions. You will feel upset and continue to try to find ways to balance your self-concept with your outcomes. So you will try harder to get your own way. Your behavior will become more deeply ingrained.

Can you think of other qualities associated with selfishness? Impatience, narrow-mindedness, egotism, ill temper are a few. The more we practice a behavior, the more we become what we practice.

> "Concentration of effort and the habit of working with a definite chief aim are two of the essential factors in success which are always found together. One leads to the other." —Napoleon Hill, author

The more we repeat thoughts, the more we develop the characteristics that match those thoughts. Remember, our thoughts affect our actions and actions affect our thoughts. Emotions, actions and thoughts are intertwined in the circuitry of our brain.

If we want to stop being selfish, angry, depressed, impatient, or anything else, we must take action to break the cycle. Nothing happens until something moves. If you want to become patient, for example, it must become a regular word in your thought process. You must think of yourself as a patient person whether you are now or not. The object of the exercise is to feed your self-concept a new message—a new component in the picture of who you are. You want to create new response pathways in your brain to override the pathways that are currently in place and keeping you upset and stressed. You cannot be both an impatient person and a patient one, so if you keep focusing on the thought of yourself as patient, and you choose small actions at first to reinforce this, you will begin to feel positive feedback emotionally.

Mentally rehearse (practice) for situations in advance, such as when you have to drive in heavy or slow-moving traffic, or when you have to wait in line at the supermarket, or wait for a habitually slow friend or family member. In each scenario, envision yourself as unhurried and accepting of the situation. As your stress levels decrease and the benefits appear, your brain will reward you with even more positive emotional feedback. In time, you will actually become a patient person! (More about the incredible power of visualization in the next chapter.)

Any change in behavior patterns is difficult and even disruptive at first. This is natural. But eventually what you do most and what you think most, is who you will become. As you develop new qualities, both your self-concept and your outcomes will change for the better.

How Your Brain Processes Baby-Step You to I.M.Possible

Goal-setting, focus and visualization are all interrelated. Whatever we give our attention to creates an image or picture in our brain. The more we develop a picture in our mind, the deeper it is imprinted in our brain. Our brain then activates processes that direct us towards creating or accomplishing what we envision, just as a supportive coach would do if we were training to win an event. It rewards attentiveness to our I.M.Possible goals by activating our internal reward and motivational circuits. Paying attention to your goals feels good. When your behavior is aligned with a goal that is strongly imprinted in your brain, don't you feel a sense of satisfaction, pride and accomplishment?

When your sub-goal is immediate (for example, studying for an exam, working out, researching, reading to the kids before they go to bed), for each moment you isolate and build a fiber that successfully takes you in that direction, you also open up greater ability for achievement in the moment after that. Because your brain is designed to produce feelings of encouragement and reward as you work at causing your goal to become reality, each small step taken motivates us to take the next.

CREATING REALITY: LETTING IT GO   DR. KOLB

JDN: I was reading about the neuroscience of goal-setting, and how too big or too many goals can mess us up inside. Experiments revealed how hard it is for people to let go of things, even if it's trading up. Letting go of what you already have is harder, even when it's to get something of more value.

DR. KOLB: Yes, that's very true.

JDN: If you can keep them both, that's one thing. But if you have to let go of one to get the other, you'll drop the one you don't yet possess. The same is true of activities. Once we start something, it's harder to stop and switch to something we aren't yet doing, even if we know it's a more productive way to spend our time. I guess that's why it's good to keep our goals and our lives as focused as possible, so we can keep our priorities straight.

DR. KOLB: Absolutely.

I.M.Possible Moments

Who's not heard the Latin expression *Carpe Diem?* It may be more familiar to you as the popular saying "Seize the Day." While it's good advice and fun to say, I think there is a piece missing. Why is it that, all too often, what we have seized in our bag at the end of the day is much less than we'd intended at the beginning? While there are inarguably legitimate reasons that can cause our agenda to take a sideways turn, many more days have been lost because of our inability to recognize that *we cannot seize the day unless we first capture the moment.* The bigger opportunity slips because we fail to respect the power of the moment.

I.M.Possible Focus: Respect the Moment

There is a story about a fisherman who goes down to the sea early one morning and finds a sack filled with little pebbles. He idly starts tossing the tiny rocks one by one into the water and doesn't notice how long he's been at it until the day starts growing late and the sack is nearly empty. As he reaches for one of the last few rocks, he is shocked to find it is a diamond. It is then he realizes these little pebbles were actually a bag full of diamonds and he has just thrown all but a few into the sea, where he can never get them back.

Does this ancient metaphor help you understand why this book focuses so heavily on the significance of moments in our lives? Tiny diamonds may not seem impressive but if you had even a handful, would you throw any of them away? On the day of our birth, each of us is given a container holding something much more valuable than diamonds. We are given the moments of our lives. Each of the 3600 seconds in every hour of every day is precious and powerful. Once gone, these cannot be replaced at any price.

Like diamonds, the choices we make in each moment can be clustered to form a thing of beauty and value or become scattered and lost. Every choice we make that contributes directly to our goal or to its underlying foundation, increases the overall value of our efforts.

Live in the Moment vs. Respect the Moment

> "Life, we learn too late, is in the living, in the tissue of every day and hour." —Stephen Leacock, teacher

Live in the moment. This somewhat ambiguous catchphrase is excellent advice if you, with all your senses attuned, are engaged in what you are doing because you know it's the right thing, the important thing to be doing right now. You are fully present because there is a connection between where you are at this moment and what is required to move your life forward in a positive, meaningful direction. There is no inner conflict. You are committed to the experience. Each moment joins to the next to add to the sum quality of your life. You are living in and for the moment in a spirit of understanding.

But when there is a disconnect between what you are doing in this moment and the quality of your life or the quality of your future—be it immediate or distant—then you need to stop living in that moment and determine what to change in the next. Depending on the situation and the circumstances, it may be an action or simply a thought. One will have an effect on the other. It's the law of the way it is.

There is no doubt that this can be very hard to do, especially when we have already begun to invest ourselves in the moment. No one likes to think of oneself as a sucker for a bad investment, but how often have we refused to pull out of a bad investment, *even in small things*? Have you ever begun watching a

> "When people tell you time is money, they are overestimating the value of money. Time is not money. Time is life. You can't buy that back once it's gone. "
> -   Jamie DeNovo

movie or reading a book and realize after a short period of time, *"This is a waste of my time. I really don't like this at all."* But we keep on watching or reading until we are finished. Then we say, *"Why did I waste all that time and money?"* Here's why. Without realizing it, we had made an investment and decided to keep going to see it through, hoping that, despite all indications, it would suddenly pay off. And the end result was a write-off, a non-goal. Okay, we've all been there at some time or other. But the insidious thing about not learning to cut our losses in these small things is this: *The more we allow ourselves to repeat actions that lead to wasteful use of our time and resources, the more we come to accept non-goals as a comfortable part of our self-concept. One thing leads to another and another. Unless we change direction, our brain will follow that path.*

The more we allow our mind to eat up our moments feeding on useless, mindless or demoralizing activities, the more we introduce toxic waste materials into our brain network. You know what toxins do. They poison the systems to which they have access and compromise their healthy functioning. Your brain, like our body, works by processes. Your freedom of choice comes beforehand. Once inside your body, including your brain, processes take over. Whatever flows into the system –your system- reflects the qualities of the input, and impacts the nature of the output. To some extent we all have natural barriers and defenses that go to work to counteract and protect. But eventually, with time and repeated exposure to toxins of any kind, the reality you create – the outcome - will be negative. Quality time really is quality life.

CREATING REALITY: WINGING IT   **RYAN**

RYAN: It's so much easier to see things after it's too late to change it. It's so important to realize that now is the time to get serious about your life. Every hour that's passing, you're losing more of your future if you don't take advantage of doing all you can do, not just the least you can do, or not just 'winging it' and hoping something big recognizes you. I took so much for granted, without ever really coming up with a serious, well-researched plan.

JDN: When you're winging it on that level, the 'something big' that recognizes you is probably going to be something big and hungry who sees you as a plump little bird just ready to be gobbled up.

How to Respect the Moment

When we understand how distractions and counterproductive thoughts impact our brain, we have a greater ability to reset adverse thinking and behavior patterns. Despite the many things in life we can't control, you are much more than an object pushed around by uncontrollable forces. Try it. Use the fiber-by-fiber and the One-Sock processes. You can pull yourself out of impossible moments and build I.M.Possible muscle through exercises such as the following. *Action is the best antidote to despair.*

Practice until you make it a habit to stay in control of how you invest the moments of your life. Ask yourself:

- What am I doing this moment?
- Is what I am doing this moment going to change my future for the better?
- Is what I'm doing this moment contributing to new, future memories or is it something that will keep my present the same as my past?
- If I could be doing anything at this moment that would make me feel I was doing something productive to create new realities and memories, what would it be?
- How do I change the next moment to move one step closer to the thing I need most right now? Think in seconds. Think micro.
- How much better would I feel later on, if I did this, than I do now?

Remember: *Respecting the moment does not always mean staying in the moment.* If where you are in the moment is not where you know you should be, or if it's not getting you the quality of life results you need, then you need to focus not on where you are now but where you can be in the next moment. Focus on the next tiny thing you can do that takes you out of the present moment. Then do it. By so doing, you get away from the counterproductive moment you are in right now and live forward instead.

When trying to come up with ways to respect the moment, think in terms of micro increments of thought or action such as this:

1. *Can I get up from this chair?*
2. *Can I turn around and face the other way?*
3. *Can I walk out of this room?*
4. *Can I open the door?*
5. *Can I get a water glass out of the cupboard?*
6. *Can I fill it with water? Can I take a swallow of the water?*

In other words, can I imagine my I.M.Possible muscle fiber growing just a tiny bit stronger with this action?

CREATING REALITY: MOMENTARY ADJUSTMENTS   DR. KOLB

DR. KOLB: There was an interesting article written by a runner, in *Runner's World.* One of the things he talked about was the idea that, if you don't feel like doing something, do just one step at a time. Once you've begun to engage in it, in this case running, and you've gone half a mile, if you still don't want to do it, turn around and go home. Because you'll do more harm than good by persisting in something you don't want to do. He was talking about injuries in that context, but it can apply to many activities in life. When things hurt, when it's really not working, just ask yourself, "Should I turn around?" He said, "Surprisingly, it's rare that you actually do turn around when you're feeling healthy." But on those occasions where it's just not going well, his feeling was, "Okay, stop now, and don't ruin tomorrow by doing something today that clearly is negative."

JDN: It's true that once we do start engaging in a behavior—even if we tell ourselves that we have the option not to go on—once the train starts rolling, it kind of wants to keep rolling. And it takes more to stop it. But there is a time when, if you are engaged in an activity and you are getting practical signals indicating "No. This is going to be counterproductive now," it's the course of wisdom to pack it in and say, "I went as far as I could reasonably go."

DR. KOLB: Right. I agree.

JDN: It's the One-Sock Process. If you reach a moment wherein you know that, despite your investment or effort, the healthy choice is not to continue, you can then make that choice. What can I do next that is also going to be productive? *This* particular thing has reached its law of diminishing returns.

DR. KOLB: Right. That's it. Being aware that progress happens in moments can help you to be more responsive when the moments are increasingly telling you it's time to change direction.

JDN: Realize when to change the program, or part of the program. I'm reminded of your story about when you were training the horse, and realized it just wasn't the day for the horse. So you made an alternative choice of activity that was still helpful, but it wasn't flogging an unwilling horse, so to speak.

DR. KOLB: Or a dead horse, yes.

Memories: Good Servant, Bad Master

Remember this: in making choices now, we are creating our future. In making these choices, the brain depends on two things: past memories and experiences, and information you currently possess.

So here's the thing: if you are facing an impossible obstacle, and you don't choose different behavior (thoughts/actions) today than you did yesterday, you will face the same obstacle(s) day after day. You have nothing new to add to your memories or your experiences. What is more, your

I.M.Possible muscle does not strengthen enough to help you shift away from the obstacle, as it requires a foundation of sufficient I.M.Possible fibers to do so. Buying into your own past behaviors or into someone else's—father's, mother's, friend's, role model's—behaviors that led to undesirable results, or no results at all, is to buy into a future that looks very much like the past. *If you really want to change, start with the next moment.*

Questions to determine whether we are moving towards I.M.Possible in this moment, with this action or activity:

1. *How does this affect my mind? Does this send I.M.Possible or impossible signals to my brain? Does it cause inner peace or a more agitated mind?*
2. *Is it an essential I.M.Possible muscle-building activity, a needless, time-killing distraction, or an amusing recreation?*
3. *If it is an amusing recreation, is it the right thing at the right time or is it preventing me from doing something that will move me forward in my goal of building an I.M.Possible fiber?*

The choice of whether to embrace the activity or abandon it is yours. Remember: everything in life takes longer than we think, except for life itself. It's not by days or hours that we either waste or fulfill our potentials; it's by moments. The degree to which we discover just what we would be able to do if worked to our fullest potential is absolutely determined by the choices we make in each and every moment. There are no meaningless choices. Each moment of your life, your choice of thought or action is either feeding into I.M.Possible muscle growth or into I.M.Possible muscle atrophy. The way you choose to use your moments will affect your personal failure or success in ways you often will not be able to foresee for years down the road. Don't let memories of the past hold you back. Practice moment by moment and break through to an I.M.Possible future.

CREATING REALITY: POLISH THE DIAMOND INSIDE   JAMES

JDN: A lot of people say, when they look back at their pasts, *"I wouldn't change a thing."* Personally, I wouldn't say that, but a lot do. Do you feel that way?

JAMES: Yeah, I would change some things. I'm not saying that I'm not grateful for where I am. Maybe these were things I had to learn to be who I am. I don't know. But I do wish I'd had a mentor—someone at twenty-five who said, *"You're all over the ballpark, Jim,"* someone who was connected to me enough to help me have the courage to say, "This is what I love and this is what I will do." You know, that beautiful, smooth stone you can see in the stream wasn't smooth and beautiful

156

when it first came off the mountain. There was a process that smoothed all those edges and made it beautiful. It's the same way with anything. But better late than never. I'm glad I don't have to look back one day and say, *"I wish I'd done that, but it's too late for me now, it's impossible."* I'd hate that.

I wish I'd realized earlier, though, that it is acceptable to pursue your passion as your career in life—those guilty pleasures. That it's okay to do what you love.

WRITE IN THIS BOOK: *List from one to six bad investments you may be making with your time/resources/beliefs/energies. (This is not necessarily an all-or-nothing mindset, unless the activity or behavior is destructive to yourself or others. Bad investments of time and resources may include certain aspects of relationships or overkill on a particular recreational activity).*

Evaluation questions that may be helpful:
What is good about this? What is actually indispensable? What is worth keeping? Why? What is contributing to the real purpose of my life goals? What is it holding back? Why is this so hard to give up? What am I keeping myself from by hanging on to it? What do I have to lose by letting it go? What do I have to gain? What am I unable to do as long as I continue to hang onto this?

For each of the time investments listed above, list the trade-off you need to make in order to bring you closer to your I.M.Possible goal.

"The world is moving so fast these days that the man who says it can't be done is generally interrupted by someone doing it." —Elbert Hubbard, writer

"I can't believe that," said Alice.
"Can't you?" the Queen said in a pitying tone.
"Try again; draw a long breath and close your eyes."
—Alice in Wonderland, Lewis Carroll

13. I.M.Possible Visualization: See It to Achieve It

"Only he who can see the invisible can do the I.M.Possible." —Frank Gaines (paraphrased)

Take a moment and think of the word *visionary*. Who comes to mind for you? The most influential individuals, achievers, teachers, and leaders have always been referred to as visionaries. Why? Because, despite any odds against them, they never stopped visualizing a positive outcome—as if their goal were already achieved. How do they do this?

Visualization is the process of creating a mental picture of what we want to have happen. In reproducing the processes that are associated with creating the outcome we envision, our brain combines what is imaginary with what is real. Visualization is one of the most effective I.M.Possible exercises to strengthen our ability to break through impossible barriers. It is also probably one of the most under-utilized. Visualization is so powerful it is actually capable of completely changing outcomes. Today science calls this type of powerful, mentally focused projection of outcome *psychosomatics* (that is, relating to the influence of the mind on the body, and the body on the mind). Visualization is a powerful form of mental rehearsal and neuroplastic change.

What Makes Mental Rehearsal so Powerful in Creating Outcomes?

Picturing something clearly in our minds and repeatedly focusing on an image sends a signal to our brain to cause that outcome to happen. Our brain prompts us to speak, think and act in ways that will result in production of that outcome. The biggest predictor of how you will perform in any set of circumstances is your state of mind. Mental rehearsal and visualization involve the constant running through of a scenario or activity in your mind. Not surprisingly, mental rehearsal also involves emotional rehearsal. When we create strong pictures and feelings in our mind, our brain will search and capture the information needed to bring the image

158

increasingly closer to reality. Emotions come into play because the activity we envision evokes real sentiment. Combining mental and emotional rehearsals serves to strengthen our ability to accomplish the goal that is pictured.

The best-performing athletes continually use visualization to mentally practice their success before competing—often with outstanding results. They recreate their victorious performance beforehand in every possible aspect, with all the details and positive emotions that come along with it. For example, if an athlete is going to clear a high jump, he visualizes himself cleanly clearing the bar. *It is an accomplished fact.* There is no room for wavering, no room for doubt. Many times before this moment, over and over in his mind, he has gone through all the moves necessary to clear the bar. His brain is prepared in a way that has allowed him to give his all to his performance without distraction or fear. However, if even an ounce of doubt is allowed to creep in at all, the dynamics affecting his probability of success are radically changed. The possibility of failing is substantially and materially increased.

How can you (the average Joe or Joan) accomplish the same kind of outstanding results athletes do? Start by becoming a visionary. Take yourself through all the steps and see yourself as having already achieved your goal. The more intense your internal efforts and the more detailed the experience, the stronger the impact will be on your actual behavior. (Behavior determines outcome.) Visualization is also a major exercise in navigating through your discomfort zone to a new I.M.Possible zone. Keep your end purpose in mind: the good you will do, the joy of a strong performance, the satisfaction in beating impossible odds. **The visualizer will always have an I.M.Possible edge over the person who doesn't develop the power of visualization.**

The Navy SEALs use mental rehearsal as one of their Big Four techniques for operating and surviving under conditions that most of us would certainly view as impossible. Commander Eric Potterat, Naval Special Warfare Psychologist, said of the I.M.Possible exercise of visualization, *"If you practice in your mind first and imagine and rehearse what you might do in stressful situations, the next time in reality you're faced with these situations, in effect is actually the second time you've been faced with the situation, and you'll have a less stressful reaction."*

"I never hit a shot, not even in practice, without having a very sharp, in-focus picture of it in my head." – Jack Nicklaus, champion golfer

I.M.Possible Over the Odds: Stay Calm, Error Correct, Carry On

Deliberate calm. Airplane pilots call this 'the ability to remain focused on a desired outcome, and to give oneself automatic correction under stressful circumstances.' You are the pilot of your life. As you strengthen your I.M.Possible Muscle you can increasingly teach yourself to take deliberate, remedial action to refocus and override emotions such as fear and anger with calm, rational, productive thoughts. For many of us, this is not easy. But don't give up! Practice and more practice will create new connections and new patterns of behavior in your brain.

Although not as outwardly dramatic as many well-publicized disasters, I was just as surely fighting for my life as I wrote this book. There have been jungles to fight through, demons to battle, mountains to scale - up and down (often from a handicapped position); all the while

> *"I got up every morning and I said, 'I'm going to make it to breakfast,' and then at breakfast I said, 'I'm going to make it to lunch,' and then, 'I'm gonna make it through the run this afternoon.' You take it in these sort of little chunks."*
> —Chuck Pfarrer, Navy SEAl

attempting to put my discoveries on paper so that eventually anyone, anywhere, would have a reliable guide when navigating similar terrain.

Using the One-Sock Process, I was able to keep moving toward my goal despite injuries, setbacks, delays and never-ending obstacles. Through constantly visualizing my end goals, and remembering *why* I was doing the work, I was able to rebuild my faith and the mental toughness to dust myself off, treat the wounds as best I could, and get back up again after every setback. How?

> *"The clearer and more vividly you visualize a goal, the easier it becomes to achieve or acquire it. If possible, ride in it, fly in it, get pictures of it. Then list the steps to attain it."*—Gil Atkinson, businessman, entrepreneur

I just kept building the next fiber in front of me, seeking help, making adjustments where necessary as I went along. True to the nature of I.M.Possible Muscle development, this produced an extra, unexpected benefit: *I became conscious of how my brain activity changed to reward, and nudge forward, even my smallest actions towards my goal.* I no longer wrote those small steps off as insignificant. I realized that I.M.Possible muscle is attentive, responsive - ready to work with our vision and keep us moving toward it. Both the skill and the will to do more come only from *doing.* Just be prepared to objectively analyze the results and feedback, and then make indicated adjustments. With each step the brain is designed to help us keep the forward momentum going.

Just How Powerful Is Your Mind?

In 1994, Harvard Medical School conducted a study known as the Piano Study. Volunteers repetitively played a five-fingered combination of notes on a piano for two hours a day for five consecutive days. Another group only imagined playing and hearing the same sequence of notes for the same duration of time. At the end of the five days, brain scans showed that the finger maps for the volunteers who had only imagined playing the piano exercises had grown to the same extent as those of the volunteers who had actually played them.

The I.M.Possible Miracle Additive: The Power of Purpose

"Vision is not enough; it must be combined with venture. It is not enough to stare up the steps. We must step up the stairs." —Václav Havel, Czech playwright, poet

To transform a dream into a reachable goal you must first clarify the dream—bring it into focus and provide the details. Make both the goal and the worthy big-picture purpose it will achieve so clear that your brain sees its accomplishment as part of who you are. There are two steps involved in clarifying your dream.

1. *You can see it, feel it, know what you must do to achieve it and what it will feel like when you do so;*
2. *You must know why it is important to you—how does this goal contribute to your I.M.Possible vision for your life?*

How important is it to have a strong sense of purpose behind your vision? We've all heard or read about cases in which people have suddenly been confronted with a horrendous disaster, for which they were completely unprepared. In the T.V. documentary series, *"I Shouldn't Be Alive"*, episodes recreate true experiences of human survival against all odds. Their circumstances are widely varied, but each had been hurtled into life-threatening conditions, cut off from any but the remotest chance of deliverance. Situations run the gamut from plane and vehicle crashes, to natural disasters, recreational accidents, or criminal victimization. Conditions go from bad to worse to seemingly hopeless. Survivors generally had two things in common:

1. They forced themselves to visualize a successful outcome. As soon as they started to visualize a horrible outcome, all reported that they felt the effects. Physical condition, endurance, and ability to reason—would

161

weaken. Nearly all of the survivors fought down panic or defeat by pushing away every negative thought and continually striving for productive, positive, creative thinking.

2. They had a purpose for living that was greater than self. Each visualized his or her survival and return to a loving family and friends, to fulfill some great vision or goal, and to rise above the circumstances.

For these everyday people, the outcome, against all odds, was positive.

"Formulate and stamp indelibly on your mind a mental picture of yourself as succeeding. Hold this picture tenaciously. Never permit it to fade. Your mind will seek to develop the picture... Do not build up obstacles in your imagination."
—Norman Vincent Peale, minister, author

The Transformation from Dreaming to Doing

While visualizing success is essential, it is not enough to take you from dream to reality. To overcome your impossible hurdles, you need to act as well to move your vision from dream to accomplished fact.

To encapsulate: Your dream must become a visual goal to achieve. Research. How do you prepare? What knowledge or skills are required? Write down well-constructed goals, including sub-goals. Review them regularly. Visualize each goal on a consistent basis. Meditate on the reasons behind your desire to overcome and achieve. What will success look like when you get there? What will it mean to you and others?

Focus on thinking and actions that will take you towards your goal. Do you recall the moment-by-moment steps I used in developing the One-Sock Process? You can scale and modify this micro-template for navigating through chaotic waters for use in your own circumstances. Apply it with any task, sub-goal, or main goal you want to achieve.

Do you see the importance of breaking down goals into sub-goals and then into moment-by-moment fibers? By skipping the sub-goals and steps in between, you are metaphorically trying to leap to the top of the mountain in a single bound. It's just not going to happen, so your brain will continue to create a sense of ongoing stress, grief and fear around this non-achievement of your main goal.

In contrast, the brain creates feelings of satisfaction to reward and encourage even our smallest efforts towards our goals. As you become aware of this, appreciate just how responsive I.M.Possible Muscle really is - always ready to work with you, coaxing achievement onward.

Stay alert for sidetracking and small distractions. Remember, these become sub-goals that divert your focus. 'Little diversions' add up and work directly against achievement of your big victory. Can you imagine the outcome for any Olympic racer who is distracted by the crowd, the adverts, or the other racers? Fight back by moving the focus of your eyes, ears, and mind back to your vision, and on the goal of lasting value. Then *continue every step of the way, to mentally rehearse your success, with all accompanying details and emotions.*

If you practice these I.M.Possible exercises regularly, you will soon find you have moved from dreaming - to making the dream come true. What I.M.Possible Muscle fiber are you building this moment? Warm up with the I.M.Possible formula—productive thinking. You *can* do it. Start at the simplest level. Success is always a One-Sock Process.

CREATING REALITY: FIBER-BY-FIBER TO I.M.POSSIBLE   SALADIN

JDN: Give us the fiber-by-fiber process for how you wrote your first script.
SALADIN: I needed to get a clear picture in my mind of what I had to do and who I would be dealing with. That picture had to be based on what was really going on in the industry and what it would take for me to be successful. I didn't know that much about the entertainment industry so:

1. *I did research to find out how the television industry works, who makes the decisions, and who, exactly, creates the shows.*
2. *I learned about the role of the writer, network execs, agents, different types of television shows and how they're made, and I really just got interested in writing.*
3. *I read a few books about the writing process for television and how television works, and just kind of learned the lay of the land and as much as you can learn from a book.*
4. *I got online and I joined screenwriters groups and stuff like that, just to read comments from other people who were writers, and kind of learn what they were going through.*
5. *While I was in Nashville, I just started writing spec scripts. It was just sample scripts of my work to see if this is really something I could do and sit down and enjoy.*
6. *The books taught me that if you want to become a writer, you write spec scripts so you can have samples of your work and submit those spec scripts to agents or production companies or shows themselves so I just started doing it. It was kind of a fluke. At first I didn't know what I'd really use them for. My first spec script was for the show Frasier, and I really enjoyed it.*
7. *It was one of those things—I learned the stretch of a sitcom, I learned the stretch of Frasier. I ordered the scripts from the show so I could learn their format. I would sit in front of the TV and record Frasier or other shows that were good. I would go through and watch them from the VCR and pause and stop them and take notes about how they're written and how the stories were being told or how the writers of those individual shows crafted the stories they told,*

163

how many scenes they had, what sort of act breaks the stories had, if they had A stories and B stories or just a story, types of jokes.

It's just really a way of learning, emulating what successful writers and television shows are doing. It really helped me learn the craft a little better and also just gave me some tools to use and try to filter my own voice through in terms of writing spec scripts.

So I did that. I tried. I enjoyed the process, had my first script completed and was like, "Wow! I can't believe I actually enjoyed that!" I enjoyed the feedback I got from other people who read it. It was the first time where I felt, "This is really rewarding. This is something actually fulfilling."

WRITE IN THIS BOOK: *Visualize your I.M.Possible Muscle. Describe the images and mental pictures that come to mind.*

Now visualize and describe the fibers weaving into your I.M.Possible Muscle through the fiber-by-fiber process as you build toward achievement of your goal.

Describe how the building of each fiber will make you feel. (Imagine, sense and feel the changes.)

In what other ways will you use visualization to help you make way for the new I.M.Possiblity to occur? (I Make Possible)?

"Visualize this thing that you want, see it, feel it, believe in it. Make your mental blueprint, and begin to build." —Robert Collier, American author

Alas! Either the locks were too large, or the key was too small,
But at any rate, it would not open any of them.

– Alice in Wonderland, Lewis Carroll

14. I.M.Possible Reality Checks

"However beautiful the strategy, you should occasionally look at the results."
- *Winston Churchill, British politician and statesman*

I always thought it was true. "You can do anything if you put your mind to it," until I was faced with a situation that no amount of thinking or doing would change. What I wanted to do was turn back the clock and use the knowledge I had now to make different decisions. That option truly was impossible. Next, what I wanted to do was find a competent lawyer who would actually care about justice and end results more than the immediate cash grab. (Yeah, I can guess what you're thinking.) It wasn't until I finally acknowledged that I could not overcome either of these limitations that I could look at what was left and begin to create a life that would allow me to move beyond them.

When this book refers to achieving *impossible things*, the term refers to a goal or outcome that we or others may believe to be impossible because:

1. *It has not been done or proven at this time;*
2. *The circumstances are assumed to be unchangeable;*
3. *None of the barriers to success have yet been overcome.*

We already know that, by building the fiber in front of us and applying the One-Sock Process, many things once perceived as impossible can be accomplished. However, I.M.Possible does not deny the existence of the truly impossible, as brought out in the first chapter of this book. When all the evidence points in a contrary direction, it is not useful for us to deplete ourselves by hammering away at a truly delusory goal. If something is really impossible, if it is an immovable fact, acknowledge that fact and move on from there. Like the law of gravity, some things are just not going to change for you. This is one of those inevitable external realities with which we all must deal.

If someone closes a door on you, don't try to break it down with an ax. To force anyone to bend to your will using harmful or irrational means is

165

not an I.M.Possible quality, nor is it an approach that works in your best interest at any time. In fact, it is diminishing to I.M.Possible strength to keep trying to force more out of something than it's ever going to give you or that you can give to it. It is especially sad that such obstinate persistence blocks you from finding what else you really *can* do. When you remain in a place where you're always feeling impossible, you cut yourself off from other avenues that enable you to experience the exhilaration of I.M.Possible.

If conditions render something unrealistic for you, either short-term or permanently, or if there is a conflict between the activities required to achieve a goal and your core values, it may be time to re-evaluate the end goal or your methods of reaching it. Everyone must work with certain fixed realities to beat impossible odds. Bear in mind too, that what is impossible under certain conditions may be possible under different conditions or at a different time in our lives. What is impossible one day may be possible the next. What is impossible given one set of circumstances may be possible under a different set of circumstances. What is impossible using one set of tools may be possible with another set. So even though we must work with limiting factors in one way or another, remember that circumstances change over time, which could in turn alter a formerly 'impossible' aspect of our reality.

Carl Macdonald's advice to clients 'when it's just not working' can be applied to all I.M.Possible areas of life. He advises:

"When in physical training, there are times our expectations don't live up to reality. You may be in a good mood, have eaten and slept well and have made it to the gym with a solid plan. As you move through your program, though, you find that your body just isn't cooperating. Every weight feels unusually heavy, fatigue comes on much too quickly, various joints won't stop twinging or just don't feel right. Expect these days to come. Off days are a part of life, no matter who you are. But it can be just the day for looking after another necessary part of our health. Maybe progress today simply means not taking a step back. Has it been a very stressful day or week? For some, a tough workout with a body full of stress hormones is counter-productive and rest is the best thing they can do for themselves. Perhaps you find you have a limiting condition that won't permit certain exercises—do what you can, make the alterations you must. Especially in the last example, professional help is very important. Sometimes, despite doing everything right, we realize today isn't going to be the day for what we planned. We can pack it in and be dejected on bad days or we can switch focus and find progress where it may be hiding."

Whatever the endeavor—large or small—we can accomplish far more when we recognize the strengths and limitations of the tools and resources with which we have to work. We can then learn to use those tools with maximum effectiveness and creativity.

"Once we accept our limits, we go beyond them." —Albert Einstein, theoretical physicist

Make Sure You are Equipped for the Job

Achieving the impossible doesn't mean you're going to be able to do something you are not adequately equipped for. If you don't have the right vocal cord structure, you're not going to be a famous opera singer no matter how much you want to be.

> **"Stop the mindless wishing that things would be different. Rather than wasting time and emotional and spiritual energy in dwelling on why we don't have what we want, we can start to pursue other ways to get it."** —*Greg Anderson, personal trainer*

What you shoot for has got to be achievable. If indications are that you are not equipped to accomplish a goal, or perhaps not equipped to do it at this moment, then you would be wise to re-examine your I.M.Possible program. On the other hand, you may have all the ability in the world, but if you don't prepare yourself properly for obtaining the goal you've undertaken, you are far less likely to achieve it.

CHANGING REALITY: PLAY TO YOUR STRENGTHS   DR. KOLB

JDN: This book can provide tools but the reader has to fill in his or her life—what they are going to do now, the choices they are going to make from moment to moment. That's why people tell me other books don't work: because they're telling the readers to do things in a certain way, but when they try to shoehorn that into their life, it doesn't work.

DR. KOLB: No, it doesn't work. It doesn't work because it doesn't connect with their reality at some level.

JDN: This is a basic everyman's personal training guide to help anyone get to the next logical *positive* place from wherever they are now. If you're going to the wrong place or if the place you're going to won't receive you (sort of like being the wrong key to fit the lock you're trying to open), the discovery of that will be part of the journey. If it's not working anymore, if you go to climb the mountain and you lose your leg along the way, then you're going to have to rethink either the goal or the processes you are using to get there. The processes in this book are designed to help people be more realistic while helping them to achieve greater successes with their lives than they'd ever imagined they could. Those two things aren't mutually exclusive.

DR. KOLB: Absolutely. You'll realize much greater potentials in working *with* what you have, not against it. Which also means not trying to work as though you have something you don't.

When It's Not Working...

There is an ancient Greek myth about a man called Sisyphus, who was condemned spend eternity rolling a rock to the top of a mountain where, just as it nearly reached the summit, the heavy stone would fall back and roll down again. The concept behind this assignment was that there is no more dreadful punishment than futile and hopeless labor.

****

So, what do you do when you have absolutely done all the right things, and in the right way, and still your I.M.Possible goal won't materialize? If it's just not working, consider the following possibilities closely:

- Sometimes your expectations need to change. Your perspective could be wrong.

- Sometimes your attitude needs to change. Your approach could be wrong.

- Sometimes your values need to change. Your motives could be wrong.

- Sometimes you need to do more research. Your perceptions and knowledge could be faulty or insufficient.

> *"If you want things to be different, perhaps the answer is to become different yourself."*
> —Norman Vincent Peale, minister, author

- Sometimes the whole structure needs to change. Your underlying blueprint may be flawed.[1]

Have you ever heard the term, 'Garbage in, garbage out'? This is a rough way of expressing the principle of cause and effect. The quality of any end result, or outcome, is dependent on the quality or validity of the means we have used in obtaining it. What knowledge, materials or processes are you using to attain your I.M.Possible goal? If any of these are faulty, corrupt or incomplete, our outcome will likewise be faulty, corrupt or incomplete.

If, despite your time, persistence and your best efforts, the results continually send *impossible* (resistance) messages, it's time to retrace your

---

[1] Check out Jason Headley's "It's Not About The Nail" -- a humorous video satirizing the way we keep ourselves (and those who want to help us) in *impossible* mode.. *http://www.youtube.com/watch?v=-4EDhdAHrOg*

steps from outcome back to the quality of your internal or external input. A core I.M.Possible muscle exercise is to step outside our comfort zone and mindfully work with the hard questions, even the uncomfortable ones.

Impossible Origins: Looking Outside the Box

Sometimes, despite doing everything right, there appears to be a decisive flaw in a place over which you have no control. Before making a decision to carry on or change direction, a clear-minded reality check can help you identify the real barrier to progress.

An *impossible* element might have an outside origin, such as someone or something that is not suited to their role in your endeavors, much like a workout partner who appears to be encouraging you to push yourself through a tough exercise but, knowingly or not, is actually driving you toward injury. If you have any doubts about a partner, group, consultant, professional, specialist or anyone else who may hold a position of influence over you and a worthy I.M.Possible goal, get a second opinion, and even a third. Don't hesitate. A poor fit in an important relationship is going to generate *impossible* outcomes.

> "We all want progress, but if you're on the wrong road, progress means doing an about-turn and walking back to the right road; in that case, the one who turns back soonest is the most progressive." - *C.S. Lewis, writer*

Furthermore, keep this in mind: A professional designation or position of trust is *not* an assurance of integrity or ability. No matter how long you have known someone—or what explanation is given—*if there are signs that something is wrong, don't ignore the signs.* Talk to others qualified in the area of concern. Ensure they have no relationship or ties to the individual(s) under discussion. Evaluate the feedback and evidence. If your fears are without foundation, this healthy exercise will provide peace of mind. If, however, there are good grounds for your anxiety (as I have learned is all too often the case), the sooner you find out and take corrective action, the better.

Before we leave this discussion of I.M.Possible versus impossible dreams and goals, there is one other important aspect to consider. In the context of this book, we are talking about worthy aspirations, not goals that are linked with evil, with delusionary thinking or lunatic fantasies. I want to make it clear that 'what if' thinking does not in any way refer to a mindset that is divorced from all mental or physical decency or restraint. This kind of fantasizing, in whatever form it takes, is negative and harmful, despite the research and claims of those who make money promoting it as entertainment. Repeatedly entering this realm, even mentally, can lead people to act without regard for the consequences to themselves or others. In short, destructive fantasies should not leave the realm of imagination; they should not enter into the realm of possible or even I.M.Possible thinking. *If you are prone to such thoughts, it would be in your best interest to seek professional help immediately. I urge you to make this your goal.*

CREATING REALITY: NAVIGATING POTHOLES	DR. KOLB

JDN: You said that once you recognize where your potholes are in life, you don't focus on them. So, focus on what we can do, with what we've got left?
DR. KOLB: That's exactly it. And I think a lot of people tend to focus on the potholes. They miss their goal because of the potholes.
JDN: If it's impossible, recognize it and move on. Don't focus on the impossible because, if it really is, there is no sense in dwelling on it. Go to I.M.Possible. What do we have left? Where do we go now? When you're working towards a goal and you've had to make adjustments, you may feel you're still in the ballpark; you just need to proceed in a different way. And that's where the moment-by-moment, fiber-by-fiber process comes in. Ask yourself, "What can I do to forward my progress in the next moment?" If you get to a point where your answer is, "Nothing: it is literally impossible for me to use this means to get where I want to go," then, why beat it to death?
DR KOLB: You got it.

I.M.Possible Muscle: A Soul Ownership Exercise

"I shouldn't know you again if we did meet, you're so exactly like other people."
—Humpty to Alice, *Through the Looking Glass*

Your life will only be successful to the extent that you maintain soul ownership. As you work toward your dream, do not compare your goal—or your success in achieving it—with other people's goals and successes. Great I.M.Possible achievers didn't have fame or great wealth as their primary motive or goal. Rather, they were passionate about what they were doing— feeling it heart and soul. They knew *why* they were doing it. The goal was such a strong part of their self-concept that it actually became core to their personal identity.

Wilbur and Orville Wright didn't attempt to climb Mount Everest; nor did Sir Edmund Hillary try to invent a new kind of airplane. Each had a clear understanding of what they were attempting, why they were doing it, and of the work, preparation, level of skill, and commitment involved. They added rational (logical) thought and action to their passionate attachment to a higher purpose. This fuelled their confidence in their ability to reach the end goal.

The triumph of the Wright brothers' airplane, the Edison light bulb, and Hillary's ascent of Mount Everest were not the first I.M.Possible victories each of these people had achieved. Like the White Queen in *Wonderland*, they had to prepare long in advance, to practice every day. It was a matter of growing and improving until one impossible thing gave way, then two, and so on. How were they able to defy the restraints of conventional wisdom and not give in to all the setbacks? This came as a result of exercises performed so often; the qualities had become second nature in their work. Success was never a matter of luck or blind faith.

While we are in the process of *becoming*, we are largely alone in our efforts. Almost all of the groundwork for strengthening our impossible muscle happens behind the scenes, where there is no limelight. We don't have someone always watching to pull us through and pick us up, so the incentive to succeed has to be very personal and deeply rooted. We have to know *why* we are doing what we are doing. We must be willing to take ownership of the *whole process* involved in pursuing our goal.

I.M.Possible – A Private Enterprise

When you see an individual whose muscles are obviously in top physical condition, you know this person has been sweating it out in a gym most days of the week, or training in whatever way was necessary, to achieve the physique that is now so obvious to others. His or her heart is committed to the process, not just to the end result.

- The Wright Brothers' eventual success with the first heavier-than-air, machine-powered flight involved ongoing scientific research, experimentation and study. Only five people watched the historic event and very few newspapers even wrote about it.[2]

- Sir Edmund Hillary was, in his own words, *"very fit and had much climbing experience."*[3]

- Before his light bulb would work, Edison first had to invent an electric lighting system that contained all the elements necessary to make the

---

[2] www.nps.gov/wrbr/historyculture/index.htm; www.biographycentral.net/wilbur-wright-and-orville-wright.php
[3] Interview by students with Sir Edmund Hillary, www/teacher.scholastic.com/activities/hillary/hilltran.htm

incandescent light practical, safe, and economical. This involved inventing seven different and complex systems. Edison stated, *"I never did anything worth doing by accident, nor did any of my inventions come by accident; they came by work."*

Every I.M.Possible victor has had to go through a succession of moment-by-moment choices, many of which resulted in setbacks and formed part of the learning curve leading up to their ultimate victory. To take this in stride, it is essential to have an overriding, honest curiosity and commitment to results rather than appearances.

What would Edison or the Wright Brothers have achieved if they were so worried about what other people would think of them that they couldn't focus on their work? Or if they had refused to make corrections, recognize weaknesses, and examine failures?

In August of 1900, Wilbur Wright built his first glider. In one of Wilbur's interviews he said, *"For some years I have been afflicted with the belief that flight is possible to man…What is chiefly needed is skill rather than machinery."*

Agatha Christie, one of the most popular novelists of all time, was once asked by a journalist why she didn't write in genres other than mysteries. Christie replied, *"Because I do what I can, not what I can't."*

Don't let pride, impatience, or pressure from anyone else goad you into doing anything before you are ready to do it. If Edmund Hillary had not disciplined and prepared himself from the most basic levels long before he finally began his successful ascent of Mount Everest, would he have made it to and from the summit? If you read his autobiography or interviews, it will become obvious that, without many prior years of training and experience as a mountain climber, and a partner with a similar level of expertise, Hillary would not have lived to tell his tale. Many others who later believed they could do the same, died in the attempt. When asked about the 1996 tragedy in which eight climbers were killed on that same mountain, Hillary answered, *"Many people have been getting too casual about climbing Everest. I forecast a disaster many times."*

"Failure is inevitable for two types of people: those who thought and never did, and those who did and never thought." —Rev. W.A. Nance

JDN: It's so hard to let go, even of things that are counterproductive. It seems it should be simple, but why is it so hard to do when it means abandoning something we have already taken ownership of?

DR. KOLB: Certain emotions or events become tied up with [a person's] self-concept, even when it's counterproductive. Also, people in all walks of life get very ego-involved with their thinking and viewpoints. Have you ever seen the TV show *Hoarders*? In a sense these people are hoarding memories. And you can't. Or you'll just go crazy. Like hoarders, we can snow ourselves under with thoughts and emotions that are really cluttering up our ability to grow.

JDN: Great achievers are great learners because they are willing to change in whatever way is necessary to allow growth. We have to be willing to let go, or step back for a time in order to do the work necessary to climb past the obstacle to higher things.

Are You Living in the Red King's Dream?

Tweedledee: (referring to the Red King) *He's dreaming now. What do you think he's dreaming about?*

Alice: *Nobody can guess that.*

Tweedledee: (clapping his hands) *Why, about YOU! And if he left off dreaming about you, where do you suppose you'd be?*

Alice: *Where I am now, of course.*

Tweedledee: *Not you! You'd be nowhere. Why, you're only a sort of thing in his dream!*

Tweedledum: *If that there King was to wake, you'd go out—bang!—just like a candle!*

—Through the Looking Glass, Lewis Carroll

I like the above Wonderland conversation because it vividly represents how we can lose control of our own reality and be sucked into becoming nothing more than a 'thing in the Red King's dream.' Alice is essentially told that her reality is defined by the Red King's dream, and that, if he wakes up, she'd disappear. Because the king controls the dream, he also controls her. And when his interests change, he won't even remember she existed. And she, of course, will have no substance. At that realization, Alice protests. She later says, "Well, if life is just a dream, I want it to be my dream. I don't want to be a thing in someone else's dream." Do you see the parallels between Alice's situation and our own in the real world?

Your life is your dream, and it passes all too quickly. Although we all share parts of that dream—our lives—with others, we each like to think we are captain of our soul, making our own conscious choices. Like Alice, we all want to maintain ownership of our dream. However, in our topsy-turvy world where change happens faster than logic, it is all too easy to find oneself living in the Red King's dream without realizing it. It will not be possible for any of us to own our I.M.Possible dream when it is largely being created and controlled by someone else.

Who is the Red King's Real-World Counterpart?

The Red King can be anything from advertisers and big business to peers and relatives, that is, anyone whose interests center around getting your involvement or buy-in, primarily because it feeds into their own ideals or agenda. They need to ensure our participation, regardless of the consequences to us, in order to live out their dreams.

> *"So I wasn't dreaming, after all, unless—unless we're all part of the same dream. Only I do hope it's MY dream, and not the Red King's! I don't like belonging to another person's dream."*
> —Alice in Through the Looking Glass

The Red King constantly changes identities. It can be an event or habit that controls your life—anything that tries to define who you are or should be, but has no true connection with your personal well-being or core values. The Red King is living his own dream—directing the scenes, moving the boundaries and designing the mazes into which we wander from our own dreams.

Sometimes, unfortunately, the Red King can even be someone very close to us. An acquaintance recently told me that his doctor had suddenly sold his practice after many years and gone into real estate. When I asked why he would have done such a thing, the man told me, *"He hated being a doctor. The only reason he went into medicine is because his father expected him to do it. So he became a doctor and did what he thought he had to do all these years. When his dad died, he was free. He could finally live his life."* Wow. Whatever the reason for living his father's dream at the cost of his own, this impossible situation was unhealthy, and not just for parent and child. Can you imagine what your feelings would be if you discovered you were under the care of a reluctant, resentful doctor?

> *"Why should we be in such desperate haste to succeed, and in such desperate enterprises? If a man does not keep pace with his companions, perhaps it is because he hears a different drummer."*
> —Henry David Thoreau, author

We buy into the Red King's dream when we chase after those things that rob us of our own direction in life. We feel the Red King's influence when we allow outside pressure to define who we are. When we surrender to the Red King's dream, be prepared to find we've given up our own. Instead of contributing to our long-term happiness or success, we will very likely find that other dream working against us.

As we learn how to take control of our own thinking, we also learn to identify the Red Kings in our lives, and imprint and lock in emotionally on only those goals that allow us to create our own life's meaning and purpose.

174

Until we do, we will remain susceptible to those who know how to play on emotion and subtly direct our brains. The result, for each of us personally, is that we begin to tie meaningless ideals or values to our own self-concept. When we do this, we lose the chance to discover just how much more we could otherwise accomplish with our life.

If we remain under the Red King's spell, his dream will gradually replace our own, and we become, as Tweedledee said, "only a sort of a thing in his dream." Our perception of other people also becomes skewed. We evaluate them largely in terms of how close they come to filling the stereotypes and images dangled in front of us by groups of people whose interests are purely self-serving. We wander ever further out of control of our own reality as we then, unconsciously, seek the company of people who are under the same spell—living for and in the Red King's dream.

There is a striking example of this in casinos. You can walk into any casino and see hundreds of people feverishly paying into the Red King's dream. They are no doubt reassured by one another's company, but in trying to shortcut themselves to their dream, the majority of gamblers will lose it. When the money is gone, the loser is ejected from the Red King's dream as though he never existed.

CREATING REALITY: PASSING HAPPINESS   TIM

Alice (panting): "Are we nearly there?"
The Red Queen: "Nearly there! Why, we passed it ten minutes ago! Faster!"
—*Through the Looking Glass*

JDN: No one can define your success. Don't let anyone else do it for you.

TIM: The problem is, everybody tries. They're trying to measure their own success by defining yours. Because one of the things we measure our own success by is what everybody else does. So, we look at everybody else. If there were twenty people and you all had a 1000-square-foot house, but one of you had a 1200-square-foot house, we'd look at that guy and suddenly measure our success by that person. And actually there is always someone with more of anything and always someone with less. Set your own goals, not theirs. Viktor Frankl, famous Holocaust survivor and psychoanalyst, summed this up beautifully in the preface to his book (one that everyone should read), *Man's Search for Meaning*. Frankl wrote, "Again and again I admonish my students both in America and Europe: Don't aim at success—the more you aim at it and make it a target, the more you are going to miss it. For success, like happiness, cannot be pursued; it must ensue, and it only does so as the unintended side-effect of one's personal dedication to a cause greater than oneself or as the by-product of one's surrender to a person other than oneself."

JDN: I wonder, how many times do we get to success? We have it right there—a goal that would give us financial or personal peace of mind. But we get caught up in the hype of our culture: measuring ourselves by things that have more to do with keeping up appearances, with moving targets, so we just keep going. How often do we actually push ourselves to unhappiness and create a new level of problems we didn't have before? Whereas, if we had consulted ourselves [on the] inside, we had actually reached the real goal back there, before we kept going—the law of diminishing returns.

TIM: Here's how it goes. If someone says to you, "Would you be happy with a new car?" You reply, "Absolutely. I've never had a new car before. I'd love a new car." So you go out and get a new Ford Focus. And everybody else around you has a Mercedes. All of a sudden you're not happy with your Ford Focus. Because you're measuring it against other people, and it's the measurement—it's induced by other people. As opposed to: You were really happy until you became aware [of the difference]. Suddenly, ignorance is gone; you're not happy. So you're stressing and striving for something all the time. Today's society is very much driven by that. If you look at advertisements, at everything around us, society is very product and status driven.

> "Very often, happiness has more to do with what you get rid of than what you get."
> —Suze Orman, author, financial advisor

[If society says] you're really successful if you've got a Mercedes, then you're really successful. It's a car. Does it go from A to B? Yeah? Well, my 1975 Ford Pinto goes from A to B as well.

JDN: Even if you get the Mercedes.

TIM: Then, of course they say, "Aha! Is it this year's model?" Because in order to sell things, stay product-driven, those manufacturers are saying, "Oh, yeah, but this year's is much better. You really need this year's." If you look at the auto industry, that's why leasing came about. "You can't really afford it. So what we're going to do is, we're going to lock you in with these golden hand-cuffs and we're going to say to you, 'Every two years, you can have a new one of these. The bigger the better.'"

JDN: Now, if your vehicle is even five years old, you're thinking, "Oh dear. My car is five years old. What's up with that?" And that's what people have been psychologically trained for. It is trained discontent.

TIM: Because, you can't sell things to people who are content with what they've got.

JDN: Because, contentment is something you buy year by year. You've got to sell them on the idea that they never are content. They don't realize it. They internalize it and it becomes part of their schema, their way of thinking and cooperating at an auto-conscious level. Because, that's the bottom line with the big business world: Train society and our culture to never be content. You have never arrived. You will never reach a place where you are okay with the things you have. You've got to renew your lease on success and contentment every day, every month, every year by buying better things. All the time.

TIM: It's got to be bigger, better, shinier, faster.

JDN: I call that "buying into the Red King's dream," after a scene in *Alice in Wonderland.*

TIM: And that's actually what we are in today. We're living in an advertiser's dream and believing it's our own dream. We say we want to live our own lives. We want to line up our lives with people, choices and goals that really have lasting value. But how much of our life is actually based on trying to just impress other people? How often do we sell a piece of our souls without realizing it, just to fit in with something we don't really believe in? Maybe we once did, but we don't anymore. Maybe we never did. So we're living our life for something that is keeping us captive in someone else's dream.

JDN: Exactly. We're buying into the Red King's dream. So we're making *him* happy, all the while we're diminishing in our own dream. When [the king] wakes up, or changes the program on you, you're going to be so far in debt that you will have disappeared. Your life will have disappeared right into the Red King's dream. And he doesn't even remember you existed.

The Red King's I.M.Possible Imposters

Tradition, ego and crowd-following are not reliable guides to I.M.Possible success. We can have great qualities and abilities, but the need to portray a certain status or self-concept can block our thinking and stonewall I.M.Possible progress.

We can't get around the universal law of exchange; *you have to give up something to get something.* When in impossible territory, the first thing we have to give up is ego. *The way of becoming more is by first becoming less.* Tradition, ego and peer pressure, if given first priority, can take control of your dream. Hold them in check with the I.M.Possible mindset:

- *I am open to change for the better. I will do what I need to do this moment and not what I decided was best for me yesterday.*
- *Because I did it this way in the past, is not sufficient reason to do it this way today. In fact, if I think honestly and clearly, it is often a good reason not to.*
- *When the problem competes for my attention, I will focus on I.M.Possible thoughts, actions and solutions, and not dwell on the problem. I will not weaken myself by dwelling on what I would rather have or do, but will direct attention to the moment and fiber in front of me. What I need to do now is what counts.*

Ego is like salt – it's a great seasoning but should not take over as the main course. Too much is sickening and its purpose corrupted by excess.

CREATING REALITY: MOVING PAST EGO   TIM

TIM: It is a rare ability to keep your ego in check when you feel superior, stubborn, desperate, angry, fearful—whatever. Traditional approaches are, "Just because that's the way everyone in this position acts, it's the way I have to act. It's the gold standard." It's actually the standard that will keep you locked in to a certain level of failure, even if you don't acknowledge it as failure, even if it's not recorded somewhere in numbers.

JDN: We never see how many opportunities we've missed in life because we don't see what never got the chance to happen. It would be interesting if we could pull back an invisible veil to [Robert Frost's poem] *The Road Not Taken*.[4] If we could have the power, even briefly, to see just how life would have changed for us in some important aspect, if only we hadn't been so unwilling to change our mindset, most of us would probably go into shock.

TIM: I agree. Just because you were this in a previous life, or because you hold this position, doesn't actually mean that you know everything. Or just because something is sort of working this way, you're afraid to give anything up to try and make it work better. That holds true for all of us at times—no exceptions. That part of our self-concept, the ego-blinded side, so often gets in our way. There are times when, in order to be greater, you have to humble yourself first. No matter how much you've already achieved or how much better you actually are, or think you are, than the other guy, the other guy may actually have something to teach you.

"Perhaps Looking-glass milk isn't good to drink— " Alice, Through the Looking Glass, Lewis Carrol

WRITE IN THIS BOOK: *Take an I.M.Possible moment. Describe some key features in your identity—your values or the deepest roots of your beliefs about your truest self. Use the stem phrase: "I am …" and describe yourself in several main settings in your life.*

---

[4] *"I shall be telling this with a sigh, somewhere ages and ages hence: Two roads diverged in a wood, and I—I took the one less traveled by. And that has made all the difference."* Excerpt from *The Road Not Taken* by Robert Frost (1874-1963).

Reflect and imagine. How many Red Kings can you identify in your life and within your identity system? How does each make you feel? How does each Red King influence and erode your goals?

Where could your ego or fear of others' reactions be holding you back from greater success? Take the time to really think about it. Be honest, and list as many as you can think of.

What can you do in each case to maintain your I.M.Possible focus and minimize the extent to which your life is dominated by the dream(s) of your Red Kings?

As your I.M.Possible systems deepen and form part of a stronger internal foundation, how will this work toward living in alignment with your core values and life purpose? (Think one fiber at a time, using the One-Sock Process to build.)

"In all affairs it's a healthy thing now and then to hang a question mark on the things you have long taken for granted." —*Bertrand Russell, British philosopher*

"Come, there's half my plan done now!
How puzzling all these changes are!
I'm never sure what I'm going to be, from one minute to another!"
—Alice, Alice in Wonderland, Lewis Carroll

15. Discomfort Zones:
I.M.Possible Growing Pains

"It takes a lot of courage to release the familiar and seemingly secure, to embrace the new. But there is no real security in what is no longer meaningful. There is more security in the adventurous and exciting, for in movement there is life, and in change there is power." —
Alan Cohen, author

"I need to get out of my comfort zone." We've all made or heard this cry a thousand times. If you think about it though, the biggest problem most of us have with reaching I.M.Possible goals, is not with stepping out of our comfort zone. The real challenge is staying in our *discomfort zone* long enough to navigate through to the other side. We have a tendency to progress to a certain point, and then revert back to the very behaviors we were trying to leave behind, ending right back at square one.

Why Do We Stay in Self-Defeating Situations?

Why is change so hard, even when we know the change will, sooner or later, be to our advantage? One major reason is this: The more time we've spent (or invested) in a self-defeating situation, the more deeply the concept of defeat has become imprinted as part of our reality. Of course, we then also fear letting go of behaviors and responses that have become ingrained, instinctive, and protective of a reality that was already extremely fragile. As impossible as our current situation may be, we have learned to tolerate it. We have trained ourselves to expect defeat and to mistrust our own successes. If we risk changing the formula, something may go wrong, and life may become unstable in ways in which we are not equipped to cope. As a result, we either tell ourselves to turn back or we sabotage our own success before it has a chance to mature.

Another reason we have to fight so hard with change is because the experiences that created our current reality have become intertwined as part of our self-concept. The very walls we want to climb have become part of

180

who we are. The world inside those walls consists of thoughts, actions, people, environments and/or things that either consciously or unconsciously reinforce our self-defeating behaviors.

To breach those walls and change behaviors for the better means that our relationship with some of our comfort zones is going to have to change or be eliminated altogether. I think the term *comfort zone* is actually a misnomer. Often, these zones are far from comfortable. They are simply familiar actions or habits that offer immediate gratification or relief, so we condition ourselves to remaining entrapped and taking the inevitable consequences rather than put forth the effort to break free. Perhaps, if we renamed the term to *impossible zone*, we would find it easier to keep going. To leave, however, requires we make associated changes that will take us through a temporary *discomfort zone*. It is important to note that, although discomfort zones are I.M.Possible territory, I.M.Possible does not purposely enter into or remain in a discomfort zone so long that it signals threats to moral, mental, or physical welfare.

> *"I must be willing to give up what I am in order to become what I will be.* —Albert Einstein, theoretical physicist

The longer we have been familiar with a habit or way of living, even if it's self-defeating, the stronger the connections in our emotional circuits and self-concept. It takes time to imprint new behaviors on our mind, to work through the restructuring process and establish a new reality and sense of self. All of us want to be a hero to others, but we all too often fail to realize that it is just as heroic to rescue ourselves from a damaging situation, and often more difficult to do. The effort, at times, can be likened to pulling oneself out of quicksand. This is where building your I.M.Possible Muscle will help you to pull through, up, and onward.

Reorganizing the established boundaries that materialize in and around us requires courage. Recognize that, an appearance of strength is a strength in itself. Even if you are afraid, act as though you are not; in time, you will develop courage. As we make our way through life, the discomfort zones that lead up to I.M.Possible growth and strength can be scary, but once you work through them, the end result will be a wonderful new sense of freedom.

"When patterns are broken, new worlds emerge." —Tuli Kupferberg, poet

In one of my favorite books, *Notes on Love and Courage*, author Hugh Prather provides this analogy:

Whenever I take a long run, I go through one or two periods when my body feels as though it were trying to shut down. If I were to follow its lead I would slow to a walk. Had this consistently been my response when I first began cross-country running, I would never have become conditioned to last for two or more hours, and would not be able to explore out into the badlands every day, and would not have known the experience at other times of having a body with this kind of reserves. I have seen this pattern before. There have been other times when I reached a physical or creative plateau and then overrode what felt like a natural restraint. The results were that I broke into what was for me a new territory (with its own new boundaries).

Yes, it *is* true: Once you get to the other side of your personal discomfort zone, you will develop a new, true comfort zone. Looking back, you will realize that the old was really not a comfort zone at all; it was more a case of familiar demons, a type of predictable conflict or misery. On the flip side, fear of success is also the reason many of us sabotage ourselves. Do I really deserve this? Will I be able to handle the changes that would come with success? Fear is actually a very big factor in our refusal to take ourselves to a higher level.

"The man who can drive himself further once the effort gets painful is the man who will win." —Roger Bannister, the first man to run the 4-minute mile

Impossible Comfort Zones

To make the I.M.Possible happen for you, you must make way to let it happen. The way over, past, or through an impossible obstacle always involves a stretch that, much like the process of re-training physical muscle, will take us through unfamiliar or uncomfortable territory. After all, if the challenges we are facing do not involve elements of the unfamiliar, or uncomfortable (and very often lonely), we could hardly consider them to be impossible.

Achieving the I.M.Possible requires a willingness to go through the process of forging a new route through areas we had formerly blocked as Impossible. These are the discomfort zones. To get to the other side involves checking our ego, preferences and emotional security blankets at the gate, allowing ourselves to let go of something now (become less) in order to make room for something new (gain more) in the future.

"Strength does not come from winning. Your struggles develop your strengths. When you go through hardships and decide not to surrender, that is strength."
—Arnold Schwarzenegger, bodybuilder

Neuroplasticity is Effected by Varying Difficulty Level of Activities
—Dr. Edward (Ned) Hallowell

As the difficulty level of an activity increases, the brain must utilize more neurons to achieve the precision necessary to complete the activity. For example, throwing a ball and hitting a small moving target at 8 meters as opposed to 4 meters requires the brain to involve 64 times as many neurons to achieve the same degree of accuracy. What this studies [sic] example indicates is that increasing the difficulty level of a task increases the brain "efficiency" (neural involvement) needed to complete the task.

If a person has difficulty executing a particular sensory integration activity this may be because the activity is more complex than their brain is currently capable of organizing to complete. In order to avoid a sense of failure, everyone should start out with activities that are simple enough to perform and gradually increase the difficulty level. At each stage the neural networks in the brain improve their level of efficiency and organization, enabling them to be stretched to reach the next level. As the difficulty level of an activity increases, the required spatial awareness, brain hemisphere integration and brain timing precision are all increased along with it.

Source: www.learningbreakthrough.com/brain-processes-targeted#neuroplasticity

Confusion Endurance: The Gateway to Our I.M.Possible Zone

"'Confusion endurance' is the most distinctive trait of highly creative people." -Michael Gelb

When new experiences challenge or disrupt old patterns of behavior, we often feel confused, embarrassed, uncomfortable or fearful. Uncertainty can generate hyper-awareness and large-muscle paralysis. This discomfort is a sign that our working memory is seeking more information from various systems and inhibiting impulsive action until an appropriate response is determined. Some areas in our discomfort zones exist for our own physical, moral and spiritual safety and protection. If there is a valid reason for our discomfort when we hit this particular zone, we should respect the warning and back off to safety.

"The truth is that our finest moments are most likely to occur when we are feeling deeply uncomfortable, unhappy, or unfulfilled. For it is only in such moments, propelled by our discomfort, that we are likely to step out of our ruts and start searching for different ways or truer answers." – Eugene Wilson, Dean of Admission at Amherst College, President of the Association of College Admissions Counselors

The Zones

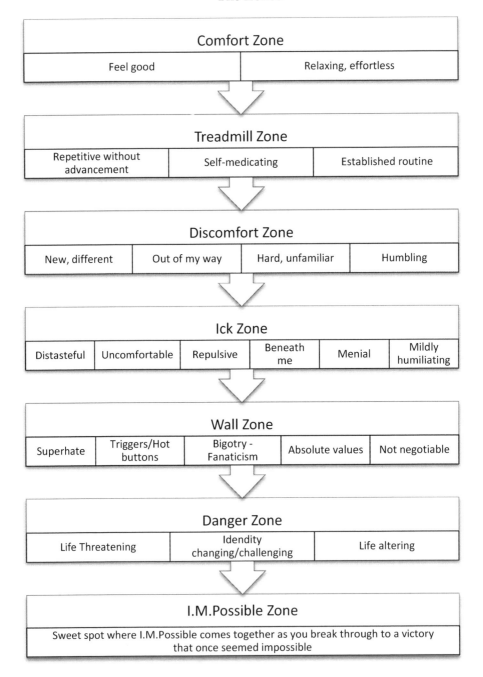

Comfort Zone	
Feel good	Relaxing, effortless

Treadmill Zone		
Repetitive without advancement	Self-medicating	Established routine

Discomfort Zone			
New, different	Out of my way	Hard, unfamiliar	Humbling

Ick Zone					
Distasteful	Uncomfortable	Repulsive	Beneath me	Menial	Mildly humiliating

Wall Zone				
Superhate	Triggers/Hot buttons	Bigotry - Fanaticism	Absolute values	Not negotiable

Danger Zone		
Life Threatening	Idendity changing/challenging	Life altering

I.M.Possible Zone
Sweet spot where I.M.Possible comes together as you break through to a victory that once seemed impossible

In his book, *How to Think Like Leonardo da Vinci*, Michael Gelb outlines seven steps in what he refers to as the da Vinci principles for innovation. One such step is called *Sfumato* [Italian, meaning, *to go up in smoke*]. Gelb defines this as *"a willingness to embrace ambiguity, paradox and uncertainty."*

Gelb emphasizes that the people who are able to overcome in order to achieve and create the most, are people who have high confusion tolerance, or even more than that, they have developed high confusion navigation ability. This means they are able to tolerate confusion and discomfort. They work through it logically, rationally and creatively in order to discover or accomplish something greater.[1] Their secret?

Great achievers are great learners. While it may sound simple to some, it is actually much harder to do, if it means abandoning something—even ideas and beliefs—in which we have already taken ownership. But the fact remains, the people who are able to overcome, to achieve and create the most—the most innovative people of all—were able to do just that. Regardless of intellect or past achievement, they successfully navigated their way through fear, discomfort and uncertainty, because the end to which they were working was more important to them than protecting an unsatisfactory status quo.

> "It's great to find a shortcuts to our goal, but keep in mind that a continual reliance on shortcuts won't build in us the mental map needed to navigate where there are none."
> —Jamie DeNovo

The truth is, however, *an aversion to personal discomfort is often a far bigger deterrent to breaking through impossible obstacles than is the risk of personal danger.* This is why so many people get to a certain point in life and, beyond that, don't seem to grow in any appreciable way. If this is our situation, we are going to face upheaval when life forces us out of our comfortable rut, as it does sooner or later.

To push through impossible to I.M.Possible requires a willingness to pay the price in more than just time and effort. Great breakthroughs require our toleration of the inevitable confusion and discomfort. It is part of the process of breaking away from the old and familiar, and laying the foundation to build something new.

If we can tolerate the discomfort, we will be rewarded with fresh insights and awareness. We will have a strengthened ability to recognize and make way for logical, meaningful change, allowing us to move above and beyond the limitations imposed by earlier beliefs and behaviors.

---

[1] Michael Gelb, *How to Think Like Leonardo da Vinci* (New York: Bantam Dell, 2004), Introduction, 9.

"I have accepted fear as a part of my life—specifically, the fear of change... I have gone ahead despite the pounding in my heart that says, turn back." —Erica Jong, author

Scott M. Peck, American psychiatrist and best-selling author of *The Road Less Traveled*, wrote regarding personal accomplishment versus the path of least resistance: *"The truth is that our finest moments are most likely to occur when we are feeling deeply uncomfortable, unhappy, or unfulfilled. For it is only in such moments, propelled by our discomfort, that we are likely to step out of our ruts and start searching for different ways or truer answers. Look at a day when you are supremely satisfied at the end. It's not a day when you lounge around doing nothing; it's when you've had everything to do, and you've done it."*

The bottom line: There are no personal guarantees in this world on the other side of anything. But if we don't keep reaching for something better, if we stay trapped in a situation that is not taking us anywhere new or anywhere good, then we condemn ourselves, untried to a life filled with impossible dreams that stay just that—impossible. Regardless of who you are, where you are from, and what lies in your past, you do not have to allow 'impossible things' to define who you can become. Keep your I.M.Possible vision firmly in front of your mind's eye, and allow the changes to happen. Remember, as with physical muscle, we must allow certain 'Impossible' muscle fibers to be broken down so they can be rebuilt with stronger material. The rewards will far surpass any temporary discomfort.

CHANGING REALITY: THERE WILL BE SWIRL   DR. KOLB

JDN: I am learning to recognize when a goal is not happening because I'm in a comfort zone I should be leaving if I'm going to make headway. Discomfort zones can begin to put you off just thinking about them. How do I navigate through it?

DR. KOLB: Not by avoidance. You get going and take the obstacles one step at a time. And work out the knots. And that's basically confusion endurance.

JDN: Dr. Turner, the psychiatrist I work with, said a lot of the most difficult obstacle to progress for most people is their inability to deal with all the new emotions and changes that come with being in a different zone—our discomfort zone. So again, [it comes down to] confusion endurance; to get through and find new ways—re-inventing yourself, allowing transformation. It's not our brain that lacks plasticity, it's our attitude—a resolve not to change any further.

DR. KOLB: I was working on a chapter to a new edition last week, one my co-author had sent me that he had done, and I experienced confusion endurance. I read it all and I thought, "I don't know how I can add to this." I felt so stupid. It was this feeling of complete loss. All these ideas swirling around and I couldn't see how they could possibly make sense. So it was only when I went back and started re-reading stuff that I'd written before, it started me thinking, "Well, yes, I can add something."

JDN: And the [ideas did make sense,] right?

DR. KOLB: Yes, they did.

JDN: So you had to allow them to swirl. If you'd given up and said, "I don't get this. I can't get a handle on it," you'd have not gotten there.

DR. KOLB: It's part of the process; you have to let them swirl…Yes, that's very true.

Write In This Book: Imagine and record an area of confusion or discontent in your life.

Come back to this section as you go through the book and make a list of means you will use to get through your discomfort zone to a place of greater contentment and productivity.

"Impossible is just a big word thrown around by small men who find it easier to live in the world they've been given than to explore the power they have to change it. Impossible is not a fact. It's an opinion. Impossible is not a declaration. It's a dare." —Muhammad Ali, World Heavyweight Boxing Champion, philanthropist

"Well! ... after such a fall as this,
I shall think nothing of tumbling down stairs!
How brave they'll all think of me at home!
Why, I wouldn't say anything about it, even if I fell off the top of the house!"
—Alice, Alice in Wonderland, Lewis Carroll

16. Failing Upward

"To succeed you must first improve, to improve you must first practice, to practice you must first learn, and to learn you must first fail." —Seneca, Roman Stoic philosopher

- *"I've tried everything but it's just not working!" "I feel like such a failure!"*
- *"How can I have made such a mistake?"*
- *"If there is any chance of failure, I'm not going to try."*

Failure! It's not a word that activates our pleasure circuits. Unfortunately, we all fail at some point in life. Have thoughts of past or future failure ever caused you emotional distress? If so, move over. You've lots of company.

At least three times a week while writing this book, I fought feelings of frustration and failure. "I'll never get this book finished. It's too big an undertaking. I don't have the resources to create my version of the perfect book. My editor is being so editorial—I'll never get through this process. The experts that have mentored me, they're all high performers who believe in the value of this project. *After all I've gone through, what if I fail?"* Despite my fears, I carried on, through confusion and discomfort. At times, it seemed Murphy's law was stalking me. But in the long run, *I did accomplish what had once seemed impossible.* The book, as you can see, has become a reality and the tools developed are being used to help you. I did fail at times. I had to struggle with making changes and adjustments. Many of those failures led to greater insights, including this chapter on how we can view failure as a means to propel us upward.

Think of something in your own life that did not, or has not as yet been the success you had hoped for. *What does failure mean to you personally? What form does your self-response take?* It might look something like:

"I failed to...be good/great at...be the best/the first/the only..."
- *to complete...succeed at... find a solution to..."*

188

Regardless of how you define personal failure, this end result this: You did not hit the mark at which you were aiming. You didn't reach the desired goal. This is bad, right? Maybe once or twice you can deal with, but three strikes and you're out. *Or are you? Do mistakes mean we're through?*

It can be difficult to keep trying again when our efforts seem inadequate to the challenges we face. It can also be hard not to begin thinking of failure as inevitable. Wouldn't it be great if you could just reach your goals without any possibility of failure? After all, failure signals nothing but pain, right? Another way to spell failure is l-o-s-e-r. It just sucks. It would be such an ideal life if we never had to struggle so hard to succeed! *Or would it?*

"The most successful people in this world often are the ones who have failed the most." —
Thomas A. Edison, inventor

The Crucial Role of Failure in I.M.Possible

How many achievements or discoveries can you think of that at one time were declared 'impossible'? Did the majority of these breakthroughs came about spontaneously – just a lucky shot in the dark? Not likely. In the absence of a more direct learning route, failure and mistakes play a critical role in any advancement process. People rarely, if ever, make big transitions against a background of faultless choices and unerring thinking. Even the best-laid plans can go wrong. Failure at some point along the way is not just possible, it is inevitable. Failures, however, can be as important as successes in opening doorways to new opportunities and new ways of thinking. The stronger our I.M.Possible Muscle, the less we are bullied by fear of making changes and the more we can view it as a personal training device.

As we've learned, the brain is designed to help us problem solve, make choices, create and achieve goals (generally tied to fulfilling a higher purpose). To do this, it ties goal attainment with who we are (that is, our self-concept), and switches gears to help us to succeed, coming up with ways and means to shorten any gaps or remove hindrances between the two. This includes the activation of processes that result in good feelings when we succeed and bad feelings when we fail. Those feelings can range from mild disappointment to embarrassment, despair, anger, horror or outrage.

If the thoughts we put into our brain are not valid in terms of actuality or fact, failure on some level is going to occur. Unpleasant feelings are part of the feedback process. What purpose does this serve? For one thing, when we fail, if we don't feel some form of discomfort or discontentment, we'd all be comfortable with failure. Those negative feelings, in a healthy perspective, motivate us *to not stay where we are*. Can you imagine what would happen if we were actually okay with failure or had no desire to solve the problem? We would be comfortable living with mistakes that would probably destroy us.

> "I have missed more than 9,000 shots in my career. I have lost almost 300 games. On twenty-six occasions I have been entrusted to take the game-winning shot, and I missed. I have failed over and over and over again in my life. And that is why I succeed."
> —Michael Jordan, basketball player

What if our ability to recognize mistakes and failures was actually a brain signal to give up? The physical part of our brain involving flexibility, imagination, creativity, conscience and problem solving would soon shrivel up and waste away. We would no longer feel motivated to use it. If we felt no discomfort at failure, there would be no personal growth, discovery or problem solving. No new inventions, no beautiful art, medical advances, ideas or advancement unless by luck or outside intervention.

Failing Upward and Onward

One of the biggest reasons people cringe at the word *failure* is because of what they have told themselves it represents. Failure is seen as a sign of weakness. Maybe it is, maybe it isn't. It's certainly a sign of weakness somewhere. The problem could even originate in someone else or in something outside your control. There are many reasons for the failure of expectations to materialize, but here is the point: Failure is a sign. However, it is not a judgment of self-worth; it is a condition or an outcome that conveys a message. *Sign* is another word for *signal*. A sign is not a stopping point. It is an indicator along a journey. Signs along the road are designed to help us make adjustments that will allow us to reach our destination as safely, effectively and enjoyably as possible. So, if failure is a signal indicating a weakness somewhere, what is the obvious response? *Identify the area of weakness*. Repair it, replace it, make adjustments, but don't be defeated by it. When you meet with a stop sign, would it make sense to sit there and refuse to move on? Or resent other drivers for then honking and by-passing you? Would you refuse to travel for fear of meeting with a sign that reads *Detour, Dead-end, Caution* or *Road Closed?* Of course not! Such adaptability is a requirement for voyaging.

> "The important thing is this: to be able at any moment to sacrifice what we are for what we could become." – Charles Dubois, Belgian naturalist

What about past failures as indicators of long-term performance? Many people who have faced disappointment and lack of success over a long period of time begin to label themselves as losers. But failure is a tricky thing (and this is so easy to forget when it affects us). How so? Regardless of magnitude, past failure has very often turned out to be a very poor predictor of future success.

While developing his vision, Sir James Dyson went through 5,126 failed prototypes, as well as his savings, over a fifteen-year period. But the 5,127th prototype worked, and now the Dyson brand is the best-selling vacuum cleaner in the United States.[1] *It is not failure itself, but our choice of behavior in response to failure, opposition, trials and setbacks that is the best predictor of our long-term outcomes.*

> *"It is Impossible to live without failing at something, unless you live so cautiously that you might as well not have lived at all—in which case, you fail by default."* —J.K. Rowling, Harry Potter author

Stumbling Block Or Stepping Stone?

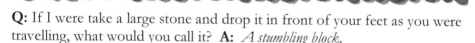

Q: If I were take a large stone and drop it in front of your feet as you were travelling, what would you call it? **A:** *A stumbling block.*

Q: If I were to take the very same stone, and drop it in front of your feet and you stepped on it, what would you call it then? **A:** *A stepping stone.*

How did the change take place? The stones have the same size, weight, composition and source. There is no difference between them, but on one occasion you fall over it and the other you step on it. The difference is in you, the way you used it! The question now becomes, how can we turn stumbling blocks into stepping stones in daily life?

Have you ever noticed that people very often relate to others problems more readily than they connect with the solutions? Note a difference in the attitudes of those included in this book. Each overcame a big problem (stumbling block) by breaking it down into small stepping stones. In this way, a potential 'mountain' was moved - or transformed into

---

[1] Read more at: www.businessinsider.com/26-successful-people-who-failed-at-first-2012-7?op=1#ixzz2BBtvTgF2

a stepping stone. The response, not the difficulty, was the final determinant. They looked toward solutions.

In order to turn personal obstacles into stepping-stones we must exercise I.M.Possible Muscle in new ways - working through discomfort zones. Fiber breakdown and repair is not comfortable, but is essential to all healthy growth. How can we begin? First chip away and break out the small stumbling blocks. Two positive results occur when we do this: The smaller blocks are more manageable. It is easier to work with one weight than a barrel of weights. Also, the big stumbling block loses some of its mass.

This chipping away can be hard to do at first. Many of those small-seeming stones are embedded in long-standing beliefs and behaviors. It is much easier to own up to unavoidable difficulties than to those which drop in front of us tied to our own faulty thinking and behavior. Nevertheless, solutions and growth don't exist in isolation from identifying weakness. *If you can't isolate the weakness accurately, you can't make adjustments necessary to transform them to strengths.* **All change follows the law of exchange.** *Something must be given up to get something else.*

Do you think you have no weaknesses or blind spots? If you're not sure, talk to people who you know will be honest and objective. They'll tell you, if you really want to know. Consider their words and insights. If you hear the same suggestion coming from numerous different people, this is probably a place to begin.

The process of turning stumbling blocks into stepping stones can take time. Long-standing or complex challenges are like big rocks that must be broken down little by little. Start the chipping process by practicing each day in some way to build strong fiber qualities of humility, curiosity, courage and endurance. This will prove to be of tremendous underlying value during these periods of extra exertion.

Had Edison let pride or discouragement stumble him, he would never have developed the light bulb, electricity, the phonograph, motion pictures and myriad other products and processes that opened up the world to a technological future. His attitude toward failure? *"If I find 10,000 ways something won't work,"* he stated, *"I haven't failed. I am not discouraged, because every wrong attempt discarded is another step forward."*

Leonardo da Vinci exemplified the dreamer-scientist mentality to an outstanding degree. An ultimate "What-if" thinker with a desire to grow in whatever he undertook or in whatever circumstances he found himself, da Vinci wasn't deterred by pride or fear. In fact, first-hand experience was da

Vinci's preferred learning method—including failure from mistakes. He wrote, "Experience never errs; it is only your judgment that errs in promising itself [outcomes that do not happen]." Da Vinci's courageous outlook led him to take many risks, some of which were pure genius, and others that backfired big-time. Either way, you've got to love this guy –

"Although generally recognized as the greatest genius of all time, Leonardo made many colossal mistakes and staggering blunders. Among his most notable faux pas were tragically unsuccessful experiments in fixing paint for The Battle of Anghiari and The Last Supper; disastrous and hugely wasteful attempts sponsored by the Signora of Florence to divert the Arno River; and a flying machine that never got off the ground. There was also a particularly hilarious failed scheme to automate Ludovico Sforza's kitchen. Asked to preside as head chef for a major banquet, Leonardo created a grand plan for sculpting each course to be served to the more than two hundred guests. The dishes were designed as miniature works of art. Leonardo built a new, more powerful stove and a complex system of mechanical conveyor belts to move plates around the kitchen. He also designed and installed a massive sprinkler system in case of fire. On the day of the banquet everything that could go wrong did. Ludovico's regular kitchen staff wasn't capable of the fine carving that Leonardo required, so the maestro invited more than a hundred of his artist friends to help out. In the vastly overcrowded kitchen, the conveyer system failed, and then fire broke out. The sprinkler system worked all too well, causing a flood that washed away all the food and a good part of the kitchen! Despite mistakes, disasters, failures and disappointments, da Vinci never stopped learning, exploring and experimenting."[2]

We've all got some da Vinci in us—some genius, some not so much. To get to the genius, to polish it and make it shine, there is always a learning curve. This includes mistakes and failures along the way. The rise of people from *impossible* to *I.M.Possible* always leaves in its wake a long list of astonished onlookers whose disbelief is replaced with the regretful words, "*If only I'd known…*"

Here are a few others who made stumbling blocks into stepping-stones.[3]

- *Today his department store chain, Macy's, is famous, but R.H. Macy started seven failed businesses before the eighth succeeded.*

---

[2] Michael Gelb, *How to Think Like Leonardo da Vinci* (New York: Bantam Dell, 1998) 78-79.
[3] Adapted, with thanks, from: www.onlinecollege.org/2010/02/16/50-famously-successful-people-who-failed-at-first/

- *Turned down for a job by Toyota Motor Corporation, engineer Soichiro Honda was jobless for quite some time. He started making and selling scooters from home and finally started his own company, today the billion dollar Honda Corporation.*
- *Walt Disney was fired by a newspaper editor because "he lacked imagination and had no good ideas." He also went bankrupt several times before he built Disneyland.*

I.M.Possible Training to Minimize Failure

While there is much to be learned from times of failure, no one wants to fail if they can possibly avoid it. As you continue to practice in the right way to train and strengthen your I.M.Possible Muscle, you will become increasing able to recognize when an effort is going to fail. You can then take action (preemptive measures) to either prevent or minimize its occurrence.

> "Action is a great restorer and builder of confidence. Inaction is not only the result, but the cause, of fear. Perhaps the action you take will be successful; perhaps different action or adjustments will have to follow. But any action is better than no action at all."
> —Norman Vincent Peale, author

Meanwhile, don't run away from your greatest potentials in fear of failure. Decide what is important to you, *look to where you want or need to go* and create fiber-by-fiber stepping-stones every day, even when it means having to work through weakness and setbacks. Your I.M.Possible Muscle will respond and eventually enable you to turn even the largest stumbling blocks into stepping-stones.

The Law of Progress: Two Steps Forward, One Step Back   **Dr. Kolb**

DR. KOLB: I'm learning as I'm training a horse, and I'm training me. It's two steps forward and one step back but I have to go through it.

JDN: It isn't just part of the process; it is essential to it, isn't that right? What we often don't realize is that the one step backward is what actually enables us to take a bigger step forward. It's part of the error correction process, because you take all those things that you now know with you. And the failures are as important as the successes.

DR. KOLB: Yes, absolutely.

JDN: Talking to you, learning how the brain works, how we learn, acquire knowledge; move forward, I'm looking differently at failures and setbacks. None of us likes catastrophe; but now, instead of allowing it to diminish us, we take the lessons and build something new on what we now know—that's resiliency. And the healing process is like the learning process: two steps forward, one back, isn't it? It's the law of progress.

DR. KOLB: And sometimes just one step to the side. That's one of the things I learned in working with my horse. I used to get angry when I'd take a step back and now I realize, "Okay, I'm not doing as well today. It's not the horse's fault; it's not my fault—this is where I am today. Let's not persist in this cause. It's not going to work today. Let's do something else that's fun with him.

JDN: That's a great way to look at it, that we don't have to quit altogether. But it's time to change and do something else for a bit. The ability to move laterally is an I.M.Possible Muscle trait. When the means to an end isn't working, change the means—even temporarily. And who knows what you might discover doing that?

DR. KOLB: You're learning elasticity, to stretch as the situation changes, not give up. Impossible is all-or-nothing thinking; it leads to learned helplessness and learned non-use.

WRITE IN THIS BOOK: *List the top three things for which you failed to accomplish your desired goal (at least the first time around) at some time in your life, big or small. What are the thoughts, feelings, memories?*

Be aware of your I.M.Possible Muscle now. What comes to mind? What did you learn from each? What do your mistakes and setbacks mean in your life?

In the context of I.M.Possible, what do your mistakes and setbacks now say about you as a person? How have your mistakes helped you become a better friend, parent, human being?

How can you reinforce, or celebrate, the importance of what you have achieved because of the way you responded to these mistakes and setbacks?

"Success and failure. We think of them as opposites, but they're really not. They're companions—the hero and the sidekick." —Laurence Shames, distinguished novelist, failed taxi driver, lounge singer, furniture mover, lifeguard, dishwasher, gym teacher and shoe salesman

The Caterpillar: Who are YOU?
Alice: I—I hardly know, sir, just at present—
At least I know who I WAS when I got up this morning,
But I think I must have been changed several times since then.
—*Alice in Wonderland, Lewis Carroll*

17. When the Dream Changes

"It's astonishing in this world how things don't turn out at all the way you expect them to."
—Agatha Christie, crime novelist, essayist, wrote world's longest running play, The Mousetrap

"That's how it used to be and I was happy then. Things were so much better."
"I'll never be happy again."
"I put my heart into this, and now that happened. It's over for me."
"This has to work like I've planned or it's never going to work well at all."
"Even though it's not working, I don't know how I can improve my situation."

A Funny Thing Happened on the Way through Life...

While researching this book, I discovered that very few individuals actually take the direct road, as originally planned, to I.M.Possible success or dream actualization . Some have deliberately chosen to redirect. Others were suddenly whirled by unforeseen events into a massive kaleidoscope of change. The road for each became the trail they had to blaze through new and often treacherous territory. Setbacks appeared, many times, to represent personal failure. Appearances, as we all know, can be deceiving— the condition of success or failure, temporary. What we deplore as failure is often, in actuality, a praiseworthy effort —and an optimal victory that opens the doorway to a new way and a new day.

Life has probably never been as fluid and the future as unpredictable as it is today. From a world-view to close up and personal, times, people and perspectives are continually in a state of change. As often as not, it is change over which we have no personal control that affects our lives and our efforts to achieve an I.M.Possible goal. An IT consultant told me about an ambitious co-worker in his company who was promoted to a high-pressure job with executive status, flown out to a stress management conference with other execs, then let go along with the entire group on their return. Sudden job loss scenarios are taking place by the thousands every day. College and

196

university graduates are finding it increasingly difficult to find employment in the area for which they have trained.

A strong I.M.Possible Muscle develops not only strength but also adaptability and flexibility. In building characteristics that empower us to shift an *impossible* viewpoint to I.M.Possible, we gain greater power to act in a productive way when circumstances indicate a realistic need for adjustment. We learn how to turn stumbling blocks into stepping stones.

Again, it is important at times like this to keep redirecting our mental and visual focus on the discovery aspects—the adventure, if you will—of inventing or re-inventing yourself. You are creating something new. This is the means through which athletes set new records for achievement and explorers brave the unknown to discover new worlds. It is the visualization and focus process that spurs on inventors when the goings gets tough. Researchers persevere through the intensive process of research and experiment motivated by their vision of what lies beyond yesterday's knowledge and accomplishments. To achieve the impossible, we must do likewise. Never lose your mental image of the purpose *behind* the means you are currently using to achieve your goal. When breaking new ground, we must not only accept and adapt to change and error correction, but expect it to be a necessary part of the process.

Self-Concept and Change

"...when you have to turn into a chrysalis — you will some day, you know — and then after that into a butterfly, I should think you'll feel it a little queer, won't you?" – Alice to the Caterpillar, Alice in Wonderland

One reason change can be so hard to undertake is because many times, the necessary alteration causes disruption in our self-concept. Of course, our self-concept is our self-identity. So when we give up leaning on old ways of responding, we give up a metaphoric security blanket that is made up of huge pockets of familiarity. Even when the security blanket becomes a liability, more ragged and less practical every day, it's tough to say good-bye.

Emotion can play a powerful role in keeping us tied to established patterns of beliefs and responses. We have created neuro-pathways supporting our determination to achieve an outcome in a certain way. It's much easier to identify where our thought processes are off track when we are observing someone else. It can be much harder to look at the picture objectively when *you* are inside the frame.

197

Much like the investor (or gambler) who keeps throwing good money after bad, there are times we have made a mistaken decision and go on sticking to it even after evidence for its failure mounts. The tendency to become increasingly trapped in bad decisions, known as *escalation of commitment*, is largely emotional. It is why many investors hold onto investments that are clearly going nowhere, and why people remain in abusive marriages and destructive relationships.

Familiar emotions and responses can also turn out to be bad investments, but the results of refusal to withdraw an unhealthy emotional investment can be more devastating than any material or economic loss. As with physical rehabilitation, there is some initial transition discomfort to change anything that has become an ingrained practice. Familiar behaviors have played a significant role in forming our reality. Change, though, is the only route to advancement and growth.

It takes intentional, concentrated effort to press forward beyond our habitual practices to fulfillment of our ultimate purpose and potentials. *It is strength—not weakness—that we will have added to our self-concept when we make productive changes.* Our brain processes may signal discomfort on one level during transition but if we train our focus to look to the end goal, to visualize the achievement of that goal in every aspect, you will find there is another kind of feedback at work urging you onward.

Don't you feel pleased and proud after you've successfully transitioned through a difficult period of time? Your brain is producing readily recognizable reward emotions at that time. During the time before you win through to your goal, however, *it is the much smaller, less obvious increments of achievement and internal reward mechanisms that cheer and urge us forward to the bigger I.M.Possible victory.*

CREATING REALITY: EXPLORATION REQUIRED   SALADIN

SALADIN: Around eighth grade, I made up my mind I wanted to be an engineer, to go to MIT. So I focused on that throughout high school. I went to a math and science magnet school. I was able to realize that first dream. Next, I applied and went to MIT for my undergraduate degree. When I got there it was a great experience but also very challenging. It was my first time being around other people at the top of their class, very competitive, who were also gifted in math and science. I really had to reassess where I fit in because I wasn't at the top anymore. There were many, many other people there that were better students than me, and understood things better than me.

I struggled a lot with identity. So much of my identity was wrapped into becoming an engineer and being the smart person in class. When that was challenged, it made me evaluate, "Well, if that's not really who I am, then who am I?" And it was a soul searching that we all go through at a time in our lives where we're trying to figure out, "What is it that I want to do? How do I want to define myself?"

I finally came to the point where I would accept that I didn't really love engineering. It was hard to come to that point because the curriculum was hard, the classes were hard and the environment competitive and harsh. Up till then I thought I wasn't enjoying it because it's just hard. I'd think, "I can do better if I just study harder and then I'd enjoy it more." But the real thing going on is I wasn't able to put forth all the energy that I knew I should because I didn't enjoy it. I had to accept that. I didn't have a love or a passion for it anymore. I had to re-evaluate, "What is it that I think I want to do? Who is it that I think I want to be career-wise?"

It was really hard to tell my parents I didn't want to be an engineer anymore because they had probably thought, "We don't have to worry about Saladin anymore. He's going to be fine. He's gone to MIT, something to fall back on." But once I took that step to leave engineering, it freed me to do whatever it is that I'm supposed to do, take this time to figure out what that is.

JDN: What was your next step in that process?

SALADIN: I was interested in human behavior so I took psychology classes, thinking I may become a clinical psychologist. Most of the people in the grad program were in their 30s or 40s. Their lives had changed in some way and they'd gone back to school. They gave me a very valuable perspective because they had an opportunity to actually live life and I hadn't. All I'd known was school. I realized that the question of, "What do I want to do?" is something that takes a while to really answer. And it's unrealistic of us to think that it's a question we should know the answer to coming out of high school or college. Often you have to experience things, meet people, try different things, fail and succeed, and take time to explore.

Optimal Victories: It's Not Failure When...

"I'd spent several years amassing evidence, studying, researching, and educating myself in every aspect to in my efforts to get justice. Days and months passed; the quality of my health and family life was deteriorating. I was losing something more precious and irreplaceable than what had been stolen already. The forces working against my success were more powerful than I, and without conscience. If I kept going, if I pulled out all the stops, I knew I could achieve at least a nominal victory, but at what cost? I had come such a long way, at great personal expense, in the face of seasoned and unscrupulous opposition. I had to make a heart-wrenching evaluation. The cost to continue on under the circumstances put me in a no-win situation. I had to pronounce that

199

particular dream impossible, for the time being at least. I would lose more than I would gain by continuing on with the means I was using. I had to find another way to begin to heal from the evil that had turned my life upside down. So I began to write a book... — *Jamie DeNovo*

The Law of Diminishing Returns

There is a world of difference between giving up and knowing when to quit. The term 'giving up' is used here in a context of defeat. Knowing when to quit—when to change direction—is different. It an optimal victory. What is meant by optimal victory? In economics, this turning point is called the *law of diminishing returns*. The law of diminishing returns refers to the point at which continuing to make an investment is counterproductive and will result in a decreasing return.

There are times when it's not terribly hard to let go and say, *"That's enough."* It doesn't upset you. In fact, it's more a relief. At other times, it's an intense internal struggle. But regardless of how deeply we have invested, if that investment is continuously eroding rather than adding to your outcomes and purpose in life, it may well be time to let go. If you are spending time and energy on something that's just not working, it's time to make some kind of change. The cost of continuing down the same avenue is higher than any return you could now get out of it.

> "Part of being a winner is knowing when enough is enough.
> Sometimes you have to give up the fight and walk away, and move on to something that's more productive."
> —Donald Trump, American businessman

We're all happy when we achieve a successful outcome. We experience great pride when we surpass our own expectations. What happens though, the moment we experience the next failure? We have a tendency to minimize what we have accomplished, don't we? Remember: Self-talk has the same effect as hearing the words spoken to us by someone else. Self-talk messages like *'I'm a failure'* eat away at your self-concept. Your whole world shrinks to the size of this thing that didn't work out, despite your best efforts. We've learned the words we choose act as focal points activating different emotional circuits in our brain. So messages reinforcing the image of a defeat or failure will strengthen inhibitory circuits and negative emotions and weaken the map for productive ones. We then get down on ourselves when we should be reflecting on what we have learned or accomplished. *It is not defeat to recognize and acknowledge when you have gone as far as you could go productively and must now change direction. To the contrary, it is an optimal victory.*

CREATING REALITY: OPTIMAL VICTORIES   DR. KOLB

JDN: Optimal victory. The concept came to mind after you described the events that prevented you from getting hay into the barn on a snowy day. You had an important goal, requiring a few simple steps for achievement: pick up a load of hay, return home, unload it into the barn. Due to a series of complications over which you had basically no control, attaining the goal within the time you'd hoped became increasingly stressful.

DR.KOLB: Yes, it was just one thing after another. I reached a point where I knew it was time to quit. I just left it at that and said, "This is as far as I can go today. The rest will have to wait until tomorrow."

JDN: Reflecting on your story, I thought, "But, look how far you'd come. You weren't defeated at all. *You found out what you could do if you did all you could possibly do that day to accomplish your goal.* Nothing went as planned. And you knew when it was time to say, "This is all I can do here and now." And you didn't berate yourself. You were at peace with that. Because it wasn't failure, it was an optimal victory.

DR.KOLB: That's a very good term.

JDN: Given what I've learned, to think in terms of *optimal victories* changes the way we think of something that didn't pan out the way we'd hoped. So it changes the effect on our self-concept. So we don't waste vital energy berating ourselves. We don't miss the positive aspects of knowing we have done all we could do in a certain direction. It's changing the feeling from failure to one of graceful acceptance. There's a world of difference between giving up and knowing when to quit. When you have taken an effort as far you can take it and you know that to carry on would be counterproductive [that it is truly time to walk away], you've achieved optimal victory. *That is not a defeat.* Hooray for you.

DR.KOLB: Very good. I like that. I'm going to use it.

CREATING REALITY: FINDING YOUR FIT   JAMES

JAMES: Sometimes there are tough realities that have to be faced. Like finding out that what you do well and what you love aren't the same thing.

JDN: So, what then?

JAMES: So what are the other alternatives? What do you like next? What else could you enjoy doing that you can do well? I have a son who wanted to be a teacher very much. But he simply wasn't disciplined enough. Then he found out he loved golf. He didn't want to compete so now he's a golf teacher. Try and find something you can compromise with that won't work against your own best interests and balance. I was very lucky. I did some goofy things and my vision caught on. But, the truth is, I'm not everyone's cup of tea. And that's okay, too. But, it's also true that the harder you work the luckier you get. The balance part, though, has to come into play.

CREATING REALITY: RESETTING OUR MAP   **DR. KOLB**

JDN: What would you say to people who feel like this: "That's how it used to be; I was happy back then. Things were so much better. I put my heart into this, and now that happened. If my life can't work just like it worked yesterday—if it's impossible—there is no use trying to make it work from another angle today."?

DR.KOLB: This metaphor belongs to my friend Jeff Kline. It's used for recovery from brain injury but it can apply to the I.M.Possible concept in many areas of life where we are trying to cope with a loss of some kind, even the loss of a goal we had our heart set on. Imagine a symphony orchestra playing Mozart. Beautiful. Now, you stop the players and you remove all the stringed instruments, or even just part of the stringed instruments, so a whole bunch of them are gone. Now, you say, "Play the same music." You can't. It's not going to work because the symphony is written for those parts, with those instruments included. So you say to the conductor, "Just practice, over and over and you'll get it." Of course, you are just practicing over and over, doing it wrong; doing something that won't work. What you need to do, instead, is you rewrite the symphony for brass instruments or whatever is left. And when you do that, lo and behold, it's beautiful again. People who've lost their violins, in whatever form that takes, but continue to practice the same score written for violins—it isn't going to work. One of the reasons rehab doesn't work is because you have people practice the same thing over and over again and they fail, fail, fail. So the real key is, *"What is necessary is to rewrite the score and make it so it's possible to create success with new basics?"*

JDN: So to get through such times of loss and change, it's important to recognize when it's time to rewrite the symphony. Who's going to achieve the most? The person who says, "We're missing the strings, so let's write the most beautiful symphony we can using what we've got," or, the one who stubbornly keeps trying to play a composition that was meant for strings?

DR. KOLB: Here's an example of something else that happens. A man had a stroke and was unable to use his right arm, and so couldn't write. What did he do instead? He got so used to using his left arm that he gave up even trying to improve his right. The effect of that is, his right got worse and worse and worse. It's a syndrome called *learned non-use.*

JDN: Like learned helplessness? We can do that in life when we go through loss. To get through a difficult phase, we all have different healing and compensation methods, maybe cocoon, or depend on someone else or some form of medication or therapy. But if we don't eventually go back and try to make the most of the life we have left, we will never know what we are missing. And the overall quality of our life will deteriorate, when it is actually in our power to make it much better.

DR. KOLB: It is a kind of learned helplessness. The treatment [in physical cases] is called *constrained induced therapy.* Even though it was years later, this man put his good limb, his left hand, in a sling. For eight hours a day he had to use his right.

We're rewriting the score because we're not asking him to pick up a pen in any particular way. Any normal person would pick it up in a grasp like this [shows me how most people hold a pen to write], but he does it like that [grasps the pen in a fist]. We don't care how he does it as long as he gets it. Within two weeks, he could write his name and it wasn't distinguishable from what it had been before the stroke.

JDN: So, what would be taking place in his brain that would enable him to do the same thing in such a different way?

DR. KOLB: First of all, there's the learned non-use. What you have in your head is a map in your brain. Within that is a map of your hand and the arm. That map had been damaged by his stroke, so part of it isn't there anymore. But the map can reconstruct itself. If you don't use it, the map goes. It's not there anymore. He had to get the map to reconstruct itself, to rewrite the score, rewrite the symphony, for the map.

JDN: It may not sound the same.

DR. KOLB: It's not going to sound the same. It's going to sound different. But is it useful? If he can drink now, if he can pick up a cup with his right hand, even though it's not with the same grasp, he's got a new symphony. And so, that's the goal—to write the new symphony taking advantage of the parts that are still there, not having him practice what he can't do.

JDN: And to accept that.

DR. KOLB: And to accept that.

JDN: If he wouldn't accept that, he wouldn't try, because it's all or nothing. We can do this when we lose anything in life. We can just begin to coast or accept defeat and say, "Well, this is all I have now and it's all I'll ever have." We wouldn't discover how much further we really could go.

DR. KOLB: No. Learned non-use talks itself into the fact that you can't do something. So you can't do it. Your brain won't automatically look to reset its map. There has to be a conscious effort—a conductor that actually conducts the new score.

JDN: You can't do nothing and expect a change is going to take place, right?

DR. KOLB: Right. Won't happen. If change takes place, that's reality. Change has to take place in order to create new reality. If nothing happens, nothing happens.

JDN: So even beginning with one little thing to break the pattern has to create a change. It can't not create a change. Back to the One Sock Process. The more you break the old pattern, the more you create new possibilities. If you do nothing— well, it's a poor sort of memory that only works backwards, and that's all you're going to have.

DR.KOLB: That's it.

WRITE IN THIS BOOK: *List one minor and one major event or occasion in your life in which you had thought of yourself as having failed, but now realize you had actually achieved optimal victories.*

What makes each a victory? List the good that came of your efforts.

What made you realize it was time to change track?

Write an example of adapting or flexing around an obstacle or significant adversity in your life. Feel the memory and describe the discomfort zone you were (are) within.

Now rewrite the example, the memory, by moving your focus to a new group of questions: How did you get through it? What was your fiber-by-fiber process?

What did you call upon and strengthen in yourself to persevere, independent of how you coped at the time?

How was your determination related to qualities of your I.M.Possible strength?

Review these questions through loss, disappointment, or any uncomfortable zone in the change process. Practice using the One-Sock Process and record the steps here to imprint the practice on your mind.

"Being unready and ill-equipped is what you have to expect in life. It is the universal predicament. It is your lot as a human being to lack what it takes. Circumstances are seldom right. You never have the capacities, the strength, the wisdom, the virtue you ought to have. You must always do with less than you need in a situation vastly different from what you would have chosen." —Charlton Ogburn, American author, journalist

"I wish I hadn't cried so much!" said Alice,
As she swam about, trying to find her way out.
"I shall be punished for it now, I suppose, by being drowned in my own tears!"
—Alice in Wonderland, Lewis Carroll

18. Collaring Evil

"There will come a time when you believe everything is finished. That will be the beginning."—Louis L'Amour, author

"I'll die of grief. There is no future."
"Evil is too powerful. There is nothing I can do."
"Fight evil with evil. There is no other way."
"This is too much. I can't get past this. It's over."

I consider myself a loyal person. I don't walk away from anyone who has proven faithful to me—even if severing the relationship would bring greater personal advantage. A number of these people turned out to be unworthy of any such loyalty. If you've ever been the victimized by serious betrayal of trust, you know the damage can go deeper than mere words can express. We'd have to coin an entirely new word to describe the emotional impact, because I've never found one that is adequate. Many of you reading this book can relate. At some point in life, you have also faced a personal disaster that left you feeling lost, angry and on some level, betrayed. We can't change the reality of what has already happened, but we have the choice of how we will ultimately respond. Some of the choices in life are taken away. But you are left with others. My grandfather, whose trait of loyalty I inherited, once told me, "When bad things happen, it hurts like hell. But holding on to anger is like drinking poison and expecting the other person to die." So the question becomes, "Will I let bitterness take over my life?" I.M.Possible answers: "No, because I choose otherwise. I choose to put up a fight. To find a way or make one. As long as I am alive, I will not let evil, catastrophe or temptation define who I become or whether I go on trying. I choose to collar the evil and make it serve good in some way. I will not die having given up. I will die trying."

It is one thing to travel a certain path, anticipate the obstacles or perceive them as they come, and then choose our responses - for good or for ill. But when we are blindsided, through no fault of our own, by disaster or (more devastating) disaster caused by evil intent, it is a whole different journey – more like being catapulted into another dimension.

When faced with life-changing traumatic events, especially when no closure or justice is available, how do we deal with the overwhelming feelings of grief and loss? How do we avoid becoming a defeated plaything of evil or circumstance? Should we give up as futile any past groundwork or future accomplishments? Or is there still something satisfying and meaningful we can build from this point, and eventually to use to help others?

No matter how strong we are, or how much we think we know, who is ever adequately prepared for sudden trauma in the form of an accident, disaster, crime or anything else that results in great loss and devastation? We can hear or read about other's situations, talk all day long about how we would react if this happened or that happened, but most of us react very differently when it actually does happen to us. Why is this? As you've learned in preceding chapters, we all have different genetics, mental make-up and life dynamics. Additionally, our personal reality is generated through various types of knowledge and experiences, including secondary means such as reading, discussion and media/electronics.. But information we read about or hear about does not process the same way as when we actually live an event firsthand. It does not have the same reality or impact.

Thus, when life-changing disaster hits personally, anyone can become overwhelmed by feelings of helplessness, despair, anger, hopelessness and sorrow. It may seem impossible to ever be happy or productive again. I certainly felt that way. It is at this very time, however, that we have the greatest reasons and opportunity to transcend. I didn't believe it at the time. So what then? I had to begin with *actions* in order to begin to believe again. And you can, too. Practice small productive, forward-moving actions, even if you don't believe right now.

"To be courageous means to be afraid but to go a little step forward anyway. Life shrinks or expands in proportion to one's courage." *– Beverly Smith, and Anais Nin*

I.M.Possible Makes Evil Work for Good

From the time we are children, when we watch a movie or read a story, we experience emotions of satisfaction and rightness when the hero defeats the villain. Triumph of good over evil is powerfully satisfying and reassuring. It's not surprising. We were created to love justice, not just for ourselves, but as an essential component of secure healthy human existence and interaction. Whether you call it - 'reap what you sow,' 'karma,' or 'what goes around comes around - every decent human being on the planet wants to believe that, at the end of the day, justice will eventually prevail over evil and injustice. Increasingly both in life and in the movies, this just doesn't happen. Such outcomes don't make for happy endings in the movies and are far more disturbing in real life. The difference is, in real life, the victims have to live with the consequences and are left to create the sequel as best they can.

In both fiction and reality, villains come in many forms. Unfortunately, the evil done by a villain can live on even after the villain is out of the picture. Who or what are the real-world villains? Any malicious force that gains power through harming or weakening innocent lives is a villain. A villain is anything that steals our courage, steals our self-respect, or minimizes human value and human life. Villains can come in forms we least expect. Villainy may come through someone we've known for years - someone we have every right to trust. If you encounter a villain, don't do anything to help it along. Don't give them any more foothold or power in your life than they may have or once had. Don't let destructiveness grow on if you can thwart it. If there is no other person available, come to your own rescue. (See also chapter 19, Die Trying) And, if it is in your power, rescue someone in need. How can you do this, if you yourself are feeling less than heroic?

From Bleeder to Leader: Flexing To Heroic

Even when we are helpless to personally change evil that has happened to us, we can do something heroic. When you are able to do that, you become a hero. When something horrible happens to you—a tragedy—you take that something and say, *"Okay, you hurt me. You hurt these people. You did this damage. But that's all you're gonna do."* And then, you put a collar around it and you go, *"You're here. I didn't invite you, but since you've come, for the rest of your days you're going to work for good. This evil will be made to serve and lift other people."* Do you know what that does to help you heal? What it does to help other people heal, or to avoid the same kind of heartache? When we collar the evil and tie it to something good, we change more than just our attitude. We regain control of our self-empowerment. We can refocus in a

> "When written in Chinese, the word crisis is composed of two characters. One represents danger and the other represents opportunity." — John F. Kennedy, 35th U.S. President

productive, positive direction. We tap into a superpower reservoir. We have taken on the impossible - and pushed through to an I.M.Possible outcome.

The Power of Good: It's No Myth

You know this principle by now: We give power to whatever we focus on. By directing the insights you've gained toward action that can make a positive difference in the life of others, you take the focus off the evil, and the pain it causes you. To collar the evil (or the disaster) and direct it toward good strips it of continuing power. When you turn tragedy on its head and make it do some good, you are no longer paralyzed in its grip. Helping others in genuine need, or devoting ourselves to a worthy endeavor, is strong therapy. It is one of the best ways we can help ourselves.

As I struggled with devastating aftereffects that were compounded by rampant professional and organizational corruption and an inadequate 'justice' system, my biggest motivation was the determination to not allow evil to win the attack on my personal integrity and value. With what eventual result? That potentially life-destroying battle evolved into a catalyst for the development of a micro-simple process to progressively reinvent myself. My decision to fight, even when I didn't believe, resulted in the creation of a way to move from *impossible* to *I.M.Possible*.

I'm writing the *I.M.Possible Muscle* series on a level I could never have done before. I've discovered that I am able to reach and connect with many more people than I would have before. I've gained insight and a scope of understanding that would previously have been impossible. In talking with people about their *impossible* experiences, a sharing and transformation process takes place on both sides – one that would not otherwise have unfolded.

Another person who made way for I.M.Possible under tragic circumstances was Ernie Tillman. His step-daughter was one of four college roommates who died horribly and needlessly because their landlord's illegal, faulty heater started a fire in their basement suite. The students desperately tried to get the window bars open to escape, but they were unable to get the bars unstuck. They perished as a result, and the landlord was let off with a small fine. What did Ernie do? He turned his grief and anger into a channel that forced good to come of evil. Ernie devoted his resources to creating window bars that could be easily accessed and removed—even by small children—in case of fire. And he did it.

When Jesus Christ said, *"It is better to give than to receive,"*[1] he was not simply referring to material possessions. Courage, inspiration, hope, information, wisdom, support, words of healing—these are all within the power of anyone to give. Giving in this way is truly powerful. Why? Have you ever been told by someone, "You just made my day"? How does it make you feel? How does your brain respond physiologically? It rewards you with feelings of pleasure. It makes positive connections with your self-esteem and self-concept. It triggers the release of hormones and neurochemicals that decrease stress and motivate you to give and to help again.

> *"Life means to have something definite to do—a mission to fulfill—and in the measure in which we avoid setting our life to something, we make it empty. Human life, by its very nature, has to be dedicated to something."*
> —José Ortega y Gasset, Spanish philosopher, writer

Our brain responds to our experiences. There is no possible way we cannot be changed by disaster or acts of evil. We can, however, ultimately control the direction in which we change. To regain a sense of purpose and equilibrium is essential to I.M.Possible victories in these situations. It is also the most powerful and effective way to find a new normal and re-invent ourselves in a positive manner.

Grief and the Process of Letting Go

In his book *Mindsight*, Dr. Daniel Siegel observed, on grief and loss, **"Grief allows you to let go of something you've lost only when you begin to accept what you have now in its place. As our mind clings to the familiar, to our established expectations, we can become trapped in feelings of disappointment, confusion and anger that create our own internal worlds of suffering."**[2]

I learned the truth of those words through hard experience. As long as I let myself go back to the wrongs that had been done to me and to my family and so many others, I was consumed by bitterness. I was stuck in the "Why?"—a treadmill question that often keeps us frozen in time and going through the same old paces to the same old pain. Psychiatrist Roy Turner stated, "As long as we stay stuck mentally, we are living in the same moment, over and over." This is an impossible waste of precious moments of your life. Choose to move on from those moments, from the thoughts

---

[1] Holy Bible, Acts 20:35

[2] Daniel J. Siegel, MD, *Mindsight*, (New York: Bantam Books, 2011) p. 6.

and actions that keep you trapped and re-living them. If we choose to be happy, we also choose not to tread that mental treadmill anymore. To build to this point, however, if you suffer from grief, depression or PTSD, please, please seek professional support. Use the fiber by fiber and One Sock Process to help you get to each new level of your healing process.

We can't completely stop traumatic experiences from hurting us at times. (If you collar a rabid dog, it will still bite if you get too close.) This is another reason that it is so important to not make the events themselves our focus. Remember – stumbling block or stepping stone? Keep your focus, your energy, forward-moving and productive and your brain *will* respond. You can rewrite the symphony, beginning this moment. (See page 202, Resetting Our Map)

Kill or Make Stronger: Impossible vs. I.M.Possible

There is wise saying, "An appearance of strength is strength in itself." What does this mean? It means that by acting as though we are strong, even though we don't feel strong, we create strength. It means we acquire a particular quality by acting in a particular way. Remember, behavior consists of patterns in time. So when we perform actions that conform to a certain quality, our brain progressively changes in that direction. Our self-concept changes as well, running true to the basic science of cause and effect: We eventually become what we do.

Stability doesn't come automatically during these times. There will be discomfort zones to work through. Often, the knowledge or the strength needed for two steps ahead comes only after we have taken the one. Your I.M.Possible Muscle will increase in proportion to the quality of your efforts. The impossible *will* give way if you don't give in. Impossible can become a platform for breakthrough because, *"I Make Possible."*

One of the clichés that I totally had to rethink during desperate times was, *"What doesn't kill you makes you stronger."* This glibly expressed ideal is based on a quote from Friedrich Nietzsche[3]—but its truth is conditional. People often respond to adversity by harming others or by drowning their emotions in drugs, sex or alcohol. Still others crawl into a shell and withdraw from life in misery. Some even kill or commit suicide.

Most of the things that don't actually kill us couldn't care less if we died. Evil, in particular, does not *intend* to make us stronger. No credit for good

---

[3] Friedrich Nietzsche, "What does not kill me, makes me stronger," *Twilight of the Idols, 1888.*

belongs to evil. What misfortune does do, inadvertently, is present us with a challenge. We are all wonderfully designed with I.M.Possible potential to search for meaning, generate new understanding and enlarge our ability to recreate ourselves and our world in a positive way. Through *this* process we become stronger and more valuable; not *because* of the things that almost kill us, but *in spite of them.*   Eleanor Roosevelt, human rights activist and First Lady to President Franklin Roosevelt beautifully summarized what Nietzsche left unsaid. *"You gain strength, courage and confidence by every experience in which you really stop to look fear in the face. You are able to say to yourself, 'I have lived through this horror. I can take the next thing that comes along.' You must do the thing you think you cannot do."*

CREATING REALITY: ESCAPE INTO ACTION	DR. KOLB

JDN: Many people have experienced a traumatically life-changing event. Disaster or evil can happen in a way that changes something in a person so drastically, it feel like you have literally died in some way. Some part of them is gone forever with the disaster. They can't let go. It still controls them. The fact that it happened still controls them, as though they never come out of shock. What can we do to break the cycle and begin the change?

DR. KOLB: I can empathize with that feeling. When I had my stroke… those types of fears and feelings come to you.

JDN: How did you handle it?

DR. KOLB: When I was in post-doc, Brenda Melnop said she'd never met anybody like me because my response to adversity was that I would escape into action. So that's what you have to do. **You have to escape into action.** I wasn't sure if I'd ever be able to read again, work again, drive again, or have a life again, really. That's pretty sobering. I also knew it would be possible to spend the rest of my life on disability. But I felt that my life would be wasted down that road. So the [new] 'possible' wasn't acceptable. I had to go further than that. I had to create a new reality out of what I had to work with. That's what your book refers to as the I.M.Possible.

Rather than sit around feeling sorry for myself, I started designing what I thought might be treatment programs for ways I might work around this, and at the same time studying myself from a neuroscientific point of view. In doing this, I was also trying to distract myself from sort of burrowing into a hole and hiding in it. As it turns out, I was able to use my own experience to further our research in the field of the brain and stroke recovery rehabilitation and recovery.

JDN: What would Michelangelo have done if someone had defaced most of his work and he had nothing left but a few paints and some clay? He would be very upset but he'd go on to create the best works of art he possibly could with what he had left. Because that's who he was. People and circumstances couldn't change or take that away. And my guess is, the result would still be amazing. Maybe more so, because there is something in a work inspired by extraordinary circumstances that comes through in the quality, regardless of the lesser resources.

DR. KOLB: Absolutely. Most of us, regardless of what has befallen us, have more to work with than we realize until we get going.

JDN: Touché. Escape into action.

> "As each situation in life represents a challenge to man and presents a problem for him to solve, the question of the meaning of life may actually be reversed. Ultimately, man should not ask what the meaning of his life is, but rather he must recognize that it is he who is asked. In a word, each man is questioned by life; and he can only answer to life by answering for his own life; to life he can only respond by being responsible."
> —Viktor Frankl , "Man's Search for Meaning."

CREATING REALITY: THE PET EXPERIMENT   JESS

JDN: When we are overcome with problems, we can't concentrate, we don't want to interact; we lose positive motivation and become very negative and frightened. We don't want to go anywhere or do anything. We don't want to face people and have them ask how we are. It is crucial to keep ourselves from giving in to these tendencies. Love helps us to take the focus off ourselves and lessen our own anxiety. Even taking in a pet we can care for and love has been shown to make a difference in helping people to transform impossible feelings to I.M.Possible.

JESS: My son would get lonely and depressed at times when he was young. When I brought home a puppy, it made all the difference in the world. It doesn't have to be a puppy, but something you can love and care for that takes you out of yourself and makes you feel good in return.

JDN: There was an experimental study in the U.S. with a group of people who were very despondent and depressed. Doctors brought in cats and dogs for pets, and people got used to it and eventually started interacting with the animals, developing an interest and concern for them. As they focused on caring for something outside of themselves, this group's morale significantly rose with time. They started coming out of depression and most were able to go off depression meds altogether.[4]

> "Give light, and the darkness will disappear of itself." – *Desiderius Erasmus*

---

[4] *Anthrozoos: A Multidisciplinary Journal of The Interactions of People & Animals* 6, no. 2 (1993), 135-138(4).

WRITE IN THIS BOOK: *Name an injustice that has occurred in your life.*

How did it cross your values?

What are the feelings? Is anger or distress among them?

Now imagine in terms of I.M.Possible. Begin to let go of the familiar images and feelings as you move your focus to a broader meaning system, like Frankl's responsibility to life and to others, or the One-Sock Process. How will you escape into action, one fiber at a time?

How can you move your sense of fear, anger and danger into an opportunity to move forward and collar evil?

"Adversity has the effect of eliciting talents, which, in prosperous circumstances, would have lain dormant." —Horace, Roman lyric poet, satirist, and critic

"I don't see how he can even finish,
If he doesn't begin."
—Alice, Alice in Wonderland, Lewis Carroll

19. I.M.Possible: Die Trying

"I don't want to get to the end of my life and find out I have just lived the length of it."
—D. Ackerman, author

✗ *"There is nothing to try for. I'm too far gone...too alone, frightened, weak, sick, spoilt, poor, sad, miserable, old... to start now."*
✗ *"It's too late for me."*
✗ *"I don't have enough time or resources in my life."*

Do you ever feel that life has passed you by? Perhaps you are at a place where you feel that it is too hopeless or too late to achieve an impossible dream or make a positive difference in the world around you. Are you: in disadvantaged circumstances, poor health, discouraged, feeling isolated or helpless? This kind of anxiety can hit at any time. At any stage or age in life, we can develop 'impossible' thinking patterns, convincing ourselves there is no need or use to strive for an I.M.Possible goal.

Odd as it may seem, no matter what we choose to do (or avoid doing), our mind has an emotional outcome in view. The goals for such restrictive thinking can be summed up as either immediate gratification or discomfort minimization—living around or giving into the moment, rather than investing for maximum performance. Apart from serious medical disorders, this might be the result of fear, ignorance, learned disuse/helplessness, selfishness or laziness. How can we make new I.M.Possible breakthroughs with such impossible-oriented goals?

To achieve a meaningful life of value requires building and maintaining a heartfelt appreciation for the value of life—your own and that of others whose lives might be influenced by yours. Don't give up. Don't give in. There is *always* a place for you. Worth is in the qualities we *bring* to the table; it is in how many others *could* be served by our example afterwards, even if we don't know them directly. It is the effort we make, how we use our time, not how soon we die, that determines the ultimate value in what and who we are and what we leave behind. *So die trying.*

215

Life is filled with impossible battles, there is no doubt about it; often more than one at a time. The extent to which we achieve I.M.Possible victories is determined by the way we face those battles, those we choose to fight *and* those that are imposed on us, not by how many we win.

People of all ages and backgrounds, whose lives were cut tragically short through no fault of their own, left the world a better place in some way because they kept trying. There are infants born who live no longer than a few hours, a day, a week—yet they struggle to survive to the end, imbued with a sense that life is worth fighting for.

Viktor Frankl, Austrian neurologist, psychiatrist, and Holocaust survivor, was in a position to understand this battle. His entire family, including his wife, were murdered by the Nazis, while he himself endured years of abject torment in a concentration camp under conditions so horrible it defies description. Frankl observed the different ways in which people of all ages responded to adversity, including those who represented the best of the human race—even when under trial by those who characterized the worst. The superficial details don't matter. The heroes and victors were those souls whose commitment to something greater and worthier than immediate personal gratification enabled them to summon strength to rise above overwhelming obstacles. They were those whose love and care for the welfare of others was unfailing despite their own conditions. Whether they lived or died the next moment, they countered the imposter—*impossible*—with I.M.Possible. Later, Frankl would write: *"We cannot, after all, judge a biography by its length, by the number of pages in it; we must judge by the richness of the contents...Sometimes the 'unfinisheds' are among the most beautiful symphonies."*

In order to feel less helpless or more important, try experiencing the power of kindness. Discover it in yourself and others just by being kind to people you pass as you go through life. Age, background, past, resources— these can't block you. How much more you can empower yourself by just being kinder every day! Don't give up on I.M.Possible. Maybe your dream will be realized in helping someone else achieve theirs. *Die trying.*

"Nobody can go back and start a new beginning, but anyone can start today and make a new ending." —Maria Robinson

---

Whatever your plight, however hopeless it may seem, you have *something* you can yet accomplish. It is not the time, place and manner of one's death that determines the success or failure of our life. It is the use to which we

216

have put the moment of our lives before death happens—the efforts we have made, the qualities we manifest, the choices we make, the number of lives our own life affects (whether knowingly or not), or if our story becomes known to the rest of the world.

Ironically, the wins often come in ways that are far different than those we had originally envisioned. And they are often much bigger and better—even if we aren't alive at the time to know about it. Nothing can take away the I.M.Possible gifts you leave behind, and there is no way of knowing how or when those gifts will benefit others.

> *"Whatever I have tried to do in life, I have tried with all my heart to do it well: whatever I have devoted myself to, I have devoted myself completely; in great aims and in small I have always thoroughly been in earnest."* —Charles Dickens, author

At the age of fifty-nine, Rita Pickering heard about a fund-raiser that touched her heart. The catch: it was a two-day, 200-kilometer bike ride through the foothills. Pickering didn't own a bike and hadn't been on one for longer than ten minutes in many years. It was mid-winter so she trained at a gym. At the beginning of the race she got caught in a knot of riders and lost her team. Intimidated by the throng (2280 riders registered) and the cold, wet weather, Rita wondered what she'd gotten herself into. "But after I climbed the first hill, I thought, bring it on," she says. Rita's team raised $53,000 for the cause.

Da Vinci is one of my favorite examples of someone who had such a zest for life that he looked at everything, even disasters, as a sort of wonderland. Whatever his circumstances, da Vinci viewed them through his own window of discovery, understanding and value. He thought productively, accepting the fact that a major part of the achievement process was a lot of uncertainty, trial and error. Everything he wanted to achieve took time, and he knew he couldn't just leap to the finish line. Leonardo da Vinci had to deal with life moment by moment, sixty seconds to a minute, like anyone else.

Says Michael Gelb in his book, *How To Think Like Leonardo da Vinci*, *"Da Vinci died at the age of 67....Vasari claims that in his final days Leonardo was filled with repentance and apologized to...God and man for leaving so much undone."* Yet, toward the end, Leonardo also wrote, *"I shall continue and never tire of being useful."* Vasari also records that Leonardo was observing and described, in scientific detail, the nature of his illness and symptoms as he died in the arms of the French king.

> *"The woods are lovely dark and deep, but I have promises to keep, and miles to go before I sleep,... and miles to go before I sleep."* —Robert Frost, poet

What You Probably Don't Know about Leonardo

No one has ever attempted so much in so many areas as Leonardo da Vinci, yet much of his work was left unfinished. He never completed *The Last Supper*, *The Battle of Anghiari*, or *The Sforza Horse*. Only seventeen of his paintings exist, a number of which are incomplete. Although his notebooks contained wondrous information, he never organized and published them as he intended. Despite the fact that Leonardo died with many of his masterpieces unfinished, his value was unarguably appreciated by many people throughout his lifetime.

That's DaVinci what if no one appears to appreciate your efforts and abilities? Vincent van Gogh would understand and sympathize. *He sold only one painting in his entire lifetime—to a friend.* Despite his discouraging situation, van Gogh continued to paint and finished over eight hundred pieces. Now everyone wants to buy or own one. They are priceless. His most expensive painting is valued at $142.7 million.

Van Gogh is very much alive through the works he left behind. Your works don't have to be material, though. As a perfect man and a carpenter by trade, Jesus Christ must have created some masterpieces. Yet none of his carpentry work survives today. Why then, has this man had more impact on the world than anyone else who has ever lived? Because of his non-material works. Because the effect he had on human beings was so profound, it changed their lives and future forever after.

It is never too late, it is never impossible to make this world better for your having lived—it all depends on how you define success. It is not about other people and what they think—I.M.Possible emerges because of who *you* are. If you are paralyzed and all you can do is think, *pray and mean it.* As long as you can think and are open to learning, you can receive new insights. New insights can lead to I.M.Possible outcomes.

Die trying. Respect the moment. If nothing else, take away those two mottos and keep them in the forefront of your mind. Live every moment so that you are able to say:

☑ *"I did everything I could in the time I had. Whether it was much or little, I didn't waste it. I made it count as far as I could and didn't hold back."*

☑ *"I had to find out what I could do with my life if I really tried, with everything I had to be, everything I could be."*

☑ *"I had to know, how far could I go? What could I accomplish?"*

☑ *"I am on earth for a purpose. I will search for and fulfill that purpose."*

☑ *"I will seek fiber-by-fiber; I will build, fiber-by-fiber, to fulfill a worthy goal."*

"What can I leave behind as an inspiration, as seeds for others to grow further? It will be something."

If you want to feel important - or less helpless, if you want to act as an inspiration, try experiencing the power of kindness. As long as you are able to move, speak, touch or smile, you can make a difference to someone in the next moment. Take the very next opportunity. Practice showing kindness and compassion, whenever possible, to people you pass during your day. You will become aware of a new inner sense of personal empowerment and self-worth that can never be gained in serving self-interests alone. Ironically, the person who will gain the most when you step away from fear or ego is you.

My grandparents lived in a tiny little house in a small town with a population of about 1000. Most of their meager income went to help other family members or anyone having less than they. There were some who shamefully took advantage of my grandparents' large hearts. They had very little money or property when they died. But they were richer than many multi-millionaires. And they never really died.

The sort of persons my grandparents were before their deaths, their deeds of kindness, and the imprint they left on others, have lived on through the 30 years they've been gone. To anyone whose lives they touched, they left a legacy of humor, wisdom, faith and love. Except for my husband, my grandparents probably had a greater influence than anyone else on the person I have become. They would not have imagined; couldn't have known just how much their many acts of love, imagination and selflessness would affect me and my children decades afterward. I wish they knew how often and fondly they are remembered; how regularly their actions and words are repeated when family gets together, or in the course of daily conversation. Both had rejected opportunities that would have provided far greater material gain. Each made choices based on reasons bigger than self alone. My grandparents truly exemplified spiritual grace under pressure. Right up until the day each of them passed away, the world was a better place for their presence. They never complained or looked back – just kept working for the good and hoping for the best. There are so many people besides myself who are grateful to these two simple, beautiful souls who died trying.

219

Have you ever known someone whose presence touched everyone around them with warmth? Make your appreciation known that person. Do you have such qualities? If the answer is *Yes*, how wonderful it is to have you in this world! If you're not there yet, don't give up. You can be.

I.M.Possible Muscle is designed to perform with greater strength when directed towards some worthy end higher than ourselves. We have a drive to seek knowledge that will result in solutions to problems. The greater the odds working against you, the more heroic your efforts to take up the

> *"I can accept failure,
> everyone fails at something.
> But I can't accept not trying."*
> —Michael Jordan, basketball player

challenge. It's easier to take the path of least resistance, but lasting success isn't found along that avenue. The world is strewn with failure rubble heaps left by those who chose not to make the effort or who quit trying. All you will leave is another sad example, another sad story.

When you are given something, *show* gratitude. Say it, write a thank you note, give back to someone else in need. When you accomplish something worthy, don't bask or self-congratulate; go on to the next thing, and the next from there. There is no finish point. If don't know where to start, look for the fiber in front of you. Sometimes it is obvious, other times you have to widen your mental scope (thinking without the box) in order to make way for it.

> *I will live my life in such a way that threat of death at any moment would not make my having lived a waste.* – Hugh Prather, author, philosopher

Although it is not the function of this book to comment on personal spiritual and religious convictions, it is fact, not theory, that we as humans are designed with mental and spiritual qualities that make us unique from all other species on the planet. Our possession of these attributes cannot be satisfactorily explained by purely survival logic or through laboratory experimentation. Among these, our comprehension of the occurrence of miracles is a concept that wouldn't be understood by any other species on earth. Humans not only look for miracles and hope for them, we actively seek ways to encourage miracles to happen. I.M.Possible Muscle is the muscle we need to build in order to allow miracles to occur in our lives. Fiber-by-fiber. Don't ever give up. You never know what good you may yet accomplish for yourself or someone else. Miracles materialize in ways and timeframes beyond imagination or calculation when you are determined in mind and heart and spirit to die trying.

CREATING REALITY: THE POWER OF VISION   JAMIE DENOVO

I grew up in a tiny farming town, in a family environment dominated by physical, sexual and emotional abuse. Despite this and the fact that I had no formal education beyond Grade 12 and was barely out of my teens, I approached a television station and talked them into giving me the chance to create a documentary on child sexual abuse. I explained that I'd never done a media film project but I was passionate about the topic, there was a huge need, no one had ever taken the approach I planned to take, and if they gave me the chance, they would never regret it. This was during the mid-1980s. None of the portable, compact technology available today existed then, and the budget barely registered past zero. My approach was absolutely unorthodox in every way. It was a subject no one talked about. How would I get anyone to open up to me? On a television show? And who was I? No past credentials. What I did have was life experience for my topic, deep compassion for others, intelligence, imagination, and a determination to elicit the co-operation necessary so I could better understand how to help. Equally important, I had found a station manager who was willing to give me the chance to prove myself.

Bottom line: *Hell is for Children*, the half-hour documentary I wrote, produced and directed, won a first prize award at Canada's Can-Pro Awards ceremony. The documentary was named Show of The Year by the city's newspaper. The editor I had worked with on the documentary told me later that the station had never before in its history received so many phone calls on a production. At the time I created this show, I was also pregnant, a mom to a two-year-old son and five-year-old daughter, and going through divorce after a young marriage filled with beatings, abuse and infidelity by an alcoholic husband. (And that's not the half of it.) Because they were unaware of my condition at the time, and such TV stations back then weren't comfortable with single, pregnant women as community leaders on-air, I was unable to accept their offer to realize my dream of becoming a talk show host.

However, in spite of seemingly impossible odds, I *was able* to offer hope, comfort and help to thousands of people—both children and grown survivors of child abuse—whom I'd never met. People who felt they were alone, suffering and had nowhere to turn. Although I was unable to achieve my I.M.Possible dream of becoming a talk show host—yet, then, or in that way—I did achieve the I.M.Possible thing that was within me to do at the time. If I hadn't tried, if I hadn't taken the first step and followed it through, I would never have known how far I could go. I would never have made a difference to all those people. I would never have had the practice that was so necessary to my ability to believe in and achieve other I.M.Possible things.[1]

---

[1] Greg Nelson, Tamara Poirier and Bruce Heinbecker, you have my eternal gratitude.

The experience seemed to me, for a very long time thereafter, a great isolated event that came and went. It was over. My life was in flux, the media decision-makers who had been involved moved on, the opportunity was gone. What I wouldn't understand for many, many years was this: even seemingly past I.M.Possible achievements have a power that somehow endures, even if we don't realize it at the time. Best of all, I.M.Possible achievements serve as antidote to bad memories. It is the kind of past that you never have to dread catching up with you.

The Man [or Woman, or Child] in the Arena

"It is not the critic who counts, nor the man who points out how the strong man stumbled, or where the doer of deeds could have done them better. The credit belongs to the man who is actually in the arena; whose face is marred by dust and sweat and blood; who strives valiantly; who errs and comes short again and again; who knows the great enthusiasms, the great devotions, and spends himself in a worthy cause; Who, at the best, knows in the end the triumph of high achievement; and who, at the worst, at least fails while daring greatly, so that his place shall never be with those cold and timid souls who know neither victory nor defeat." — President Theodore Roosevelt, speech at the Sorbonne, Paris, France, April 23, 1910

WRITE IN THIS BOOK: *Write down something that means so much to you that you will never give up trying to accomplish it. Why is it so important to you?*

Will it leave a legacy? If so, what is the legacy, and to whom will it be left?

If you were to die tomorrow, for what quality would you most like to be remembered?

List 6 actions of any kind that you can take to practice demonstrating this quality.

"Dream as if you'll live forever. Live as if you'll die today." —James Dean, 1955 movie actor and teen idol, who, died at the age of 24 in a car accident with his new sports car

The Unicorn (to Alice): "Well now that we have seen each other,
If you'll believe in me, I'll believe in you. Is that a bargain?"
—*Through the Looking Glass, Lewis Carroll*

20. Circle of Influence

"What we need is more people who specialize in the impossible." - Theodore Roethke, poet, Pulitzer Prize winner

An old man was walking down the beach just before dawn. In the distance he saw a young boy picking up stranded starfish and throwing them back into the sea. As the old man approached the boy he asked, "Why do you spend so much energy doing what seems to be a waste of time?" The boy explained that the stranded starfish would die if left in the morning sun. "But there must be thousands of beaches and millions of starfish," exclaimed the old man. "And there'll be more when the tide comes back in. How can your efforts make any difference?" The boy looked down at the small starfish in his hand and as he threw it to safety in the sea, he said, "It makes a difference to this one!"

****

Have you ever dreamed of being a hero? Who do you think of when you think of the word *hero*? Superman, Batman, Ironman? Or closer to home, someone whose picture and brave act has appeared in the newspaper or on the cover of a magazine? Perhaps it's someone famous who has given some of their wealth towards a good cause? What about the rest of us ordinary souls? Do we have any hope of qualifying for hero status? Absolutely. Every person who has ever achieved an I.M.Possible goal against impossible odds is a hero and an inspiration to everyone in their circle of influence. You might doubt that right now, but read on.

The media and movie world are bigger than real life. Too often, though, much ado is made about nothing and no ado about something. Heroes, too, are bigger than life. They appear in a flash of light and sound, take up the stage, perform a breathtaking deed or give a big check (while we cheer and applaud), then disappear from public view to inaccessibility unless it's time for the spotlight again. That's the kind of stuff that makes heroes. Oh, really? Think again.

Too easily, we unconsciously buy into a media mindset and assume that fame, fortune, public acknowledgement or single death-defying acts (successful or not) are necessary to qualify as a hero. It is hardly surprising that, for many of us, hero remains a role for *special* people; someone we dream of being but could never be. *Me? A hero? Impossible! Or is it?*

Have you seen film producer Tim Burton's remake of *Alice in Wonderland?* In the movie, Alice didn't emerge as an obvious and recognized hero until she fought and slayed the Jabberwocky. All of Wonderland cheered as she achieved that sixth and biggest impossible thing. But, long before that moment in the movie, the audience identified with Alice. Some felt for her while others cheered for her. Why? Because, on some level, most could relate to her emotional struggles as she left behind familiar realities and safe choices to achieve something greater. We could emotionally relate to what she felt because we've all been there in some way. We know what it feels like to find ourselves in unfamiliar territory. We are aware of the discomfort zone we must conquer in any struggle to become something more and to achieve a personal victory despite odds against it.

When facing seemingly insurmountable challenges, have you at times felt very small in comparison with the task before you? We feel like anything but a hero when we are engaged in a battle within. However, in the movie, we could see and feel that struggle in Alice. Even though we see obvious weaknesses, we are drawn to her as we recognize the inner work taking place to rise above them. To fight the fear within is heroic. *To help others when you are scared to death yourself is heroic.* That is as true of us in the real world as it was of the fictional Alice. We fight to slay the dragons *inside* before we can take on the Jabberwocky out in the world.

Could You Ever Be a Real-Life Hero? You're Right There...

It's easy to get discouraged and fail to realize your potentials to a greater degree, when you've bought into mythical ideas about what it takes to be a hero to people around you. It's high time to recognize and maximize your own qualifications right here, right now, when facing real world impossible situations. It's amazing how often many people underestimate their own true value long after they've arrived in a place where they deserve to be wearing a cape. I'm not talking about egotism, but rather about building a clearer perspective, one which will give you greater I.M.Possible power.

You will be able to do more and do it faster, with greater confidence, compassion and positive energy. As we practice in small ways and become more aware of just how much power we really have at this moment to influence and impact the world around us—right here and right now—we gain a greater ability to rise above our insecurities and the need to make comparisons, withdraw, criticize or to self-medicate.

When the pressures of life weigh on us, or conversely, when we are doing very well and living the good life, it's tempting to increasingly focus on ourselves. We become 'self-centered'. We can forget just how much of our own progress comes about as a result of other people who have taken the time to help us in small ways. Even heroes and heroines need support and encouragement to win through at the end of the day. What role was played by the minor characters who lent support to the main hero in the *Alice In Wonderland* movie? *Each represented another type of hero.* They were all, in various forms, I.M.Possible power sources! Little things are easy to undervalue until you have to do without them.

Imagine you are climbing a steep and treacherous mountain. You are trying to reach the peak far in the distance. Around you others are also trying to climb. Suddenly you miss a step, lose your foothold. As you begin to slide down, a nearby climber reaches out and steadies you, helping you to that missed step. Eventually you reach the top! Who is the hero at the top of that mountain? It is you and the one who reached out to help with the step, and anyone else who helped or made way for you along the way. Even if one of those people were to fall the mountain or turn back after giving you a hand, would that nullify the service to you or make it any less valuable? No! Do you get the point? No one is a lone hero. Every great heroic deed is a composite of the support given by lesser heroes to the superhero(s) in the limelight.

Ponder the big picture of your life. Stop and examine the details that lead to your greatest or most important accomplishments. Did the victory arrive with one big performance, an all-inclusive

> Meaning changes with the context. My meaningfulness is here. It is enough that I am of value to someone today. It is enough that I make a difference now. – Hugh Prather

package deal? Did you have all the answers and abilities within yourself? Of course not! I.M.Possible victories involve a journey that must be taken in steps: some big, some small, some forward, some back. But nobody gets through, up, or over all the obstacles without help. As we come to appreciate the value of the little lifts we receive from the actions of others, our realization of our own I.M.Possible power and our circle of influence will expand. It is by helping one another in the little things that big things are accomplished.

I.M.Possible Heroes Spot the Opportunity

When building physical muscle, part of the weight-lifting and training culture involves spotting the person next to you. *Spotting* is a physical training term used to describe the action of helping someone lift through a portion of an exercise that they cannot or might not manage singlehandedly. Its intent is to help the person doing the exercise avoid getting injured and complete the exercise activity. For example, if you are pressing weights on a weight bench, and the weight becomes too heavy for you to lift, the spotter will help by exerting some of their own power on the bar of the weight to lift it just enough to help you complete the exercise safely. A spotter can be a regular training buddy, an acquaintance or a complete stranger.

In building I.M.Possible Muscle, the same principle holds true. There are times when we will spot for other people and there are times others will spot for us. It doesn't require a lot to be a spotter—just a willingness to contribute to the well-being of others as you would like done

> *"People will forget what you said, people will forget what you did, but people will never forget how you made them feel."*
> —Maya Angelou, poet

for you. Very often it costs us little to do that, but as in the gym, the comparatively small amount of time and effort contributed by a spotter may mean all the difference to the outcome for the individual trying to lift the weight.

We all have within the capacity to aid or encourage someone during the course of a day. Often, it is help over one small hump or to the next step or level in an undertaking. Assistance might take the form of providing a contact, opening a door, or taking the time to listen and offer sound advice if we have greater knowledge or experience. Too, never underestimate the power of sincere encouragement and praise. Your kind words can make all the difference to one whose heart may be heavy and confidence lagging.

There are times when others will act as spotters for you. True, you will have had to do most of the work on your own whether outwardly or from within. But how far would any of us really get without a little help along the way? Did someone open a door of opportunity for you? Give you a referral? Help you find a resource? Lift your spirits with praise and encouragement when you were discouraged? Invest some of their own time, money or other resources to forward your efforts? Give you a break you badly needed?

If you meditate carefully and honestly, you can unquestionably recall many times when the I.M.Possible Muscle that helped you surmount an obstacle did not belong entirely to you. In fact, many of the fibers which give our I.M.Possible Muscle the strength to push through impossible to I.M.Possible are actually composed of an accumulation of small kindnesses, courtesies or breaks that we have received along the way.

How can you act as a spotter and assist someone else to break through an impossible barrier? Has your heart ever been touched by an act of kindness or generosity from somewhere unexpected? Pay it forward. Don't stop with one person. Why set a limit of one good deed for the day? Maybe you're already a regular at a gym or fitness club. You soon come to know other regulars who are always willing to lend a hand and spot for someone else when needed. You also come to recognize those who are ego-driven and look out only for themselves. Who are most highly regarded? Given a choice between the two, who would you be more likely to volunteer to help? One who readily acts as a spotter for others will readily find others willing to reciprocate. I.M.Possible is a reciprocal force. The more you do and give, the stronger your underlying I.M.Possible Muscle foundation will become and the more lives you will steady and lift on the way up life's mountain.

Hero by Example

As was shown in the chapter 'Die Trying', most people underestimate the power of example to act as a game changer for one life, or many, in their circle of influence. Richard Merritt, who today owns of two of the busiest physiotherapy clinics in Calgary, Canada, recounted his experience with the power of example.

Once a hard living, loser bad boy; Richard took on the long, hard fight against himself. He reformed and eventually transformed into a respected physiotherapist, family man and philanthropist. What caused him the dramatic change in thoughts, actions and outcome? Richard attributes the turning point in his life to the example set by a good friend who played the role of hero without ever knowing it.

"All I wanted to do was drink, play sports, chase girls," Richard told me during our interview. *"That's all I wanted to do. I wasn't interested in doing any type of school work whatsoever. I knew I wasn't dumb. I just wasn't concerned about doing anything with my life. I flunked at two universities, came out west and worked in Waterton Lakes Park. I met a girl whose father owned a successful car dealership, so I kind of got a taste for what money can buy—a beautiful house, a lake cottage, and one in Whitefish,*

Montana. I decided to go back to school but soon got back into the habit of drinking, partying and staying up all night. A friend of mine happened to attend the same university. We both played on the soccer team. He was captain, I was just a player. At nine o'clock, after our first game, we were all partying, but he just walked upstairs saying, 'Okay, goodnight.' I yelled, 'Where are you going?' He said, 'I'm going to study.' I said, 'What do you mean, you're going to study? It's the first week of school.' He goes, 'Yeah, but I want to keep up.' I just said, 'Oh.' And I went upstairs, and eventually took my 1.47 GPA from the last school I flunked out of, to almost 4.0 so I could get into physio. It seemed like it would be impossible at times, but I did it. I was not a good student. I didn't know how to write a paper properly. I didn't know how to study. Nothing. But my friend helped me.

My parents were shocked. I went from doing nothing, born to lose, to doing an about-face, becoming a successful physiotherapist. My buddy, the same guy from whom I learned how to study, gave me the feeling that, maybe I should try to keep up. He didn't lecture me; he just set the example. I'll always be grateful. It changed my life."

"There are people whose feelings and well-being are within my influence. I will never escape that fact." —Hugh Prather, author

---

Hero Is a Choice

The world today is changing quickly. Our battles in the everyday world are relentless. Faster than a New York minute, life can blindside us like a train hitting a motorcycle. Chances of survival seem impossible, never mind becoming the hero. But there are people who do it. They not only survive the collisions and train wrecks in life, they rise above the debris and create a new vehicle that will help others survive train wrecks as well. These people are heroes, whether or not anyone else has acknowledged them yet. I.M.Possible creates heroes. It is the territory of heroes and champions.

> "Do not let what you cannot do interfere with what you can do."
> - John R. Wooden

Surviving under impossible or horrific circumstances is not enough to make a person a hero. There is nothing inherently heroic in the instinct of self-preservation. Even insects have the instinct to survive. There are those who survive only to put other innocent people through misery. Some survive by sacrificing or minimizing the lives of others. Obviously, heroism means something beyond surviving hardship or beating the odds. What is it, then, that makes you a hero? True heroes do more than survive. They transcend. By that I mean someone—anyone—who chooses to rise above the circumstances, regardless of what those circumstances are, to become something better, stronger and more compassionate. You don't need special equipment. You don't need the spotlight. All you need is a willingness to pass the torch or light the way for others that come within your circle of influence.

"I cannot do everything, but I can do something. I must not fail to do the something that I can do." —Helen Keller, deaf, blind author, teacher and activist

The reality is this: In the real world, heroes do not appear in movies; they appear in moments. They can be of any age, background, color, creed, economic status or culture, and have any physical appearance, shape or size. They can come as a friend, a stranger, or even from inside of you. When I was young, I had to be my own hero many times. There were also heroes in my life who never knew they were. They were everyday people who had no idea of the true worth of their actions. That is because, so often, rescue is a quiet deed performed not in moments of obvious peril, but unconsciously, as part of daily living.

A hero may come in a voice on the phone, a word in passing, a sentence in a book, a gesture. After death, a person may even be a hero when something he or she did is remembered and lives on to lift others up. Everyday heroes are what life is really made of. Once you become aware of it, it's hard not to feel both empowered and humbled. It becomes an unconscious way of being and thinking. You never know where a single act of rescue starts and stops. Even in yourself.

A crowd might not applaud. Your name may not appear in lights. You may not get the key to the city in this world. But real heroes…they don't need keys—they can appear anywhere.

Are you underestimating the hero in you?

CREATING REALITY: CIRCLE OF INFLUENCE   SALADIN

JDN: Saladin, you write for an incredibly popular television series. You are also a spiritually conscious person, which I can appreciate because that's the mainstay of my life as well. What is the impact of your spiritual side on your work?
SALADIN: I have no idea how people navigate the [television and film] industry without having some sort of faith and a belief that, at the end of the day, God is still able to orchestrate things. If you don't have faith and don't believe that God is ultimately still in control you're just totally dependent on the whims of someone else in this industry. It has been the saving grace for me, definitely. I try to keep it

in mind that we all have a purpose for being here. Because I'm in entertainment, I do understand that there is stuff I do or say or write that has an impact way beyond me and just my inner circle. It's a responsibility to be aware of the influence and impact your work could have, and to take that seriously so there won't be any inadvertent damage done. But people also have to understand how it can be used to spread more positivity.

CREATING REALITY: BEING A HERO   JESS

JESS: Until I made a conscious effort I didn't realize how much impact a compliment from my heart would have on this person whom I didn't really like. But a few kind words just snowballed to good feelings all around. The guy just needed to hear that something he had done was a wonderful thing. He needed to realize he had special qualities, too. I would never have guessed it.

JDN: Sincere praise is so powerful. We all need it, and you just never know how much someone needs to hear something that takes you no effort to say. The world can really beat us down. The good in us is often minimized and mistakes magnified. When we bestow sincere praise or a kind word on someone, it's a kind of power you've chosen to use to lift up another being. Oxytocin is released and it activates networks in our brain that create feelings that bond us to other humanity. We get that affirmation back when we give. We were designed to feel a reward of pleasure and happiness, both when we give as well as when we receive: a double helping of satisfaction and fulfillment. How can you help but feel happier, when you've just lifted up another human being?

CREATING REALITY: RISING ABOVE   RICHARD

JDN: How important is it to you to help other people? What role does that play in your life?

RICHARD: I think that's a huge part of my whole idea in life. To help people. My wife, sometimes I drive her nuts. We had a massage therapist who was struggling. He was [Canadian] First Nations. He was gay. From a lot of people's viewpoints, these were major drawbacks. I took him under my wing as my own son. I said, "You know what, bud, you had a rough life. I'm going to help you out." And I got screwed in the end, but that's okay. I was ready to do a lot of things for him, lent him a lot of cash. My wife said, "You're nuts." I said, "Yeah, but this is how I feel. I need to help him." I was going to buy him a house, put down a down payment, but he wasn't in a place to appreciate it. So I had to cut him loose.

JDN: Wow, you're incredible. Can I be your adopted sister?

RICHARD: Yeah, sure.

JDN: At the end of the day, it's not about who someone else turns out to be. It's about who you are.

RICHARD: That's it exactly. I feel better when I help people.

230

JDN: The biggest way of getting out of myself when I'm down is to say, "What can I do that might make a positive difference somehow for someone?" I hope to get through to people that this is possible for anyone. If you've got nothing, the one thing that you have, even if you haven't got money, you've got a mouth. If you can make a positive gesture through words or actions, you've empowered them.

DR. KOLB: As a neuroscientist, I give so many talks my colleagues say, "Why are you giving all these public talks? You don't need to do that." Because I look in the mirror. I haven't got a lot of time left. I need to make a difference. And so, yes, *it's I.M.Possible.*

I.M.Possible People You Can Connect With

Every person who has ever achieved a worthwhile personal goal against impossible odds is a hero and an inspiration to everyone in their circle of influence. But heroes are also the people who are in there fighting fiber-by-fiber, who refuse to give up in their struggle to become something more. Every step is part of the process. Every step you take towards I.M.Possible is a victory, no matter whether it is successful at first or not. A battle is always easier when you know there are comrades battling beside you, looking out for you as you do for them.

The I.M.Possible Muscle book series is being created to give as many people as possible a means to tap into a new energy source. Throughout, you have encountered examples of everyday people who have proven that I.M.Possible Muscle is real, that your ability to make impossible become possible can be developed progressively, fiber-by-fiber. If you have questions for any of the people whose interviews have been included in this book, you can connect with them through the website: http://www.jamiedenovo.com.

Have you found a particular point or thought in this book that is helping you change an impossible thing to an I.M.Possible one? Share an I.M.Possible hero experience with us. Let us know how you've used the One-Sock Process to build your I.M.Possible muscle and push through an impossible challenge to the next level. Even the small steps count. You never know how many lives you may lift —including your own.

You have everything it takes to be a hero. Why not begin in the very next moment?

"For the first time in my life I saw the truth as it is set into song by so many poets, proclaimed as the final wisdom by so many thinkers. The truth—that love is the ultimate and highest goal to which man can aspire. Then I grasped the meaning of the greatest secret that human poetry and human thought and belief have to impart: The salvation of man is through love and in love." —Viktor Frankl, Austrian psychiatrist, Holocaust survivor

WRITE IN THIS BOOK: *List six ways you can be a hero in the next six days. These can even take the form of saying hello or complimenting someone who looks like they could use a kindly greeting, giving someone a helping hand, showing forgiveness, asking for forgiveness, spending time with one who needs you, being patient when you could easily lose your temper—there are no limits to what a hero can do.*

"Never worry about numbers. Help one person at a time, and always start with the person nearest you." —Mother Teresa

"There ought to be a book written about me,
There ought!"
—Alice, Alice in Wonderland, Lewis Carroll

Excerpts From: The Interview Files

"One of the greatest experiences in life is achieving personal goals that others said would be impossible to attain. Be proud of your success and share your story with others." — Robert Cheeke, famed vegan bodybuilder

Part One: Excerpts from the Science Files

Included in this section are excerpts from some of the fascinating discussions I had with Dr. Kolb on building our ability to wrest I.M.Possible victories from that bully, *Impossible*. You will soon come to appreciate why this particular neuroscientist was such a good fit for a book about transforming the *impossible* to *I.M.Possible*.

FIBER-BY-FIBER: PIONEERING NEUROPSYCHOLOGY   DR. KOLB

DR. KOLB: The other thing that happened early on in my career which really made the break was when I was teaching at McGill University and wanted to find another job. So I thought we should have a course in neuropsychology and I went to the [Department] Chair in psychology and said *"I want to put this course out."* And he said, *"No one would take that. There's no such course."*

JDN: Define the course on neuropsychology.

DR. KOLB: Basically, a course on how the human brain works. I said, *"Here's the reading list. This is what I'd do."* He said, *"We'll put it on, but you have to have at least eight students."* I said, *"Fine."* He told me, *"You're not going to get eight students."* Meanwhile, I thought, *"Hmm, why don't I just send this course to every university in Canada and say, 'I've got an idea. Here's a course that students will like, here's the reason why.'"* Well, I got six job offers based on this course, including the one here. So I ran to the Chair, gave him an apology and told him, *"You can cancel the course, because I'm leaving."* He said, *"You can't cancel the course. We've 175 students enrolled."* I said, *"Oh no…"*

JDN: (laughing) You're a victim of your own success.

DR. KOLB: Yeah. So I helped teach it. Flew back and gave lectures. They hired somebody from Oxford to come over and take my place. Then when I got here to Lethbridge, they said, *"We're going to have this course, but we need a book."* I'm twenty-eight years old; I have no business writing books on topics that don't exist. So I said to Ian [Dr. Ian Wishaw], who's eight years older than I am, *"We're going to write this book."* He said, *"I don't know anything about this book."* I told him, *"You're going to come and sit in my class."* So he did. The first time I taught it, we fought through the entire class.

JDN: To the students, it would have been like husband and wife or siblings arguing in front of the company.

DR. KOLB: It's true. The students had a great course. And so, for each lecture, I'd write out sort of what the book would be, so that, by the end of the semester, we had an outline of the book and then we wrote it. Now that's not how you do things. You're supposed to get a publisher first, and then write a book. We didn't do that. We just wrote it and then we sent it out. It was mimeographed, if you remember mimeograph. We had friends at U. of A. and Michigan so we convinced

234

them to use the book and teach this course. On the basis of student feedback, we altered it. Meanwhile, we sent it to every major publisher in North America and they all said the same thing. *No.* We didn't send it to Freeman because I thought they'd never do it. "There's no such field, therefore, there's no such course, therefore there's no such subject, therefore there's no such book."

By this time, Ian's getting pretty annoyed at me. *"You just wasted two years of my life."* Then he said, *"Well, we should send it to Freeman."* So we sent it to Freeman Company. Two days later the editor called me—his name is Buck Rogers—he said, *"Don't sign with anybody else. We'll do this book."* I said, *"We've had a lot of offers."* He laughed and said, *"No, you haven't."* I said, *"No, we haven't. Why is that?"* He said, *"Because they would say in this field, 'No such course, no such book.'"* So I asked him, *"Then, why are you doing it?"* He asked me, *"Are you a member of the field of neuroscience?"* I answered, *"Yes."* He said, *"Well, this is the future. I took it to my next door neighbor who's a big shot in neuroscience and he told me, 'Well, there is no field. They'll define what the field is.'"* So we wrote the book, they published it, it did really well. We're now in the 6th edition, thirty-some years later and it's used all over the world.

JDN: So it went from a course for a field that didn't exist to a textbook for universities and behavioral neuroscience in one of the world's most popular fields of research.

DR. KOLB: Yes. It started out as a sort of second- or third-year book but it's slowly gone up to 4th year and graduate levels, and is required for most students who do anything related to people and the brain, [etc.].

JDN: So you and Ian founded the neuroscience center here in Lethbridge and put it on the world map. You created the world's first neuropsychology course and textbooks. That must make you feel a great sense of accomplishment—to spearhead all that, from ground floor, against all odds.

DR. KOLB: Against all odds.

JDN: And did those victories prepare you for other I.M.Possible battles you didn't know you were going to have to fight in the future?

DR. KOLB: Absolutely.

Change Facial Expressions - Change Your Emotions

JDN: I have a friend, Leslie, who told me that, when she is feeling depressed, she makes herself smile for at least thirty minutes, regardless of where she is or what she is doing. She said it often turns her mood around. I tried it myself and it's true. When you're feeling really down, if you make yourself smile, it does make a change. Why is that? Has science done work on even the power of smiling?

DR. KOLB: Yes, researchers are trying to study that area of neuroscience with scanners. The question is, if you engage in a behavior such as smiling, it seems like a simple gesture. Think about what's required to smile. You've got all this musculature in the face that has to be configured in a certain way. So it's correlated with a pattern of brain activity. The brain activity that takes place in making the expression of a smile also networks to feelings related to smiling. So, just like the feeling of disgust is broader than [typically] described, linked to taste and so on, you've got this muscle activity that is the feeling of happy. When you can get that muscle activity going, you're now tapping into that bigger system related to happy. Facial expression, the way you carry your body, the way you feel—it's all a network of connections. It's all a dance. Similarly, when you want someone to pretend they're sad, you have them get into a body posture that's sad, their facial musculature has to change and that's going to start making you feel that way.

I don't know how actors do this, but for actors to actually feel and to turn emotions on and off, they're going to have to be able to get into that space where they're turning on the muscle activity and doing other actions to mimic what they'd look like. That's going to affect the brain and thus their experience.

JDN: Fascinating. So that muscle activity affects our brain which, in turn, triggers different emotions and our outlook on whatever is going on at the time. Straightening your posture, for example. If your posture is all sad and droopy, someone is more likely to have an expression to match. If you are standing straight and tall and looking proud and confident in expression, does it also work the same way?

DR. KOLB: It does. Exactly.

I.M.Possible: Getting Equipped, Getting Help, Getting There

JDN: How effective is anti-depressant [medication] in helping you through a time of depression as opposed to taking practical measures such as what you were doing in recovery from your stroke?

DR. KOLB: Well, I think you might need both. I'll give you an example. I've had several knee surgeries. The last one I had a new knee put in. You have to have the drug, pain killers, in order to be able to do the exercises, but if you just take the drug, you're not going to be able to walk on that leg. It just makes it tolerable. It's the same with depression or anything else in the healing process. There needs to be a combination of behavioral therapy or cognitive behavioral therapy or whatever promotes that part of the process.

Drugs allow the brain to be in a state that is more receptive to therapy, whatever that therapy is. As we design treatments for stroke, as an example, we try different drugs, but in no case do we just give the drug and nothing else. Because that isn't going to work.

JDN: Is this a fair comparison? Sometimes to heal or get rid of a headache which is caused by stress, you do need to get rid of whatever underlies the stress. But the headache gives you even more stress. So if you can lower that pain, that additional stress is lessened. While you don't have the additional pain, you also need to address whatever it is that was causing you the stress in the first place or you're never going to get rid of the problem. The headache will keep coming back.

Nowhere in this book do I say you can do everything and anything just by using the I.M.Possible processes alone. These work in conjunction with any other intervention required. There are people who need professional help, or augmented drug or treatment therapy, but whatever situation you're going through, if you understand how your brain works, you understand more how to develop and direct it.

DR. KOLB: That's right. Other things can help but the best pharmacy in the world is in your brain.

JDN: I can think of an analogy using Edmund Hillary. Hillary needed certain equipment to help him climb Mount Everest, but simply being equipped didn't take him to the top of the mountain. He was now prepared, but he also had to do the research, the practice and the actions it took to climb the mountain.

DR. KOLB: Yes, that's right. I like it.

JDN: You've got to put in the effort and then you can really say, *"I did it,"* even though you did have help. You still did it.

DR. KOLB: Yes. You know we have to have help in many ways through our whole life so it's no shame. None of us gets through life without help.

Part Two: Excerpts from the I.M.Possible People Files

No life story is as simple as it sounds on the surface. Each person I interviewed has fought from a disadvantaged position, not only in ways you will read about, but in many other ways at various times in their lives. You will recognize familiar challenges and parallels to your own past or present. None had any guarantees of success when they first started out at the bottom of their mountain. It wasn't until they had done something that didn't work and recognized that it wasn't working, that they were able to make adjustments. Each contributor hoped some part of their story would be of value to you in transforming *Impossible* to *I.M.Possible*.

As you read excerpts from the interview files, try to identify the One-Sock Processes used to get through small steps. You should be able to identify how each person has been able to accomplish greater goals by building first on one fiber, then the next. Their I.M.Possible Muscles were exercised in a way that helped them eventually to break through the obstacles that were standing in their way. Note how often each of these individuals discovered the next step they needed to take only after they had moved to a place where the information could become available.

You can follow the impossible to I.M.Possible muscle building patterns and do the same. Then, why not share your impossible to I.M.Possible story? We'd love to hear about your success at any level, small or large, as an individual or a group. Let us know how you applied the fiber-by-fiber or One-Sock Process to get to the next level.

Reader experiences and input are the subject of another series of books. Everyone whose input is used, will be acknowledged. It doesn't matter who you are or what your I.M.Possible challenge may be. Join the circle of influence. Share the hero in you!

ONE-SOCK PROCESS: CLIMBING OUT AND UP   **TIM**

JDN: In climbing back up from the ground floor to your current success, as persona non grata in a new country, what was the biggest factor in your ability to succeed against the odds?
TIM: One of the things I believe in, that absolutely works, is that you should give yourself small wins. As opposed to, *"I want to win the war."* Let's concentrate on a couple of small battles.
JDN: (laughing) Maybe let's get some small wins first.
TIM: Yeah, right. Chunk it down. That's it. Let's use a metaphor. If you're going to build a house, that's a long project. Chunk it down. Let's get the land. How am I going to get the land? Chunk it down, one step at a time—one moment at a time. Tick off each tiny win. Then one day you find yourself going, "Hey, I've got the land. That's one I've won. Great." Tick in the bigger box. That's why lists work. Because what you're doing is you're chunking it down. Every tick in the box is a win. It's all on the table. I can do this first thing. But if you make those things too big, they become overwhelming. If you take that big project, chunk it down to small pieces, chalk up the wins, and then all of a sudden you're making progress. To overcome our impossible situation, Irene and I used that same formula. "What's the big project? We're in a big country where we don't know a single person, no one. And there is no one going to help us but us. So we'd better get started—this moment."

FIBER-BY-FIBER: A FAIRYTALE   **JAMES**

JDN: You are a recognized master of fantasy art and have achieved success in an area you obviously love. When did you start painting?
JAMES: Believe it or not, I didn't do my first oil painting till I was in college. I was born in 1942 and didn't sell my first print till 1985.
JDN: Tell me a little more about some of the fiber-by-fiber steps it took to finally get where you wanted to be.

JAMES: When I was a little kid, I always liked the magical stuff, like you find in fairy tales. Fairy tales are a big source of inspiration to me. When I went to college, I didn't have any grandiose plans. I was an art major but I had no idea what I was going to do with it. I was a responsible person though, so I graduated with my master's degree and took up teaching art. I loved to teach, but I worked all the time. So every night I painted no matter what. I think I was too dumb to be discouraged. I figured as long as I had a job, one of those socially defined 'jobs', I could do art on the side. It didn't occur to me at that time that I could make a living from my artwork. I mean, I had those same feelings of insecurity about the value of my work as anyone else [does about their own].

My 30s were the "anything for a buck" years. I was an illustrator for advertising and editorials. I didn't really like that, but it was a living. I hated painting horses most of all, which is hard to avoid when you are dealing with western themes, cowboys, Indians and all that. But I did become an accomplished drawer and taught art at university. I'd do fantasy art after hours. I took on jobs I didn't really like because that was work in the accepted sense. This fantasy art—painting a fish coming out of someone's mouth—that was self-indulgence. I didn't think anyone else would be interested, not in a commercial sense.

JDN: You mean there was a time when you weren't sure if your work would appeal to people?

JAMES: Oh sure, a long time. I would think, *"Is my work that good? Is this piece worth anything?"* If people bought things, wonderful. It was validation. But I didn't sell lots. And it's funny, but my work at the time wasn't fantasy. Fantasy was always there, but for me it was a guilty pleasure.

JDN: So what influenced you to bring your fantasy art out of hiding?

JAMES: I went home and said, *"I'm thirty-eight years old. There's no me. I do all this freelance working-art and it doesn't mean anything to me. I've never done what I really love to do."* I also remember one of the characters in a great movie I watched who said, *"There are two things in life that are important: doing what you love and knowing what you do really well. If the two of them are the same then [life] is smiling on you."* So I started painting fantasy and taking the chance on realizing my real love in what I do for a living.

JDN: Do you feel you still have challenges to face today?

JAMES: Definitely. One thing is, after you've had some success, it's one thing to be true to yourself when you're alone. But once you've got others to think of—publishers, galleries and so on—how do you keep fresh and honest? In the back of your mind, there's the niggling thought, *"Will this sell?"* Things that I did that were freshest and had most appeal were things I did for myself. It's harder now to fool around creatively.

JDN: If you could leave our readers, people from around the globe who are reaching for some dream or struggling to overcome a major obstacle, with a last insight from your experiences, what would it be?

JAMES: Follow your passion, embrace the fact that it's more important to love what you do than it is to make a lot of money. Now having said that, I have to qualify it. As important as that is balance. If you asked me what the most important work is I've ever done, I'd say it is properly caring for my family. I have a wife with whom I have a wonderful relationship and five kids who are good people and have never been a disgrace to society. I would trade every painting I have ever done or will do for that. Of course, if you can do both, hey, it's heaven. But you've got to be willing to pay the price. Following the passion also means it's not hard to pay the price because you love what you do while you're paying it.

ONE-SOCK PROCESS: IMPOSSIBLE TO I.M.POSSIBLE   SCOTT

JDN: Scott, your line of work is extremely complex and pressure filled. How do you keep from being overwhelmed by challenges that initially seem impossible?
SCOTT: It really comes down to the One-Sock Process you describe in your book. I'll give you an example. My other techs were already out in the field, so I had to hire a new technician to come with me way up north into no man's land where we were going to install closed circuit television systems at many different sites. There was so much gear that we couldn't fit it all into the pickup truck. We had to put it in a big trailer as well as fill up the truck cab. The trailer was packed so full, it just appeared to be a huge mess. There was so much stuff the new tech was completely overwhelmed. He kept looking at it, very concerned about it, very worried. He said, "This is impossible. How are we going to know where anything goes? How are we going to know when we get to a site what goes where? There's so much stuff, we'll never be able to do this."

What he didn't realize was that I'd already spent a lot of time with all the paperwork, going, *"Okay, so here's site Number 1, and I need one of these and one of those and a box of that and a couple of these."* So I piled them up and put them in a corner. There, that site is done and accounted for. I did the same for all the other sites. Then I went back through all the paperwork and double-checked to make sure I had the right number of bits and bobs for every site.

When my tech showed up, we just piled it all into the truck and trailer and although we tried to make it orderly, you couldn't put dividers into the trailer to mark it Site A, Site B, Site C, and so on. We piled up all of one type of equipment so it didn't get broken and we just kept piling stuff up as it fit. Even for me when I stepped back after we had it all loaded, it looked overwhelming. And the more I listened to my tech going, "I don't see how we can do this or figure it out," the more it started to wear on me.

I had to just tell him, *"It's not a trailer full of stuff that we'll never figure out; it's all just one box at a time. That's all it is: one piece at a time. Trust me, we don't need to go over this anymore. When we get to site Number 1, we'll take out the piece of paper and it'll have a list. We need Part Box 1. We'll go in there and find Box 1, take it out, put it in on the floor. Then we'll*

240

find five of Bit #2, and we'll take those out. And we'll just keep going till we have the pieces that we want for Site 1. Then we'll install them, and then we'll pack up and we'll go to Site 2. All it is, is one box at a time."

He somehow couldn't get behind that. All the way up he was saying *"There's so much. I don't know how this is going to come off the way it's supposed to."* He was full of questions and rightfully concerned, but he hadn't spent all the time doing the preliminary work that I had.

I kept telling him, *"Just relax. Don't worry about it."* By the time we got to the third site he was completely relaxed. He knew he didn't have to worry. He knew that each site we get to is just one thing at a time. Take out each item as we need it, put it into the site and then screw one camera to the wall. Then get the next camera and screw that up to another part of the wall. That's all you've got to do. You keep repeating this till you have all the cameras up. Then you put the recorder in its place and then you pull cable from the recorder to Camera 1. Then you pull cable from the recorder to Camera 2. It's just one small, simple job at a time. Once all those simple things are done, you stand back and go, *"Wow. That was a very complex, big job."*

It was impossible to look at it as a whole and tackle it that way. But it was very possible to do one small thing at a time. So that was how we went through and successfully completed the job.

JDN: Now, when at first the tech was going on about how impossible it was, and he was fearful, you mentioned that it had some kind of initial effect on you.

SCOTT: It made me feel negative, too. Even though I knew logically that I'd already gone over everything, when I started looking at it and listening to him, I could take a look at that entire trailer and think, *"Yeah, that is overwhelming,"* or, *"Gee, I wonder if I forgot something? What if...?"*—even though I'm a very step-by-step person. I'd done all the preliminary work weeks in advance, I knew it was okay. But until you actually start the installation you never know what bugs you'll run into. Although I've never run into a situation I couldn't solve.

JDN: And why can you solve the bugs? Why do you feel so confident?

SCOTT: Experience. Like anything else, you just break it down into small things. There's always a way and the first few times, you're very scared about it. But I solved them the first few times and then, as projects continued to come along, I didn't need to worry, *"What am I going to do?"* because I had confidence. I've always solved them before. From the beginning, I do as much research as possible to be as prepared as possible. But Murphy's Law always comes up somewhere.

JDN: The more you do it, the more you know you can do it. And then you can.

SCOTT: So as long as you take a positive approach and don't fall into, *"Forget it. I can't do it,"* and walk away. Just keep looking. You'll find a way.

JDN: But your tech had to take it moment by moment to start feeling I.M.Possible, to go from "Impossible" to "I.M.Possible. This can be done."

SCOTT: True, but I don't want to play down the fact that we couldn't just load a trailer full of stuff without having done all the preliminary research. It wasn't like trial and error, or try anything sort of thing. We couldn't just rush off and decide, yes, I.M.Possible, and do this. I did research. I talked to other professionals and got their input. They helped me along. My very first system of this nature was quite a big system and I had to figure out how much I'd need of everything. So I got help. I talked to people who'd done it before and got as much info as I could. I even practiced the first few times before I ever went out on the job. I had to learn how to put the proper connectors onto the cables. So in the comfort of my shop, I spent some time stripping cable, putting connectors on, checking their integrity, making sure I knew how to do it before I got to the customer's site and had to figure out what to do.

JDN: That's the reason you could convince your tech to relax and take it step by step, because you knew in yourself that you had laid the foundation.

SCOTT: That's the bottom line.

ONE-SOCK PROCESS: MAKE MINE A CHOCOLATE BAR   LYNETTE

JDN: You have a really interesting example of how the One-Sock Process could be adapted to help you change a very simple behavior. And it helped you avoid a very big temptation. You called it the 'Chocolate Bar Process.'

LYNETTE: Yes. I eat healthy most of the time, but there are instances when I sabotage myself by making less-than-desirable food choices. My weakness is chocolate. I know that once I cave in and have chocolate, I give myself permission to have more. I tell myself, "I have already had a chocolate bar, what is the harm in having another?"

JDN: So did you use the Chocolate Bar Process to fight your cravings?

LYNETTE: Instead of caving in to what I think I want, I asked myself, *"What two I.M.Possible actions can I do first?"* Before I give in and eat the chocolate, if I do two I.M.Possible actions, I can still have the chocolate bar if I want. So, instead of eating the candy right away, now I ask myself, *"Can I walk over to the cupboard and get a glass?"* Yes, I can do that. *"Can I fill the glass with water?"* Yes, this is a start. I know that I can still have the chocolate bar if I want it, but I'm refocusing my attention to my real goal, not a temporary distraction. So I switch over to, *"I can even add fresh lemon juice to the water it if I choose. Lemon juice is a powerful blood cleaner. I am healthy and love the feeling that my body is clean inside."* Next I ask, *"Can I take a sip?"* Yes. *"Can I drink just half of the glass of water?"* Yes. *"Can I drink the rest of the glass of water, one sip at a time?"* Yes, I can do this. I know that I can still have the chocolate bar after if I want, but my focus is changing and I'm feeling good about the messages I'm feeding myself and the actions I'm taking.

JDN: But what if you still have a real craving for something sweet? **LYNETTE:** The One-sock process again. *"Can I go to the fridge and get a nectarine?"* Yes, I can do that. *"Can I go to the sink and wash it?"* Yes, I can do that. *"Can I go to the cupboard and get a plate?"* Yes, I can do that. *"Can I go to the drawer, get a knife and cut it into pieces?"* Yes, I can do that. I still know in the back of my mind that I can still have the chocolate bar if I choose to. *"Can I take the second slice of nectarine and dip it in the almond butter and eat it?"* Yes, I can. As I am doing this my craving is slowly going away.

JDN: You're already starting to feel like a success because you didn't cave in to your cravings.

LYNETTE: It's a poor sort of memory that only works backward. You see? I have tools I can use so I don't feel so powerless anymore. I am going to keep using this and the other skills I am gaining through working with the I.M.Possible Muscle program to reach goals.

JDN: Incidentally, how does the word *impossible* make you feel?

LYNETTE: Worthless, shut down, contracted, hopeless, powerless. Like I don't even want to try.

JDN: How does the word *I.M.Possible* make you feel?

LYNETTE: Like I have a chance. I can make a difference. Hopeful. Positive. Expanded. Ready to take action. Powerful. Like I can succeed. I love it.

CREATING REALITY: START SMALL, KEEP MOVING   JESS

JESS: I know exactly how the One-Sock Process works from my experience with depression, which landed me in the hospital. I'm not joking when I say this, but being able to do all of the other things in the healing process started with putting on one sock.

JDN: What do you mean?

JESS: When you're going to the hospital for psychiatric care, when you're depressed, the nurses say, *"You don't get breakfast until you get dressed."* Because they know that in the process of putting on one sock, you go to the next step in the process and you feel more like going to the next. Pretty soon, you're dressed even though you thought you couldn't even get out of bed. They tell you, *"You're not just going to 'get better'. You have to help yourself. This is the first step in helping yourself even though you're feeling like you don't want to do it. The medication alone isn't going to do it."* The doctor told me, *"You're sick and you don't know how to get better. I'm telling you, This is how you get better. You sit up from your bed, and you get dressed. That's the first step.'"*

JDN: Because it gets you taking action. It changes the patterns of your thinking. Break the pattern, break the cycle.

JESS: Absolutely. Then after a little time, they start giving you privileges. If you do that for a week, then you get to go out of the hospital on a day pass, but the whole

243

time it's really about getting you back to just living. So, as long as people can do that on their own, I guess that's why they don't end up in the psych ward.

JDN: But if you let yourself go down the road too far and don't break the pattern that is keeping you in a self-defeating mode...

JESS: Then you end up in the hospital. Someone usually checks you in because you try to kill yourself. So you end up in the psych ward. So now you think, *"Okay, people are going to be understanding and leave me alone."* They don't. Because isolation and inactivity is not how they get you better.

JDN: They don't baby you, or you'll keep going back to the same place.

JESS: They can't, otherwise you'll be dead. And they tell you that. And that's not being mean. That's helping [people on the psych ward] to live. If they don't do that, they will die. When they get out of the hospital again on a day pass, they will kill themselves or do something crazy and end up back at square one or worse. It's not like they don't try to help you as well. They have your therapy sessions and they help you with those things that you need to discuss, but they don't let you stay in that place. Because they also know how the brain works. They know if you stay there, you'll die.

JDN: So there's a lesson here for all of us. There are times you can't just be allowed to flow or allow yourself to flow along on the path of least resistance. There are times you have to go against the flow. Because if you go with the flow, it'll take you out to sea and you'll never come back. It works that way with anything in life. You've got to keep moving in a productive, positive direction and a lot of times that means swimming against the current. That's what I.M.Possible Muscle helps you do.

JESS: In the hospital, they use the processes you talk about in *Six I.M.Possible Things* to help people overcome their Impossible feelings. If you can't change your thoughts, they start by changing your actions because your actions will change your thoughts. If your *thoughts* link to your actions and your emotions; in the same way, changing your *actions* can alter your thoughts - which can change your *emotions*. It's really about learning to break old patterns.

FIBER-BY-FIBER: THE LIVING YEARS   **KASHA**

JDN: You are so happy and confident now. Except for your obvious kindness and compassion, it's hard to believe that for twenty years you lived in circumstances that made you believe you were hopeless and helpless.

KASHA: My ex-husband was very physically and emotionally abusive. He made me feel like I would never amount to anything if I left him. I didn't have any money of my own; he took anything I made. I didn't have anything, including my soul, I could call my own. I was scared to death, but I finally got up the courage to do it. I was forty-two years old and have always wanted to be a veterinarian—all my life. I almost talked myself out of going for it. I was thinking, *"It's going to take you seven years by the time you save the money, go to school and get trained and do all the stuff it takes to actually become a veterinarian. Not only are you too stupid, you're going to be forty-nine years old."* Then, I thought, *"Seven years is going to go by anyway, so I may as well spend it doing what I really want to be doing. At the end of it, I'll be a vet, not a shell of a person wondering what might have been."* So I did it. It didn't take me seven years but it wouldn't matter if it had. I have my degree. I have a career I love. More importantly, my children are safe and secure and they're learning from me about getting up the courage and doing what you have to do. And you know what else? I finally bought the first pair of glamorous shoes I've ever bought in my life. I look back and shudder to think about what it would have been like; if I'd let a bully who refused to change scare me into thinking that he was the best I could do with my life.

CREATING REALITY: YOUR LIFE, YOUR MOVIE   CARL, RYAN, JAMIE

CARL: One of the things I took away from this book is how much of life we waste without our realizing it, moment by moment. Just like editing your movie, Ryan, putting it together piece by piece to create that little piece of pseudo-reality that people watch for a couple hours on the screen. Ironically, it's the same way we create our real-life big picture.

JDN: We can cut away so much long-term value in our life just living in the wrong moment. What we need to do is really work our I.M.Possible Muscle—push ourselves mentally to push through into the next moment, changing what we're doing. We make things stay the same or make them worse by doing the same unproductive things over and over. We repeatedly keep or put ourselves in time and resource-wasting positions. There will be a price to pay for that somewhere down the line. Every moment is a piece of your real life movie but instead you're creating real reality. No one wants to watch the same movie over and over every day. You don't want to waste any part of it making stuff that's the same as yesterday or putting yourself deeper into a hole when you could have been doing something phenomenal. It's so exciting to be able to have the chance *every day* to try to create something more that might actually be lasting and life changing. No matter where I am right now, I can start being something else. Even if I have to start at square one.

RYAN: That's a powerful notion. I can think of a real-life example right off the bat. Sometimes, in Hollywood-land you can really re-invent yourself when you go out and about in this industry. It's interesting to see how you go to one party one night and you're a certain way and nobody really notices that you're there, and you go to another party and you act a different way and it's like you light up the room. I remember about a year ago, I had Gene Simmons from Kiss come up to me and he said, *"Who's this guy? He's the life of the party! How come all the beautiful girls are with you?"* And it just has to do with who I decided to project that night. I was a different guy that night obviously 'cause I was at other parties where no one paid much attention. I mean, both of them were really me. It wasn't anything phony. It was just that, with one attitude I created one reality and, with another attitude, it created another reality. Two different outcomes to the same type of situation, just by changing your attitude—or I guess, as you put it, your thoughts.

*"We have only this moment, sparkling like a star in our hand...
and melting like a snowflake.
Let us use it before it is too late."*
- Marie Beynon Ray, author

For more information, or to contact myself or anyone connected with this book, please visit www.jamiedenovo.com or www.i-m-possiblemuscle.com. If you would like to be interviewed, please email me through the contact form on my website: www.jamiedenovocom. I'd love to hear from you.

Made in the USA
San Bernardino, CA
10 February 2015